MYTH AND CREATIVE
THE SELF-RENEWING SONG

DEDICATION

——— ◆ ———

To students of my 'Myth and the Creative Process' course at Essex University; and to my myth teachers, Robert Hill, and Dudley Young, whether they like it or not.

Thanks to poet and teacher Hilary Llewellyn-Williams, and to Philip Langeskov.

MYTH AND CREATIVE WRITING: THE SELF-RENEWING SONG

◆

ADRIAN MAY

Routledge
Taylor & Francis Group

LONDON AND NEW YORK

First edition published in Great Britain in 2011 by Pearson Education Limited

Published 2013 by Routledge
2 Park Square, Milton Park, Abingdon, Oxon OX14 4RN
711 Third Avenue, New York, NY, 10017, USA

Routledge is an imprint of the Taylor & Francis Group, an informa business

Notices
Knowledge and best practice in this field are constantly changing. As new research and experience broaden our understanding, changes in research methods, professional practices, or medical treatment may become necessary.

Practitioners and researchers must always rely on their own experience and knowledge in evaluating and using any information, methods, compounds, or experiments described herein. In using such information or methods they should be mindful of their own safety and the safety of others, including parties for whom they have a professional responsibility.

To the fullest extent of the law, neither the Publisher nor the authors, contributors, or editors, assume any liability for any injury and/or damage to persons or property as a matter of products liability, negligence or otherwise, or from any use or operation of any methods, products, instructions, or ideas contained in the material herein.

British Library Cataloguing in Publication Data
A CIP catalogue record for this book can be obtained from the British Library

Library of Congress Cataloging in Publication Data
May, Adrian.
    Myth and creative writing : the self-renewing song / Adrian May.
       p. cm.
    Includes bibliographical references and index.
    ISBN 978-1-4082-0464-1 (pbk.)
    1. English language–Rhetoric–Study and teaching. 2. Creative writing–Study and teaching. 3. Myth. I. Title.
    PE1404.M375 2010
    808'.042'071–dc22
                                                                    2010017071

ISBN-13: 978-1-4082-0464-1 (pbk)

Set 11.5/14pt Garamond MT by 35

CONTENTS

◆

Publisher's Acknowledgements	vi
Preface: Mythic Intentions	vii
Introduction: The Mythic Writer	1
Part One: Myth and the Creative Process	11
1 Starting Creation	13
2 Birth Myths	24
3 The Truth Lies	35
4 Mythic Navigation Devices	47
5 Dark Matter	58
6 Late Heroes	67
7 Happiness Writes	80
8 Myth Madness	89
9 Modernising Myths	99
10 The Daily Myther	112
11 Dooms and Dead Ends	122
12 Myths of Fame	139
Postscript: Theories and Fairies, Myth and Magic	148
Part Two: A Mythic Subject Dictionary	157
Bibliography	207
Index	213

PUBLISHER'S ACKNOWLEDGEMENTS

———— ◆ ————

We are grateful to the following for permission to reproduce copyright material:

Text

Extract on pages 29–30 from Taliesin by Hilary Llewellyn-Williams, with permission from the author; Extracts on pages 40–42 from *The Bacchae and Other Plays*, by Euripides, translated by Philip Vellacott (Penguin 1954, Revised 1972) Copyright (c) Philip Vellacott, 1954, 1972, reproduced by permission of Penguin Books Ltd; Lyric on page 43 from *Horrible But True*, Nigel Burch, with permission from Nigel Burch; Extracts on page 52 from *Ovid: Metamorphosis* translated by A. D. Melville, with an introduction by E. J. Kenney (Oxford World's Classic, 1992), by permission of Oxford University Press; Poetry on pages 54–55 from *Scintilla*, 6 (2002), poem 'Actaeon' by Hilary Llewellyn-Williams, with permission from the author; Lyric on page 77 from *There isn't any Superman*, Jim Eldon, Golden Arrows (1991), with permission from Jim Eldon; Lyric on page 88 from *I'm Happy*, Ivor Cutler, with kind permission from The Estate of Ivor Cutler; Extract on page 93 from *The Oresteian Trilogy: Agamemnon; The Choephori; The Eumenides*, by Aeschylus, translated by Philip Vellacott (Penguin Classics, 1956) Copyright (c) Philip Vellacott 1956, reproduced by permission of Penguin Books Ltd; Poetry on page 134 from *An Essex Attitute*, Wiven Books (May, A. 2009), with permission from Wiven Books; Poetry on pages 118–119 reprinted by permission of United Agents on behalf of: The Estate of Adrian Mitchell from a collection *Heart on the Left (Collected Poems 1953–1985)* published by Bloodaxe Books; Poetry on pages 135–137 from *Oulipoems 2*, Ahadada Books (Terry, P. 2009) poem 'Dante: Inferno I', with permission from Philip Terry.

In some instances we have been unable to trace the owners of copyright material, and we would appreciate any information that would enable us to do so.

PREFACE
Mythic Intentions

———— ◆ ————

Who is this book for?

This is a book for all serious writing students, because it is about something that works to make our writing deeper, more connected to the human condition and connected to the past, present and the future of all writing. These are grand claims for myth, in its broadest sense, all of which will be explored more fully in the Introduction. By 'serious writing students' I mean anyone who takes writing seriously: teachers, undergraduates, MA and PhD students, students in adult writing courses and groups and the amateur, by which we mean (paying mythic attention to that word) anyone who loves to write. The book is based on my third-year undergraduate course at the University of Essex, but it is also my own method of working, developed over years as a songwriter, fiction and essay writer and poet. Because of my interest in many genres, the book is not genre specific, but rather concentrates on what all writing has in common. For me, this is the mythic interconnection which links all serious writers, all serious students of writing.

There are many books which, quite rightly, concentrate on the craft of writing, but, at essence, this book concentrates on the process of inspiration, the process of writing and the process of working with mythic material. Other books deal with craft, technique, theory, genre and academic debates, but we dive right into the darker sides of writing. The book is a source-book, to help writers find their own depth, methods and connections, while it has many suggestions and exercises which serious students will want to try or adapt. The book is for those who want to get into the 'creative' bit of creative writing.

The hard work aspect of writing is often emphasised by serious writers and this should never be underestimated. The hard work aspect of myth might look more like seeping ourselves in and absorbing the material until inspiration takes over, but there is hard work for us serious students nevertheless. Researching and comparing material, finding elements of contemporary use in old tales and making narrative structure function well are all vital activities. However, the book is for those who want to build up their depth and understanding of the creative and the mythic processes, so that the hard work is towards some rewarding end.

How can we use it?

The book can be used directly, as the processes are explored through practical application of the ideas. There are suggestions for writing accompanying every chapter, which will build up our understanding of the themes and provide some suggestions of how myth can be directly useful. Each chapter contains many examples of old and newer mythic material and how it has been or can be used now. There are suggestions for reading too, after every chapter, with something from old mythic material, a newer example and something which explores some of the ideas discussed relating to the creative process. These are labelled old, new and critical.

A creative process is explored in the way the book progresses. We delve into the inner world, starting from the sense of creativity, gradually moving, through key archetypes and big myths, towards the outer world and towards an audience. This can be used to build up a picture of how myth works as a structural device and as a birth-to-death metaphorical view of psychological processes and changes. Once we begin to find these connections – between thought and birth, between writing and the depths we need to explore to do it, between the heroic and the everyday – our own ideas can then come into focus in a mythic way.

As well as directly and in the connection between myth and the creative process, the book can be used to help us get our own ideas and inspirations. It can, I hope, inspire us to be inspired to find examples and instances in all media, both old and new, and to see the mythic dimension everywhere around us. Part Two, the Mythic Subject Dictionary, demonstrates this element, offering some writing and research ideas and an understanding of how a mythic view of the subject might help in our work.

What is the book (and title) saying?

The way writers work is itself mythic. As writers, we go into the depths of our thoughts and of ourselves and bring back the treasure, just as a hero in a mythic adventure does. The first chapters of the book deal with this in much depth. We do a mythic job, trying to tell a different kind of truth about what it means to be human – different from the news or the analysis, different from the theory or the cold facts. Myths for us are not falsehoods and definitions are discussed, especially in the Introduction. We try to create something living, which tells us something about living.

The creative process is mythic. The story of how a piece of writing emerges, which is a combination of idea and structure, heart and head, skill and perhaps wild abandon, is patterned like myth. It has paradox, change and the working towards some meaning, which can reveal itself as if by magic. Understanding the process can help us make it work. Myths are stories about how change happens in the mind and in the world. We create and return to creation. The process is like a life being recreated.

The Self-Renewing Song means the song, or the myth, which recreates its own energy in a new form. Myths have connections with songs. Scholars say that the old mythic epic poems, like *The Odyssey* were originally sung and, in the United Kingdom, the old ballads, still sung today, are often mythic tales. The Bible begins, they say, with what was a song or chant and the old, enchanted truths old tales tell us still self-renew and haunt us like songs.

In participating in the creativity of renewing the old messages for today, we writers also renew ourselves, as mythic beings and creative adventurers. So *The Self-Renewing Song* is the song that renews itself and ourselves, as writers and as readers. Writing, like myth, is about shared experience, or at least about sharing it with our readers.

[handwritten margin note: How ← self-indulged]

The book is also saying that myth is useful in all these aspects. It is useful in inspiration, in the growing of the imagination and of creative insight. It is useful in the writing process, where we will understand the mysterious journey and labour of creating a successful piece of work. It is useful in terms of the content of our work, including the connection between themes, narrative structures and patterns and in finding old material that can make our writing new. It is even useful when we think about being published or being famous.

Dealing with creativity, rather than with the craft or the teaching of the subject, this book is written in a relaxed and informal style. I am telling a mythic tale in the old tale-tellers' way, by talking directly to you, the reader/audience. Its mythic intention is to demonstrate its own purpose and be a *creative* book about creative writing. So my passion for mythic, creative ways of thinking will show through and I hope readers will understand if I do not always tone this down. With all that in mind, I have occasionally used pieces of my own creative work as examples of some ways of using myth. I will indicate these by using my initials: A.M.

Here then, we will take the widest view of myth and hope we can find mythic and symbolic connections in all things. Join me in my song of renewal. Myth is about how we cope with change, what we share, what happens and what we need to say to the world. It is how we make the personal universal and how we can make our writing better.

INTRODUCTION
The Mythic Writer

◆

Why writers use myth

[handwritten: Like an intrusive narrator]

The secret that writers know is that they are part of a long tradition of storytelling and word work, whether they call it mythic, intertextual, interactive or original. Exploring the mythic nature of writing, where these connections are revealed and where the writer is also seen as a mythic adventurer, is a way of finding close links to what it is we demand from literature, which is something to do with the essences of human nature. What is remarkable about knowing some of the oldest stories in the world is how little the basic problems of living have changed and, consequently, how modern these old things can be. It is true that writers will be, by and large, more sympathetic to this than critics, but the popularity of the mythic, in contemporary writing, film and children's literature, means it deserves serious attention. Returning to the source for renewal has been a pattern in the history of writing, which is a kind of going back, better to go forward. Discovering and revivifying the stories that tell us best about ourselves helps us connect with ourselves and with our readers.

The concept of myth is famously difficult to define, containing from the start a number of paradoxes. One sure thing that can be said is that myths are narratives of some kind, but when the *OED* goes on to say they deal with the 'supernatural', but also with 'natural . . . phenomena' we are already in two minds. Myth is, then, you could say, being usefully in two minds at once. In meaning 'b.' the *OED* has it being 'untrue', while myth fans tend to think of myth as containing some kind of universal truth. It certainly seems to be about some kind of narrative, or contingent truth, or, as the old definition, from Roman writer Sallust, goes, 'things that never happened, but are always'. My favourite definition is one quoted by Edmund Leach in *Genesis as Myth* (1969), from J. Schniewind: 'The expression of unobservable realities in observable form.' While this could apply to any metaphorical thought perhaps, it does allow for a wider definition of the mythic which could include fairytales, folklore, legends, history, jokes and stories, which is the way I want to use the term. Dudley Young, my myth teacher as an undergraduate, once told us that myths tend to be 'short, violent, unintelligible and insane' therefore 'difficult to read'. I would add that their meanings reward those trying to find them and that those meanings seem inexhaustible and responsive, with a power of their own to show us what we are inclined to ignore. In this way myths can be maps of what we choose to forget. Myths often deal in difficult or problematic situations, with what is taboo, in the sense of being both forbidden and special. They deal with death, with rebirth, and change is at their heart.

To define the indefinable will be an on-going aspect of what we will be doing in this book, so I will offer a definition of my own, based on the *OED* meaning: *Stories that embody the symbolic mysteries of nature, human nature and magic.* The word 'myth' is closely related to the word 'mystery' and also to 'mouth'. The Greek 'muthos' means both speech and narrative, so speaking the story, or writing it, is close too, as is the mystery of telling. Myths are common to all cultures and have been dismissed as pre-science explanations of the world or discussed as religious rituals. It is characteristic of myth that the meaning changes to suit our needs. My definition has the caveat of 'symbolic' which then allows me to use the word 'magic', without too much scepticism.

Other discussions put 'Mythos' versus 'Logos', which is story versus logic, and these oppositions are at the heart of myth too. Myths deal with opposition, with death and rebirth, with truth and lies, as we shall see. Explaining the difficult to grasp is something writers do. How else can a tragedy be uplifting? How else can a comedy make you think? We use myth so as not to deny the difficulty and paradox of living.

At a simple level, and myths deal in natural, life-and-death simplicity too, the classics are the old source stories of myth, but I would want to include all and any kinds of *useful* strange old tales, jokes and bits of narrative we all live by. Things in our lives become legendary. We all knew someone who we like to tell stories about, because they say something to us about what we need from the world. At the end of the Introduction, there is a list of some essential primary myth reading and some essential critical reading to help you use this book. We will find the myths and find that the myths are inside us.

Myths, in my sense then, are the stories which are part of us. They can help us in the urge to be objective without losing the subjective, circular without losing linearity, rooted without being against progress, connected but still able to act personally, and inclusive without being adrift in a sea of relativism. These are strong pulls for writers, which show that myth is not only used as an urge towards escapism. Myths are not just old Greek stories, separate from life. Stories are all around us and within us, too. We live by stories which

Oh look, my entire personality

attempt these balances between what we know and what we feel. Laurence Coupe, in his book *Myth* (1997), quotes 'the myth of mythlessness' to describe how even an apparently sceptical writer like Philip Larkin constantly calls on renewing images of nature in his poems. If nature is mythic, as it is, then we only have to look to the source of a word like 'pollution', which can be traced back to the Greek 'lume', which means 'a soiling', and to think of the environment, to know we live in times that struggle with the mythic in an urgent and pressing way.

The use of myth now, in popular as well as literary writing, in film and television, in music, both popular and classical, is ubiquitous. A look at the bestsellers will show you J.K. Rowling or Philip Pullman. Literary writers like Marina Warner and A.S. Byatt in the United Kingdom use myth continually. *a bit on the nose there* Poets like Derek Walcott and Seamus Heaney use myth, while contemporary UK poet Simon Armitage has published a version of the Arthurian mythic poem *Sir Gawain and the Green Knight* (2007). Myths are about testing the human spirit in its quest for truth and these old/new themes are with us always.

Myths tend to come back and are often themselves about something ignored, surprised or forgotten coming back and this, from the outset, links myth with the creative process. The oldest written-down story, *The Epic of Gilgamesh*, is about a green man having to be created by the gods to balance the corruption of mankind. Obviously, it could be about now. One of the appeals for writers is that they, like myths, were once perhaps more central to life, as they performed their mythic reminders. In an age where we have stopped trusting pure materialism, we might feel that writers want to, or need to, be important again. Myths can help us stand up for non-material wealth and the mythic is the place to start to discover what is more enduring and, potentially, a gift of infinite value.

How writers can use myth

Writers can use myth to help get beyond the merely personal. The biggest problem for new writers can be the very thing that makes them want to write. This desire wells up from inside, in a way which is demanding and personal. It is the externalising of a need for what we suppress to be expressed, which has the intensity of a physical response. Just as it is, it is a good thing, too. Those of us who are serious about writing do want to take it further. We want this feeling of release to relate out towards other people, even out into the world. The urge towards writing comes like a call from the Muses, a breathing in, or inspiration, of a need to express something. The patterns of myth can aid this connection, as they often address such things.

The idea of personal originality can get in the way. It is a twentieth-century notion to be hung up on being original and new in writing. We all know that 'new' often just means the packaging. However, we demand to be individual. This kind of self-ego can be useful, especially to the advertising industry, but it has its limits. We have all heard of the 'me' generation, the greed and materialism of some aspects that underlie Western cultures. Shakespeare never bothered himself about original plots, yet the voracious nature of the media-culture demands 'new' ideas, as if they were really new. But this is really novelty, rather than real newness, real renewal. It is easy to mistake the trivial for the genuinely innovative[To be really innovative, you have to know what you are improving on] Depth is attained by other methods than the demands of fashion.

Even Hollywood found the idea of constant novelty redundant after a while and has looked towards the mythic. Most writers in film would now know about the mythic work of Joseph Campbell, via Christopher Vogler's *The Writer's Journey* (1992; revised 1996). They found out what serious writers had known all along. The human spirit has much in common from person to person and the stories we all tell can talk the same language through the ages.

If we start from the personal, as we must, there can be no serious challenge to the uniqueness of the individual, however. Uniqueness is a given. Your writing can never be other than a part of you. We all say it differently. The things we have in common, which is where myth can help, are what we tend to take for granted. These deep connections do not challenge the self, but enhance it. We have more in common than we know and this can help us writers reach an audience. Like many things about writing, there is a duality here, which is a widening of vision, not a narrowing to the self, alone. It is not getting beyond the personal but, again, taking it further. 'The message is: Widen the area of consciousness', as poet Allen Ginsberg (1961) says, on the last page of his collection *Kaddish and Other Poems*.

It is a mistake to see myth as merely formulaic. 'No new thing under the sun', it says in Ecclesiastes (1:9), with a kind of cosmic despair, from a passage that is, paradoxically, both personal in tone and exhilarating, if you look at it another way. The best mythic work is both personal and communal. To connect the personal to the world is to take writing as a very serious thing to attempt. Myth gives us the key to reach from one world to another. At best it moves beyond the surface of its strangeness towards a universal wisdom. Here the self becomes bigger and more deeply connected, more deeply humane.

As well as getting the personal to include the world, myths can help you be innovative. They can challenge us in unexpected ways. Many writers find old stories, myths, folklore, fairytales, traditional poems and songs attractive, but it is important to remember that while they might fascinate us, at the same time they are often alien to us. They are full of potential, but full, literally and metaphorically, of dangers. Writers pay them serious attention and respect to get the best from them.

As a very young writer, I'll admit that I failed to see the point of them, myself. I had to be shown that they were not just for children, or for posh classically educated mythologists, and not just anti-realist. I had to discover that they were subversive and spoke to our mythic, archetypal inner culture. Originality, so often sought, writers realise, means to do with the beginning, the roots, so it does not necessarily mean absolute newness. If we take new to mean *renew*, we move towards something more cyclic and natural, and more fruitful, creatively. Stories begin 'Once upon a time', which is both now and timeless.

In 'Tradition and the Individual Talent' (1919), T.S. Eliot says that if we have a sense of the past, we can use 'the timeless as well as the temporal together, [which] is what makes a writer traditional. And it is at the same time what makes a writer most acutely conscious of his place in time, of his own contemporaneity.' We only know where we are now, if we know how we got here, in other words.

Eliot was a great admirer of James Joyce's novel *Ulysses*, which is known to be both modern and mythical. It is worth noticing how much Modernism in the arts is traditionalism or myth in disguise. Stravinsky's *Rite of Spring*, and the paintings of Picasso, are two examples. The influence of the primitive nature, the immediacy of traditional, mythic material, cannot be overestimated. This 'nowness' of the old stuff is part of myth's appeal in, for instance, the translation work of poets like Ted Hughes and Tony Harrison. The use of stock phrases in blues, for another example, give us the story fast: 'I woke up this morning' with the blues. We know where we are. We have to know the old story for immediacy and for depth.

We live now, as always, in narrative, as we are story-telling creatures. As Dudley Young says (Intro. to *Origins of the Sacred*, 1991), we have to do this:

> [The] potential tyranny of the fictive is often poorly understood these days ... we take little mythic instruction ... But in the *absence* of an authoritative myth or poem, the lights simply go out and the soul is closed down: no name, no game. In other words, we *have* to play; if we refuse, our robotic bodies are simply wired up by this week's television commercials.

The better the stories we tell, the better we are, if 'we *have* to play', and we have to make it work for us now, to renew what is there.

Writers use myth to deepen their sense of the symbolic significance of life then, where an old story gives us a pattern. We can use myth simply to turn an idea into a narrative. If we want to talk about a pop star, we might choose the Greek tale of Orpheus, charming all with his song. We can disguise it, so no one can tell the source, but when we get to him trying to bring his girlfriend back from the dead, we will know that we are learning that success can be fatal, remembering how he ended up in a bad way, in pieces.

If we do not use the story directly, we can always have a character knowing an old story that sheds light on the one they are in. Shakespeare and *Star Trek* both do this. They make their stories layered with other stories, to add that symbolic and mythic truth. The patterns of myth are discussed later, especially in Chapter 4, Mythic Navigation Devices, and are used by many as blueprints for crafting stories. There are overall patterns of how myths and tales work and also patterns of individual myths that might relate to a subject or tale we have in mind.

Using myths in these creative ways gives writers narrative and symbolic force and also helps us develop our own mythic muscles. Then our ideas will tend to flourish and show themselves in a multifaceted way and we will begin to think mythically.

Reading *The Self-Renewing Song* is designed to help in this way and also to help in your own process of creation. Myths map a creative approach to life and we can find ways of connecting the process of writing with the way myths show their process of change and renewal. We will tell many tales along the way, symbolically charting the creative journey into the world of creativity, which is the world of myth. If this sounds too mystical for you, don't worry. Plenty of practical examples will guide you through, to help you see what myth can say about how life and the symbolic writing life unfold. We will move from creation, through darkness, towards light, bringing with us the fruits of our symbolic life.

Writers use myth to be useful, to give life back to life. Like the hero, they bring fertility to enable the world to flourish. Our writing can flourish in the same way.

Danger, mythic traps ahead

An aspect of the mythic worth reinforcing is the tendency of myth to hide its power until it receives our serious attention. Myth is easily mistaken for escapism, for example. The truth of myth can be invisible, but not to the mythic writer, who seeks to use the secret power in writing. From the outside, mythic material can seem too playful, too distant, merely whimsical or totally irrelevant. The serious mythic writer does not pander to this trick of appearance. If we know the dangers, we can avoid them. Here is a list of some traps, which might be there, ahead.

1. Use of myth can make you seem humourless and over-serious, if you don't use it lightly. Robert Bly was accused of this in a review of his book about masculinity, *Iron John* (1990). I do not agree with the reviewer, but still know that we should make sure myth is not an excuse to assume superiority, in tone or topic.
2. You can appear to be mad if you go too far with magic and old theories. Myth needs to be grounded in the real, to be useful, which was its original role.
3. You can seem merely whimsical, perhaps like some writing for children, and some mythological fantasy sci-fi, with its unpronounceable names, clichéd plots and pseudo-archaic language. Some seem to think that myth equals a pastiche of nineteenth-century literary language. If we want our work taken seriously, these traps are best avoided.
4. The primitive can seem trivial to some. Most pop music is primitive but *very* often trivial, although it really need not be so. Myths can do simplicity well, but make sure this is not mistaken for being simplistic.

Conclusion: reading, writing, key myth texts

'There is no final system for the interpretation of myths, and there never will be' (Joseph Campbell, 'Epilogue' to *The Hero with a Thousand Faces* (1949), 1. 'The Shapeshifter') → Better you than me, pal

All our thoughts, dreams and minds, all our actions, adventures and plans are narrative: we are narrative. Our thoughts, feelings and intuitions come from and towards narrative. Even the most abstract kind of thought-works, or maths, are thought-stories or equation stories, for example. Myths could be defined as the stories we live by, to call their presence to hand here. To call them in this way is to engage with the world in an intense way, just as any writer aspires to do.

As Dudley Young suggests (see above), we have a choice of the stories we live, and we need, like we need food and water, to get the best and most nourishing stuff. Mythic stories, I believe, are the truest, weirdest, most potent, most challenging, surprising, pointed stories we know – ones that deal with change, with human nature and moral resonance. These kinds of stories have an accumulated potency that can enhance our lives. Mythic stories repay our attention over and over – they are a form of inexhaustible wealth that can work for us now.

It might seem, then, an obvious thing to say, but, if someone else had written this book, it would have been different. A book about myth and its creative use, however, must insist on its difference as a principle, both of its purpose and nature. The self-renewing and adaptable aspect of old stories and symbols are their magic and their message. If this comes across, the book has served its purpose in passing on that sense of power, with its potential to sing, to sing again and anew.

My emphasis will always be from a writer's, practical point of view, aimed at all writing students and enthusiasts, to encourage them to find their own ways of discovery and enrichment. Feel free, then, to ignore me if I get too pedantic or prescriptive. Insist on creativity for me as well as for yourself.

This is a statement of freedom as much as a caveat. Beware anyone who lays down the law about writing and beware more anyone who lays down the law about myth. My story is for the same purpose as any good story: to open the mind to possibility.

Writing

Write down a 'strange but true' story from you or someone you know. What does it tell you about change, about human nature, about the wild and the tame, the known and the unknown?

Reading

The Epic of Gilgamesh (old); Dudley Young, 'Introduction' to *Origins of the Sacred* (new); *Myth*, by Laurence Coupe (critical).

My top ten key myth texts

Soak yourself in these and add your own favourites:

1. Any good book of Greek and Roman myths.
   My favourites are Michael Grant's *Myths of the Greeks and Romans* (1960) and Robert Graves' *The Greek Myths* (1955; revised 1960).

– Russian

2. Books of myths from other cultures.
   These should include all and any you can find, even books of the World Myth kind, which give you a snapshot of many. Choose especially ones close to you, or your own interests. *– British*
3. A Classical Dictionary.
   Lempriere's (1864) is great, if you can get a modern reprint, and also find a good modern one.
4. Ovid's *Metamorphoses*.
   Any version, but perhaps try an old one too, like Golding's, which was Shakespeare's favourite myth source book.
5. Books of fairytales.
   Grimms, Perrault, Joseph Jacobs' *English Fairy Tales, Andersen, Aesop's Fables, The Arabian Nights,* etc. Many of these are available on-line for free.
6. Books of local folklore.
   Books about your area, country, or others that interest you. Search your local library for local history and legends.
7. Sabine Baring-Gould's *Curious Myths of the Middle Ages* (1866).
   Loads of strange stories, including the Pied Piper and the Wandering Jew.
8. A good Dictionary of Symbols.
   Try the one by J.E. Cirlot (1971) or by Tom Chetwynd (1982).
9. The Bible and other religious texts.
   These are full of great symbolic stories.
10. Chambers' *Book of Days* (1864).
    A personal favourite, full of folklore and seasonal stories associated with each day. Modern selections are around and other books of days, or seasonal lore are useful.

Key texts to help you use *The Self-Renewing Song*:

Dorothea Brande's *Becoming a Writer* (1934).
The classic book of insight into the creative writing process.
Joseph Campbell's *The Hero with a Thousand Faces* (1949).
The greatest guide to the use and relevance of myth.

a But to pain read

Part One

◆

MYTH AND THE
CREATIVE PROCESS

Each chapter concludes with suggestions for writing, and for readings of old, new and critical texts.

Chapter 1

◆

STARTING
CREATION

CREATION MYTHS

The Tongue of Mist (by A.M.)

Driving home at dawn
I pulled over to a lay-by
because a tongue of grey, silvery mist
was curling around the river Colne
waiting, its dark body gone with night
close by, the pallid movement of cars,

what a surprising, lovely word choice.

On cue, the sun appeared
and, having spoken its ethereal mystery
of the ordinary, miraculous day's arrival
in a breath of light, the tongue of mist
vanished away

Who am I to deny
being bespoken fresh
in Remembrance Avenue
beside the dumb intention of traffic
on just another Monday morning?

This poem of dawn, perhaps a most obvious theme, nevertheless attempts to give a sense of the wonder of creation, of the mystery of life itself, embodied in a natural image. The language of creation is one of wonder, of dark and light, of experiencing something beyond, but close to, the bounds of normal human experience. This is the language of myth and the language of religious myth. Writers, in their attempts to make the world fresh, take part in the same ritual enactment, the same 'tongue' which speaks the world into existence.

Listening to Leonard Cohen's song 'Love Itself' (*Ten New Songs*, 2001) likewise gives us a sense of the wonder and mystery of creation, of life itself. Watching motes of matter in a shaft of sunlight, Cohen uses familiar words of creation stories, as he talks about light and form and naming, as if the world is again speaking itself into creation, a process which the writer shares. Creation is bringing shape from what is shapeless and identity to what is unknown, showing the mystery and the difficulty of negotiating these boundaries between what we are and how we got here. Far beyond any scientific or religious ideals, we feel the need to give voice to this first question, to acknowledge and rehearse its careful move into life and to re-enact its strangeness, and the feeling that we are in a state of continual becoming.

If that was a bit too mystical, I make no apology. Creation, despite our endless attempts, embracings and rejections of it, is what we are trying to do, and what, despite us, must retain its urgency and mystery. We want the flower to grow, the bird to sing, so we must move to the mythic tune, like it or not. Creation is both familiar, in the sense that we do it all the time, and properly strange, so that it gives freshness and wonder, even by a main commuter road, on a dull, busy morning. We are existing and creating, however small and seemingly insignificant the signs of this seem. The use for this feeling to writers is to show us how crucial attention to detail is, how we must slow down and allow things to emerge and how to see things as strange. Literary criticism calls this 'defamiliarisation', which is a translation of the Russian Formalists' 'making strange'.

Creation texts remind us too of how it is to write and know writings; both familiar and strange. In the West, this is especially true of Genesis in the King James Bible. Even if we do not know it directly, our culture is still saturated with Genesis' imagery, so we feel we know it somehow, just as we feel we know the cadences of the wonderful use of language by the translators of the King James' version. This is true, even if the contempt of familiarity is often more palpable than a useful possibility of wonder. If we do remember this text, we might see it merely as a kind of statement of authority, with a commanding and dogmatic tone. But the 'in the beginning' bit, which began, we are told, as a chant or song, is also full of a sense of goodness, fertility and the richness of life. 'And the Spirit ... moved upon the face of the waters ... Let there be light: and there was light. And God saw the light, that it was good: and God divided the light from the darkness' (1:2–4). The wonder in this song reminds us that, as writers, we must take it mythically, see it as strange as it is, whatever else we see or do not see in it.

Man is soon to be made as an 'image', in chapter one, as an idea, a likeness of creation. The whole beginning is full of a kind of innate goodness, before the creation of evil. We might feel divided in our ideas about our own, sometimes disowned creation story, but 'division', workable opposition is both a source of creativity and a presence in chapters one and two of Genesis. We writers need to find the tensions in our subjects. *dust & ashes*

A few verses into chapter two, it can be a shock to see that, despite our prejudices, we get a very different, second creation story, where man, reminding us of Cohen's song, is made 'of the dust' (2:7). We are the result of division, which is the move from chaotic stasis towards the possibility of change and growth, of definite and growing existence. Like the editors who assembled Genesis from various texts, we are 'in the beginning' and sometimes in two minds. We are material and materialists, in 'dust' (second Genesis creation) and we are our story of ourselves, in 'image' (first Genesis creation). Our ambivalence, our comparative way of thinking and writing, our minds and our bodies, our 'image' and 'dust' are no small things. These first stories feel like all stories, full of resistance and possibility and our scepticism is part of the process. We are like the editors, trying out alternate stories. Creation might need to be authoritative for us, where we work with these wonderful ambiguities, as we split from oneness into movement, into growth. The state of continual creation is growth and rebirth.

The world is full of change, of creation and we writers must notice the continual movement away from the static in opinion and in time. Writers try to explore and explain the changes the world is full of, in its state of creation.

Looking at the less familiar, in Hesiod's *Theogony*, the Greek classic of the gods' creation, we notice the language of creation recurs. In Dorothea Wender's translation (*Hesiod and Theognis*, 1973), the request for a 'sweet song' gives the sense of goodness and richness from the first line, which asks the Muses to 'celebrate' the creation of the gods. We have 'the beginning', the 'Night' and 'the Sea'. 'From Chaos came black Night/ And night in turn gave birth to Day and Space': this gives us the sense of division. The seventh meaning of 'division' in the *OED* gives a fourteenth-century musical term 'divisions' as being the art of variation on a theme, what we might call improvisation. This came from playing longer notes instead of shorter ones, to make playing easier, and then dividing the notes became the art of variation. The space was available to create within. This is what a modern musician might call 'breaking it down' to recreate the groove. Creation is the art of selecting, of dividing, of recombining, seen this way.

The same kind of language and divisions give us a sense of wonder through the song, the night and the sea, plus we can take from here the idea of combining strange things, with an infinite sense of possibility.

Evil soon appears in the *Theogony*, as it does in Genesis, but much earlier, and evil is seen as a kind of return to chaotic stasis. Giants and monsters appear, a whole other subject, but often there shortly after creation. Evil seems to be trying to stop or control creation here and the weird nature of creation myth shows itself in the harvesting of the controlling male's genitals (misused tools of creation) and the birth of a goddess of love, the renewal of the earth and creativity. In this strange tale of innocence and experience, love and the feminine triumph and the sense of possibility is palpable, as it is in Genesis. Creation is for awe and wonder at life and its mysterious arrival. For writers, it is a reminder that to bring our work to life, we need to take part in the ritual of creation. With change, as we describe it, the possibility of evil is always present, as possible as good. Creation can give us writers the sense that innocence and evil are always near at hand, as perhaps they are. In creation, they are always there for us.

Turning to Ovid, we find that the great Latin poet's collection of old myths also begins with a creation story. His *Metamorphoses* calls on the Muses, as Hesiod does and talks in the familiar language of chaotic unity. In A.D. Melville's translation (1986), there is 'chaos', everything is 'all one' and 'undivided'. From a writer's point of view, negatives are used to define the great absence before life begins. Verse two of the opening of Genesis says that 'the earth was without form, and void', while Ovid does his 'ex nihilo' (out of nothing) thing too: 'No foot could tread, no creature swim the sea.' Imagining what is *not* would be a useful starting place for writing. Describing what is not is very evocative and very useful: 'No love, no hope, no *beer*', we might write. A world of stasis is a world without the possibility of change, division, creation itself.

Ovid, like us, is uncertain about gods, but names 'whatever god it was', using his sophisticated Latin ambiguity, before having man created as image again 'in the likeness of the gods', as 'the unknown form of humankind'. The double mystery of form, as dust, and image, in 'the unknown' reminds us again of the dividing negotiation of creation.

As Karen Armstrong says in her exploration of Genesis *In the Beginning* (1996), we keep on dividing and we keep on creating in the flow of creative movement between our night of dust and our day of image. The uncertainty

Read

life & death

is part of the movement and the process, like the uncertainty of the writer starting a new work. Writers can write usefully about the divide between conflicting states, when idea and reality conflict.

As can be told from the above, it is hard to talk about this stuff except in its own terms, but when we talk about creation myths, we talk about writing. In Dudley Young's, *Origins of the Sacred* (1991) chapter one: 1, among other vital things, he speaks of science as being concerned with the known, while myth deals with how we work, or think, or write and 'the intersection of the known with the unknown'. 'Science', he says, 'is uneasy with beginnings', while myth explains them in process and tells us, significantly for writers, *how* to start. Science has a problem with ending too, and the facts need their process of happening, which is their story, or myth. Scientists must respect the creating writer for asking awkward questions of it, with our older, mythic mode of understanding. 'Once upon a time', Young says, is our 'way of bridging the gap between non-being and being' and makes us wonder, as all good creation stories do, about losing our sense of wonder. Writers have to begin and end and have to feel some wonder, however ambivalent it might be. 'Life takes on meaning and value in the light of death', Young says and the division here is echoed in the 'liberating' and 'disturbing' qualities of science, which takes us into space and yet can take away our wonder, until we feel that 'if "anything goes", the nothing need do'. This kind of modern banality, or empty certainty means 'we are encouraged to forget that we owe the gods a death'. Scientists themselves remind us now that there is a limit to our story, and that pollution, a very ancient word and one of the 'home truths' of the 'primitive mind', still counts, or even counts more today, and we need to attend to our creation of the world and to our sense of creativity.

Scientists are good characters to use to explore these creative conflicts, as much sci-fi has shown and science can show both the open mind and the closed in internal battle, which might be the battle of our time.

Before suggesting some direct ways of moving towards the creation of creation, I will leave the last word of this section to part of Tom Chetwynd's entry on 'Creation Myths', full of awe and warnings, from his book *A Dictionary of Symbols* (1982), which, like Dudley Young's work, has much to say on the subject. Chetwynd again reminds us how creation is an essential part of our being and about how we see ourselves in the world. A writer, or a character created, can seem to lose control, shrug off the stasis of pre-creation and be transformed and re-create the self. When we move to write, we move to create, to bring ourselves into being, or back into being.

We owe the gods a death

The work of bringing unconscious content into the light of consciousness also transforms man's dark negative feelings of being lost in an alien cosmos. Man orientates himself by means of mental concepts such as order, direction, boundaries, which transform his experience of the cosmos from being terrifying, confusing, or just strange: and relate him to his environment.

But this systematising can be overdone, and it may be that modern man needs to rediscover the impact of direct experience. His conscious control is so tight that the real experience of life eludes him: he is no longer disturbed by sleep where space and time dissolve and slip away into nothing, to be partially replaced by the chaotic disorder of the unconscious otherworld of dreams. He is all too sure of his limited Ego world, and so can hardly grasp his precarious position semi-stuck to a big ball of fiery mud, spinning through endless space and time. But in reality his position is no different from that of primitive man, only his focus of attention has changed.

Creation lists

Creation is the movement from unknown to known, from unconscious to conscious.

You can use these lists as an overview, and/ or in the way the italic instructions after each of the three indicate.

Types of creation myth:

1. Primary (worlds/ universes/ from chaos/ *ex nihilo*).
2. Secondary (man/ second being/ fall/ monsters/ giants/ evil/ Eden).
3. Creativity myths (about art/ expression/ suppression/ fertility).
4. World/ cosmic order myths (Utopia/ dystopia/ ideal/ underworlds/ heavens/ politics).
5. Anti-creation myths (destruction/ Armageddon/ apocalyptic/ end of world).

Choose one, or combine two or more, to create your own creation myth.

What are creation myths for?

1. Awe: where does life come from? The World, and beyond the material.
2. Seeking meaning through stories.
3. Relation to seasons and nature/ birth/ death.
4. Relation to self and other.
5. Sense of connection.
6. Newness.
7. Enjoy and endure.
8. Celebrate creativity/ mystery of life.
9. Imagination creating the world.

10. Something to compare ourselves with.
11. Abstract to concrete/ division.
12. Understand chaos/ sex/ violence/ power/ omnipotence.

Choose or combine meanings to convey through your myth.

Some elements of creation myths:

1. Order from chaos/ abstract to concrete/ beginnings.
2. Division/ night and day/ earth and heavens/ seasons.
3. Grand, poetic language, repeating motifs/ phrases, invoking the Muse(s).
4. What is *not* there before.
5. Beings created.
6. Nature/ natural order.
7. Giants/ monsters/ evil comes into the world.
8. Perfection/ innocence at the beginning.
9. Image/ clay/ imagination/ reality.
10. Cycles of life/ death.
11. Second being/ huge being(s) divided.
12. Poetic language/ big symbols/ violent/ sexual imagery.

Choose or combine the elements you will use or combine to use.

WRITERS BEGINNING

Trouble's Coming Home (by A.M.)

Hey Layla, Goddess, Princess of song
Sing me one of Trouble, the Changing Man
Big T, what a priceless bastard he was!
He went off in all directions
after he'd smashed the Troy-boys in the War
He met everyone, he *knew* everyone
he went everywhere. Nearly smashed himself
in the giant freak waves far out at sea
Cos he's trying to get him and his mates
to coming home from the War
Trouble's coming home but his mates
never made it. The mad fuckers ate
someone's sacred cows for real and
that was them bolloxed for good
Sing us all this mad but true stuff
Daughter of God, whatever
way you want it . . .

To talk about creation is to talk about beginning to write and the writing of beginnings. How Homer begins the *The Odyssey* is a classic, epic opening, a 'proem', an invocation of the Muses and has many elements of a good beginning for a writer of a mythic tale, which survives even in the above, deliberately provocative version. It starts in the middle, as epics must. 'In medias res', from Horace's *Ars Poetica*, means 'into the midst of things'. Odysseus ('Trouble' in the version above) has been away ten years and it will take him ten years to get home. Here is a character sketch of a cunning, troubled man, a build-up, a summary of the story, an indication of the themes of war, seafaring, journeying home (a creative redefining of purpose), adventures to come, trouble with the gods and with his comrades. If we can get all that in ten lines, in the original Greek, as expanded to seventeen above, we are doing well in our own start of creativity. The language and the character are obviously heroic, big, 'priceless', the tone of the whole is there from the first and a world is created for the reader to explore.

We must be brave and creatively bold in our creative beginnings. Practise by finding a famous beginning or classic quotation and brutally rewriting it, to see what can happen, or write a boastful, 'who' did this, and 'who' did that introduction to a character, for example.

The invocation of the Muse is a whole subject in itself, but is a feature of epic poetry. For writers now it could represent the help needed from the mysterious, for what is other to us, in creation. 'Layla', probably after Eric Clapton's song, is the modern form of 'Leila', a dark and mysteriously inspiring Arabic muse-like figure, which seemed a current equivalent to use in the 'Muse, tell through me' opening, which could be a more literal translation of the start of *The Odyssey*. We summon help from the unknown, from the unconscious. This is the first connection between myth and the creative process, that of the Muses who create, metaphorically or for real, the kind of spell or trance we need to get to our creative selves. Writers can invent or include their own muse characters. We need someone who invites mystery and that could be the most unlikely person perhaps. Try inventing one for any writing being worked on, to use in creating, or within the work itself.

There are many explorations of great openings of texts. For example, David Lodge's *The Art of Fiction* (1992) has a good section on this, and we can choose our own favourites to see what they are doing and perhaps try to emulate one (see *Writing* below). But it might be a useful comparison here to look at a recent novel and see how it creates its world from the first paragraphs. There is a Greek proverb which says 'Well begun is half done' and

UK novelist Lindsay Clarke once told me that 'beginnings are fateful'. Doing them well is vital.

A 1996 UK Harvill Press paperback version of *Independence Day* (1995), the second in the Frank Bascombe trilogy of novels by US writer Richard Ford, quotes in its blurb from the deceptive opening lines, a picture of suburban tranquillity, without acknowledging that Ford is actually mocking us.

> In Haddam, summer floats over tree-softened streets like a sweet lotion balm from a careless, languorous god, and the world falls in tune with its own mysterious anthems . . .

From this, we might think he had read my opening section here and was determined to fake it so well that I might laugh, but be impressed. Right on both counts, as he even evokes a 'languorous god' of suburbia to help, like a Muse summoned and a dream of 'balm' for every ill, which tells us, albeit so quietly, that this is a utopia or Eden, about to be undermined by evil arriving, as in all creation myths.

Sure enough, we do not have to wait long. On the second page, just like Genesis, we get a whole different creation of atmosphere, although this time we have a space to indicate a change of gear.

> Though all is not exactly kosher here, in spite of a good beginning. (When is anything *exactly* kosher?)

The unbracketed sentence here, separated from the previous sentences by a space in the text, is not even a whole sentence, as if it connects, which it does by the ambiguity and division of creation, to the opening. This is an irrevocable fall, a fall from grammar, and a Fall from innocence. The use of 'kosher' also gives us a hint of Old Testament beginnings, as does the bracketed, extra caveat of divided double-think, which invites modern scepticism in early and with an emphasis on the imperfect world and the impossibility of anything being '*exactly*' innocent anywhere. Creation of innocence and the breaking of it is a classic creative beginning for writers. Creation myths are great for satire too, as you will by now have realised.

Ford has also introduced us to the mind of his hero/ narrator, Frank Bascombe, in his 'off in all directions' mind-split of the ex-writer determined to be a realist and not quite making it. He also, like Trouble, the name for Odysseus in the poem above, wants to find his home and is stuck halfway: halfway between Eden and irony. This is the comedy, as well as the division, of the struggle for creation. Comedy and creativity, absurdity and expectation, dust and images are meat and drink for writers.

Every time we write, from whatever materials we make our new creature out of, we are engaging in the same task as the writers and imaginers of new worlds and new works. We work with our own images and our own dust.

The creation game

This game can be played alone, but works best in a round-the-room form, adjusting the number for extra group members via the years, minutes, seconds, nanoseconds section at the end. The intention is to lighten the weird and weighty elements of the subject, explore some of the tropes and language in a silly way, and 'play God', as writers must do. Read out (omitting the numbers, left here as a guide to how far it will go in a group) and ask the group to add a word in turn. Creative laughter is the aim.

1. ONCE UPON A TIME THERE WAS A WORLD CALLED ****
2. AND THE GREAT GOD ****
3. CREATED THE WORLD FROM ****
4. AND ****
5. AND THEN SHE ADDED SOME ****
6. THEN SHE DIVIDED THE ****
7. FROM THE ****
8. AND THE FIRST OF THESE SHE MADE EVIL AND THE SECOND SHE MADE ****
9. SHE TOOK FROM THE GROUND SOME ****
10. AND MIXED IT WITH HER ****
11. AND CREATED THE FIRST BEING WHOSE NAME WAS ****
12. THEN SHE THOUGHT SHE MIGHT ALSO NEED A MALE BEING, BUT
13. SHE DECIDED TO ****
    BUT SHE MADE ONE ANYWAY
14. SHE TOOK SOME ****
15. AND, FROM THE FIRST BEING, A PART OF ITS ****
16. AND CREATED A MALE CALLED ***
17. AND THEY MATED, BY JOINING THEIR ****S TOGETHER, AND ALL THE ANIMALS AND SEASONS WERE CREATED,
18. INCLUDING THE STRANGE ANIMAL CALLED ****
19. AND ANOTHER ONE CALLED **** (*add more if needed*)
20. AND THE NUMBER ****

WAS THE NUMBER OF YOUR EARTH (YEARS/ MINUTES/ SECONDS/ NANOSECONDS etc.) THE WORLD LASTED TILL IT VANISHED INTO THE MYTHS OF TIME . . .

Writing (see also the creation game)

Write, in any genre, something inspired/ derived from some element(s) of creation mythology (see creation lists). Examples: you could write a lyric poem about the darkness of chaos, or create a sci-fi new world's myth of origin, or a comic sketch of how an imaginary being was created and its dialogue with a god.

Write a list of absences, before creation: for example, 'No walk, no bones, no best friend, no pet, no greeting at the door, no wet nose . . . no dog.'

Choose a beginning of a text you admire and copy the way it is done to make a beginning of an opposite or vastly different world from the one created therein.

Write with a fresh eye and a sense of wonder about something which seems ordinarily mundane.

Reading

Old: Genesis, King James, or Authorised Version of the Bible; Hesiod's *Theogony* in *Hesiod and Theogonis*, translated by Dorothy Wender (1973); 'Creation', in Ovid's *Metamorphoses*, translated by A.D. Melville (1986); Homer, *The Odyssey*, first lines.

New: *Watership Down* (1972), by Richard Adams has a creation myth; Leonard Cohen's 'Love Itself', from *Ten New Songs* (2001); 'Towards a Supreme Fiction', Wallace Stevens' complex creation poem, quoted by Dudley Young; the opening of *Independence Day*, Richard Ford (1995).

Critical: Karen Armstrong, *In the Beginning* (1996), Dudley Young, *Origins of* ← *the Sacred* (1991), 'Perceiving the World: Science versus Mythology', 1. Tom Chetwynd, *A Dictionary of* Symbols (1982) entry on 'Creation Myths'.

Chapter 2

◆

BIRTH MYTHS

Infant Sorrow

My mother groan'd! my father wept.
Into this dangerous world I leapt:
Helpless, naked, piping loud:
Like a fiend hid in a cloud.

William Blake's enigmatic poem, from *Songs of Experience*, contains in this stanza something of the trauma of existence, the natural anxiety we seem to be heir to, 'the existential angst', as it is sometimes called. Beyond that, though, with Blake, we get the ambiguity of the courage of the 'infant', who has 'leapt', 'piping loud', 'struggling' and 'striving', despite everything, 'into this dangerous world'. He could be writing about the creation of poetry, where 'piping' is playing the traditional pipe, as well as protesting as infants do, for nourishment and comfort. In the first poem of the opposite *Songs of Innocence*, 'Introduction', we are introduced to the poet 'Piping songs of pleasant glee'. The frontispiece of *Songs of Innocence* shows a child above the piper, like a miracle of birth, a self-renewing rebirth. In this mirroring *Experience* song, there is an intention amid the 'Infant Sorrow'. Despite the groaning and weeping, there is the potential of a courageous song, like that of innocence, being given birth.

In creative writing courses and in instructional self-help books which concentrate on craft skills for the writer, some of us do talk of courage, even if it is a 'c-word' not much mentioned outside that sphere of education. A few of us even talk of inspiration, and maybe you could define inspiration as the courage to embrace some depth of the 'naked, piping loud' imperative of a creative work, which is not often written of in how-to books or taught in class.

One person who did seem to teach courage and the possibility of magic and depth in writing is, paradoxically, the author of a how-to book, who I call 'the divine Dorothea'. This is Dorothea Brande, in her *Becoming a Writer* (1934). Once, when I was being interviewed for a job, I was asked if such an old book was relevant to modern teaching. I should have answered that I was not alone and that the UK critic and writer Malcolm Bradbury said it was 'a living classic among those who are interested in creative writing', in his Foreword to an edition published in 1996. Previously, the book has been republished with introductory essays by novelist John Braine and most recently by the influential US creative writing teacher John Gardner. The reason Bradbury, one of the founders of successful creative writing teaching in the United Kingdom, gives is this: 'It's about what must happen before' most how-to books, namely 'the mysterious process of first becoming a writer', which is 'a psychological matter: at once a conscious activity and an unconscious one'. This might be the habit of being 'naked', you could say, while still leaping into 'piping loud'.

Brande's exceptional gift is that she addresses this mythic duality, which is the double nature of the writer. In the rational world of science and the enlightenment, Romanticism gave back individual expression and Freud, who clearly influenced Brande, gave us back the inner world. The crude sketch of the last sentence might, I hope, indicate a kind of split between the outer world of facts and things and the inner realm of dream, repression and desire. Our writing is often born from this tension of opposites in Blake's 'dangerous world', between innocence and experience, between hope and harshness. The writer, the artist, must negotiate both realms and make them bear fruit together. Brande does not talk of Jungian archetypes or of myth, but her approach connects strongly with these ideas.

In Brande's own 'Introduction', she talks of a breakthrough moment, when she was trying to teach fiction writing. She realised that the 'basis of' her 'discontent' was that what her students were being told, by the 'top-heavy literature' about writing, missed something. It was something that writers needed to know in their naïve, or 'naked' desire to obtain 'some magic', 'some trade secret' that would make their 'piping loud', or their writing good. Brande made the courageous leap to see that the 'top-heavy' stuff and the 'discontent' and desire for 'magic' were linked by a dynamic of opposites, in psychology's idea of the conscious and the unconscious. 'There is such a magic, and . . . it is teachable', she says.

Her first chapter addresses the difficulties that writers commonly have. She argues for the need to be serious and the need for creativity and yet, despite this, tells how authors often suffer from lack of flow, inability to repeat success, periods of creative barrenness and unevenness. All these problems amount to versions of what is usually called 'writer's block'. If the opposites do not become dynamic, do not join up fruitfully, no good writing can be born.

This leap, the confident piping of fluency that most of us will recognise, has been discussed by Daniel Goleman, among others, in his widely known book *Emotional Intelligence* (1995). In chapter six, in a section called 'Flow: the Neurobiology of Excellence', he describes the state 'where excellence becomes effortless' for athletes, as well as artists. 'Even filing clerks' can experience this flow, which is 'when . . . work is at its best'. He continues

> it is a state in which people become utterly absorbed in what they are doing, paying undivided attention to the task, their awareness merged with their actions. Indeed, it interrupts the feeling of flow to reflect too much on what is happening – the very thought 'I'm doing this wonderfully' can break the feeling of flow. Attention becomes so focused that people are only aware of a narrow range of perception related to the immediate task, losing track of time and space.

Emotional confidence again seems required, as does the help of the unconscious. Emotional intelligence itself seems to be a way of being 'attuned to the emotional mind's special symbolic modes: metaphor and simile, along with poetry, song, and fable, all are cast in the language of the heart', as Goleman says in an earlier section from chapter four, called 'Plumbing the Unconscious'.

In 'What Writers Are Like', chapter two of Dorothea's classic, she begins to show us how to achieve this flow in writing. She warns us against the image of 'wild-eyed bohemianism', which to her sounds like 'the artist's personality gone wrong', but instead offers this view:

> The picture of the artist as a monster made up of one part vain child, one part suffering martyr, and one part *boulevardier* is a legacy to us from the last century, and a remarkably embarrassing inheritance. There is an earlier and healthier idea of the artist than that, the idea of the genius as the man more versatile, more sympathetic, more studious than his fellows, more catholic in his tastes, less at the mercy of the ideas of the crowd.
>
> The grain of truth in the fin de siècle notion, though, is this: the author of genius does keep till his last breath the spontaneity, the ready sensitiveness, of a child, the 'innocence of eye' that means so much to the painter, the ability to respond freshly and quickly to new scenes, and to old scenes as though they were new . . .

This vivid passage gives us a positive view of the artist as the self-inventing child, but her central point, and the thesis of her book, is in the balance of this side with 'another element to his character, fully as important to his success. It is adult, discriminating, temperate and just. It is the side of the artisan, the workman and the critic rather than the artist. It must work continually with and through the emotional and childlike side.' The writer must 'balance' these two 'aspects'. Here is where her 'how-to' strategy begins to look revolutionary, and is still relevant now. 'The first step', she says, towards this 'integrated character' will be 'to split them apart for consideration and training'.

Here she begins to prefigure Goleman's idea about 'flow' being the inspired, childlike aspect of the writer, balanced with the critical intelligence to recognise and use what is borne, or born, from the fluency of the imagination. She talks of the experience of fluency after a 'second wind', when things come right. These are the 'everyday miracles' when work or life has a spontaneity often lacking when we begin to try too hard. It is where we allow help to come from our less-controlling side. My favourite quotation about this topic is from songwriter Neil Young, who, when asked if it was easy being as prolific as he normally was, reputedly replied, 'It's easy, as long as I don't try'. Birth has to happen like an instinct and we know it is best to have a natural birth. It is easy to neglect this in creative matters, but the essence of creativity is not made without both sides of the innocence/ experience dynamic.

In chapters three and four, she advises the writer to let the 'unconscious flow freely', as a first step. Another songwriter, Bob Dylan, talks himself of learning to allow the spontaneous to flourish in his work. In his early career, he had done this instinctively, but must have felt he was floundering a bit. Then, just before his arguably key, second breakthrough album *Blood on the Tracks* (1973), he went to art classes with teacher Norman Raeben, as recounted in chapter twenty-one of Clinton Heylin's *Bob Dylan Behind the Shades* (1991). Dylan says that the painting course taught him to do consciously what he used to do unconsciously. To do this, it seems we must allow the unconscious its proper place. The best ideas happen when we allow them to come to us, when we relax and are able to go with our own flow. Try stopping 'working' on some writing and go for a walk. Often a strong idea will present itself when your mind is not so consciously engaged.

Brande outlines techniques for allowing the unconscious to work for us. The most famous of her techniques is that of free-writing, done first thing in the morning, letting this habit become the place where the unconscious can bring forth its riches. The purpose here, though, is to remind ourselves that the creative process is just this move from one side to the other of the creative self. The freshness required comes from our being able to allow the birth of the possibility. The journey to the inner world is one of mythic adventure and what is required is a particular kind of creative courage. The writer, as she says in chapter two, creates their 'own emergency and acts on it'. In other words, for writing to happen, imagination leads to action. The action of free-writing can release the imagination to move towards a creative whole.

The split personality of the writer is epitomised in Henry James' short story, 'The Private Life' (1892). Here the writer Clarence Vawdrey is depicted as chatting wittily in a bar of a hotel, while he is, at the same time, writing away, in darkness, in his room. It is obviously a tale of the uncanny, and this is a sure sign that we are entering the mythic realm of the mysteries of birth. The opposites meet and something useful emerges.

There is a link here with a form of bipolar disorder, or what used to be called 'manic depression' and the connection seems to be the source of the old saw about genius and madness. To anyone interested in this link, the book *Touched with Fire*, by Kay Redfield Jamison (1993) explores how writers 'have always sailed "in the Wind's eye" and brought back with them words . . . to "counter-balance human woes"', as she says, quoting Canto X of Byron's *Don Juan*.

However, as Brande points out, the division of tasks is not always 'psychopathic'. For me it seems that, for us writers, these ways of being *mad* can also be ways of being *sane*, if they are handled properly and not undertaken without a sense of purpose and balance. Writing is a form of handling the double nature of the human mind and imagination in a sane and productive way.

When we look to go into the dark writer's birth chamber, with James' Vawdrey, we are likely to encounter problems of resistance, often identified as 'Threshold Guardians', especially as outlined in Joseph Campbell's essential book for all creative endeavour, *The Hero with a Thousand Faces* (1949). 'The hero goes forward in his adventure', he says at the beginning of part one, chapter four, 'until he comes to the "threshold guardian" at the entrance to the zone of magnified power'. He warns us that 'beyond them is darkness, the unknown and danger', but it is also the place where the power is to be found, where the task is achieved and the boon brought back to be born to the world.

The Roman god Janus, often seen as a negative image, is one representation of such a threshold figure. Four-faced, or two-faced Janus, seen more positively, is not an image of deception, but could be seen as the artist or writer, able to look in both directions, having both in mind, in balance, being the midwife in the midst of the creation. We are our own threshold guardians and the Janus-writer is the creative self and the renewed self in potential. The unconscious can be seen symbolically as being behind a forbidden, or hidden doorway, where everything is reversed. But here also is the place of the possibility of the boon of good work. Janus is depicted at doorways and gates with a key and a stick. The stick could be said to show the dangers of the creative adventure into the unconscious, or the discipline which is needed to access the unconscious, while the key is the safe and purposeful turning from one state to the other, where new life or meaning is achieved.

The power and purpose of the creative is illustrated with a witty, trickster-like quality in the Welsh story of Taliesin, as adapted and retold by Hilary Llewellyn-Williams. Another aspect of the two-faced guardian of the threshold, where the right password, the right attitude must be apparent from the seeker after the creative, is the playfulness of the situation. Here is the testing of our ability to play, to imagine, which might be part of whether we get the key or the stick. We must be Janus-like, moving freely between two worlds, like a Trickster figure who balances the danger and the ways in and out, balances the courage needed with the craft, the risk with the intention. We have to be up to facing the tricky nature of life that Blake shows us.

TALIESIN (adapted by Hilary Llewellyn-Williams)

Ceridwen sat outside her house stirring a cauldron with a long golden ladle. In the cauldron was a magical brew of her own devising. She had a son, Afagddu, who was extremely ugly, and although she couldn't give him the gift of beauty, she planned to compensate him with the gift of wisdom. Into the cauldron went herbs and incantations, and if the spell worked as it should, whoever drank from the brew would instantly know all the wisdom of the world, and would understand the speech of all the creatures on earth. But the brew had to be stirred for a year and a day, and Ceridwen had other work to do. She had her herd of pigs to tend to, and the grain of all the world to grow from seed.

So she appointed a blind dwarf to tend the fire with bellows, and she sent for a young boy, an apprentice of hers called Gwion, to stir the pot. She instructed him to stir the mixture night and day, but warned him never to taste a single drop. He obeyed her, thinking the brew to be poisonous: but she was afraid that if he tasted it all the power would go from the potion intended for Afagddu, her son.

The year and a day drew to its close. Gwion stirred the cauldron, thinking that soon his long task would be over: and just then, three drops of the scalding mixture flew from the pot and landed on his hand. Without thinking,

Gwion put his hand to his mouth; and immediately he was filled with all the knowledge of the world. And he understood the speech of the birds in the tree above his head, who called to him to beware Ceridwen, and flee: because by her sorcery she would know what had happened, that he had stolen the magic meant for her own son. Because now he had tasted the drops, all power had left the brew, and was now in Gwion himself.

He began to run stealthily from the place; but through her arts Ceridwen spotted him, and with a great cry of rage she came running after. And she was gaining on him with long strides. So little Gwion made use of his new powers, and turned himself into a hare, and ran very swiftly. But Ceridwen turned herself into a greyhound, and ran swifter still. Then Gwion became a lapwing, and rose into the sky; but Ceridwen became a hawk, and hunted him. He plunged into a lake and became a salmon; but she became an otter and swam after him. He leaped from the lake and became a roebuck; but she became an arrow from a bow. Just before the arrow struck he became a mouse, and ran towards a barn. She became a cat and chased him, but he reached the barn first. There he transformed himself into a tiny grain of wheat, and hid himself in a large piled of threshed grain. 'She'll never find me here!' said Gwion to himself.

But he had reckoned without the cunning of Ceridwen. She turned herself into a hen, and began pecking among the grains of wheat. Soon she spied him, although to ordinary eyes he looked identical to all the other grains. And she cackled with glee, and picked him up in her beak, and swallowed him.

This was not the end of little Gwion, however. He now became a baby in her womb, and she carried him for nine months. At the end of this time she gave birth to a beautiful child with a light shining on his brow. She had intended to destroy him at birth, in revenge for what he had stolen from her son: but when she saw him she relented, and she placed him in a leather bag, and put the bag to float in the sea.

After a short while the bag with the baby was washed up onto the shore, and a prince called Elffin saw it lying on the sand, and opened it. When he saw the baby he knew immediately from the light on its brow that here was a magical child. So he took the child home, and called him Taliesin, which means 'shining brow'. Taliesin grew to become a mighty poet, with knowledge of all the secrets of earth; and he understood the language of all creation.

This then is the story of the birth of Taliesin, the first and greatest Bard of the Island of Britain, who had the power of shapeshifting. And this is part of his song:

Primary chief bard am I to Elffin,
and my birthplace is in the region of the summer stars . . .
I was with my Lord in the highest sphere
On the fall of Lucifer into the depth of hell . . .
I know the names of the stars from north to south,
I have been on the galaxy at the throne of the Distributor . . .
I have been eloquent before learning to speak . . .
I am a wonder whose origin is unknown . . .

I am a stag of seven tines,
I am a wide flood on a plain,
I am a shining tear of the sun,
I am a hawk above a cliff
I am the fairest among flowers,
I am a god with fiery head,
I am a battle-waging spear,
I am a salmon in a pool,
I am a hill of poetry,
I am a boar, ruthless and red,
I am a roaring in the sea,
I am a wave upon the shore —
I know the secrets of the stone tomb . . .

I have been a word in a book
I have been a light in a lantern,
I have been a boat on the sea,
I have been the string of a child's swaddling-cloth.
I have been a sword in the hand . . .
I have been the string of a harp,
Enchanted for a year
In the foam of water.
I have been a poker in the fire,
I have been a tree in a covert.
There is nothing in which I have not been . . .

I have been teacher to all intelligences,
I am able to instruct the whole universe.
I shall be until the day of doom on the face of the earth;
And it is not known whether my body is flesh or fish.
    Then I was for nine months
    in the womb of the hag Ceridwen;
    I was originally little Gwion,
    At length I am Taliesin.

(Adapted from *The Mabinogion,* and from Robert Graves' *The White Goddess* (1961))

In Hilary Llewellyn-Williams' story, the cauldron is an image of inspiration at work, of brewing or cooking, where the nourishing material is prepared, where it must ferment and mature. It is the magical place of enhanced power and heat, the place of transformation, where transformations of short-comings, as in the ugly son, are possible. The mix is 'of her own devising', just as any creative work must be. The cauldron is creative birth to balance the danger of 'ugly' birth. Here the practice, the use of the cauldron, supports the original ingredients which are added, to create something new with the old power. To 'understand the speech of all the creatures on earth' is to gain insight into the ways of the world, to ways of being. This is an example, as Hilary Llewellyn-Williams says in her notes to me, of 'myth as a metaphor for universal truth'. Here the brew will give us the ability to transform, through creative endeavour, into anything we please. This is both birth and rebirth from the cauldron of inspiration. The power of writing is embodied here.

In the second paragraph we are introduced to the innocent, respectful boy Gwion, who is the unexpected, 'unformed, beginning writer, patiently stirring away without really knowing what he's doing', as she says, despite his fear. He becomes her creative son, her work, which takes off on its own energy.

Gwion's sudden and unexpected inspiration seems like an accident, but he is the one ready for change, after his patient devotion to the task. Ceridwen seems to be a pitiless Muse, who drives him on to write, to greater acts of knowledge and power. He is inspired with the essence of creativity and full of wisdom, but the world is after him and it is hard to hold the strength he has found. The fairytale trope of competitive changing is a familiar one and it is a test, or ordeal, that the becoming poet must pass. He keeps being reborn. Eventually Gwion becomes her baby and has a second birth, becoming Ceridwen's son, whether she likes it or not. His next rebirth into poetry also echoes the creative process, where the delving into the depths and the tests of transformation are rewarded. The theme of abandonment and rescue are also common tropes in fairytale and again are metaphors for the process of accessing the unconscious. For us writers, this gives the sense of endless power and possibility, if the creative cauldron is kept in process, in labour.

For the combination of innocence and diligence, coupled with passing the tests of the underworld, Taliesin is rewarded by being rescued by Elffin the prince, who recognises the gift and who allows the poetry to flourish. He is always writing, always starting again, always being born.

Llewellyn-Williams says of Ceridwen that she is 'the dangerous and pitiless force that spurs us on to write and makes us scared to fail. She is the cruel fate that gives us material to write about: losses and mistakes, misfortunes and yearnings, fears and angers. She is death that drives us on to create something of life. She takes us into the dark place of writer's block and angst and depression, only to give us something shining and better than before.'

So, in this tale we have both the ease and brightness, in Taliesin, the 'shining brow', and the difficulty of writing and the courage needed in the labour and birth, which is discussed more fully in Chapter 3. The story also links with creation myths and Chapter 4, where division is a large part of what creates worlds. The dive into the unknown, into the unconscious, into the unexpected, is, with Brande, a division to achieve transformation, to induce the birth of change, energy and fluency.

The boasting of the inspired poet might be seen as a thing of the past, as here in Taliesin's song, until we look at hip-hop and rap poetry. Public Enemy's first album *Public Enemy* (1987) gives us a good example, in 'Public Enemy No. 1' (C. Ridenhour and H. Shocklee), of a boast about the power of poetry, which is typical of the genre.

What these rappers claim is a power akin to the 'magical brew' of Taliesin! The adventurer-writer will go into the depths, where the flow of magic is available and bring back the child, the boon to the world. Then the professional in the writer will take over, helped by such poet's birth stories as that of Taliesin. He is a proto-poet or first poet and his story is there to open us to the fresh courage of each journey. Do the work, combine the ingredients, unite the depths with the world and we can feel the exhilaration writers strive for and feel the natural flow being born in us.

Writing

Hilary Llewellyn-Williams suggests: 'Using the "I am"/ "I have been"/ "I know" formula of the Taliesin boast-poem, write ten similar lines, based on your own interests: events in history, characters, heroes, stories, animals you like or fear, places real and imagined, activities . . . Exaggerate! Make it as outrageous as you like. In identifying with all things you are laying claim to them. As a writer, you can bend them to your will and transform them in your imagination any way you please.'

Another way she suggests to do this exercise is for 'each student to write one line, beginning "I am" or "I have been", then read quickly around the group. Repeat, until all have ten lines. Then read the whole thing, one line at a time, in a big circular incantation. Each still has a ten-line boast-poem to keep for themselves.'

Write about what is behind a forbidden doorway, or barrier (e.g. a thick hedge) you need to pass through.

Write a narrative which usefully combines a spontaneous person with a careful one.

→ { Write, in the first person, a defence of being two-faced, like the god Janus. }

Write about a 'rebirth', or write a comic story of a false case of being 'born again', which you could call 'There's one born again every minute'.

Reading

Blake, 'Infant Sorrow' (*Songs of Experience*), 'Infant Joy' and 'Introduction' (*Songs of Innocence*), *The Mabinogion*, tales of Taliesin, from various sources (old); songs by Public Enemy, 'The Private Life' (1892; in *The Aspern Papers and Other Stories*; all stories here about writing) by Henry James (new); *Becoming a Writer* (1934), Dorothea Brande, and *The Hero with a Thousand Faces* (1949), Joseph Campbell (critical; both essential background reading to this book).

Know the concept & you know the book

Chapter 3

◆

THE TRUTH LIES

Are his stories accurate and true? I myself never inquire about their veracity. I think of them instead as fiction that, like so much fiction, provides the storyteller with the lie through which to expose his unspeakable truth.

(Philip Roth, *Operation Shylock*, 1993, p. 58)

And it came to pass, that when Jesus had finished these parables, he departed thence. And when he was come into his own country, he taught them in their synagogue, insomuch that they were astonished, and said, Whence hath this man this wisdom, and these mighty works? Is this not the carpenter's son? Is not his mother called Mary? And his brethren, James and Joseph, and Simon, and Judas? And his sisters, are they not all with us? Whence then hath this man all these things? And they were offended in him. But Jesus said unto them, A prophet is not without honour, save in his own country, and in his own house. And he did not many mighty works there because of their unbelief.

(*King James Bible*, Matthew 13:53–58)

The title of this chapter could be hyphenated, to give another definition of myth: the truth-lies. The relation between what we believe and what is true is a complicated one, and myth contains this paradox. Myth explains, but still contains the unexpected. This is an example of the seriousness of using mythic material. There is a view that sees myth as mere whimsy, allusiveness. What do all these old stories, with strange names, have to do with us now? In the opening pages of *Healing Fiction* (1983), psychologist James Hillman claims psychology as a kind of myth-making which heals and it is well known among writers that narrative truth is different from factual truth. The overall meaning of a tale can be multifaceted, compared to a list of facts. Any form of writing can be escapism, but to delve into myth seriously is to be a more serious writer, even a more personal one.

Myth can mean both false and true together then, but the connection with the duality of the last chapter is unmistakeable. The double nature of the creative process, moving from the unconscious to combine usefully with the conscious, is mirrored in the trick of the lie that reveals the truth. Myth always works creatively on these two levels. If we tell a lie about ourselves, it reveals a truth of desire about us. Tell the truth and, if it is not acceptable to the unthinking conventions of the day, you will not be believed. The psychological truth, as revealed in dreams and imaginings, is creative lies, coming from within, containing a strange echo of deep human traits. This is close to the magic, or deep or seemingly supernatural elements of myth, achieved through our descent to the depths. We are suddenly tuned to a deeper truth, which connects the unconnected. Understanding the darker nature of the writer and of writers' truth is the next stage, and a further liberation, in the mythic creative process.

The double effect of the true world and the world which might lie, in its narrative being supernatural, or made of the imagination, connects directly with the use of the conscious mind coupled with the use of the unconscious. To make a pointed pun: the imagination, helped and informed by the unconscious, lies beneath the surface world of 'fact'.

Kathryn Hughes, writing in the *Guardian* (27.10.2007) tells how novelists had recently been criticised for writing about what they do not know, in subjects like real murders, '9/11', Islam, etc. But, as she points out, politicians would avoid these kinds of things as much as possible. It's fair to say that myth has always gone near the big taboo topics: murder, destruction, religion. Try Sophocles' *Oedipus*. Hughes writes admiringly of Doris Lessing, who was 88 when awarded the Nobel Prize in Literature, and made a politically challenging speech. The writer, especially the mythic writer, must go where others will not go, to bring back some other kind of truth, which may not be as easily palatable as the way politicians are said to speak, blandly and avoiding anything controversial. Confronting an easily held orthodoxy is a stimulating thing for us writers to attempt.

A writer must be able, like the wise fool, to blurt out the real, mythic, scary truth behind the news and also be prepared to be attacked. Writing, using myth, is not a soft, distant option, but a way of being more present. The trickiness of the fool, of the Trickster, of the writer in the unknown, is a serious thing. Myth is about extremity, not generality, finding and testing truth in its depth and slippage. Only writers know where the truth lies.

How are we to get there? Dorothea Brande says this, in the opening paragraph of chapter five, in *Becoming a Writer* (1934): 'the first step towards being a writer is to hitch your unconscious to your writing arm', adding that, with appropriate ambiguity, she hopes 'psychologists will forgive us for speaking so airily about "teaching" the unconscious'. Just as we dream of ourselves as heroes when young, the reverie of the writer is a childlike quality. Moreover, this utopian dreaming, this narrative of improvement and adventure is the basic stuff of fiction. These are the embarrassing lies we tell ourselves when young, but the source of the truth, of what is truly resonant, comes from the same source. This is more childlike, more primitive, more passionate, more violent, more sentimental – but somehow more *true* to itself and its fundamental source than any considered statement. Our bravery comes also from our childlike selves.

Getting into the habit of writing freely, allowing the true lies to flow, un-judged and promiscuous, only writing, not reading back, and doing this regularly is Brande's way of accessing the unconscious, of setting it free and letting it come to the idea of helping us. Other methods work too. An artist friend of mine talks of 'doing some bad art', getting that flowing, to get, eventually, to the good stuff. Another friend, comic songwriter Chris Wager, used to write a miserable song first, so that his whole being would flow towards cheering himself up and he was able to write something comic and life-enhancing. Personally, after Brande's time, I find the quiet padding of the keyboard and the little screen of lies the computer affords us is, once you are used to it, a nice place to slip into fluency without conscious thought. Obviously, from reading much web material, we can see the mistake some make is to say that this is the finished product. But a file I can save, but never see in solid form, as it exists only on screen, can, in its fluid, virtual way, beat the notebook or printed-out draft.

One of the problems discussed in the Introduction is the fear that myth might make you less 'original' in your writing. In chapter twelve, Brande tackles this head on. Learning from others, imitation, is how we learn craft and how we also learn the language of another's intensity with the truth, with their depth and how they achieve this through art and artfulness. Other writers give us not only their surface, their craft, but also communicate, if they are good, to something in us which is prepared for the shock of the unexpected, the deep, the raw. Try out their riffs. They speak to our unconscious too. Is this a challenge to our originality? To imitate might be like a lie, but it could be another lie which tunes us into the truth.

Our individuality is a given. Brande is right when she emphasises the fact that 'everyone is unique', so if we write honestly, using our true depths, we will not produce stories which are faked in imitation, but take a good model of how to be courageous in depth from the writers who influence us. All the best writers are *fans*, but not fans of form alone. Brande's chapter twelve has a section entitled 'Honesty, the Source of Originality'. 'If you can discover what you are like, if you can discover what you truly believe about the major matters of life' – what I might call the mythic matters – you will be able to write works that are 'honest, original and unique'. Seriousness, bravery and honesty and not being frightened of the extreme and unexpected are heroic, mythic qualities. These will make us, like the hero of *The Odyssey*, someone 'of many ways', which might well find us 'out there', as we say now, or out on a limb, with a dumb world tugging on the branch. The extreme truth can be as shocking as a lie, and will often be called a lie.

Those of us who understand myth will know by now that the way we tell the story is the key thing, as is the way we take the mythic patterns and what we make of them. Originality is a by-product of truthful work in the area of slippery realities, not something, as might be believed from the superficial world, that we can decide in advance.

The results of this work on the writing self, according to Brande in chapter sixteen, is to be able to approach what has been called 'genius'. Her 'many ways' have now led her, towards the end of the book, to what she calls 'the third person' to add to her two parts, the delver into the unconscious-self and the editor-self. She comes close here to a mythic method, where the alignment of the two sides can give access to the deepest kinds of insight and inspiration. The idea of 'flashes of insight' comes close to this extra quality. The given line, which is 'la ligne donée' of French poet Paul Valéry, means it comes from the gods, God or the Muse, Nature or elsewhere – maybe the unconscious. Writers often speak of inspiration as, partly at least, a gift from outside. Poets have the line, and fiction writers often 'the given scene', as I call it. All these are approaches to genius. What Valéry meant was that we get some small piece, as of a jigsaw, then it is up to us to fill in the rest by hard work. The two sides of the writer working together will 'learn to use' this third element, the flashes, the gifts, better, so 'genius cannot be taught', as the old saw she quotes goes, but it can be used and accessed better if the depths are available to us.

How do we get these precious flakes of useful genius-gold, which seem beyond ordinary truth or lie? A simple method of working with the unconscious has proved useful to me on a number of occasions. When I was trying, at the keyboard and sat at my desk, to think of a title for this book, I could find nothing save pedestrian stuff about myth and creativity, arranged in different orders of the various terms. *As soon as I stood up and stopped thinking,* however, a better title came to me fully-formed and *unbidden*. It was as if, having asked the question and left it alone, my practised unconscious provided the answer *in its own time*. I often also sleep on a problem of writing, asking myself for help as I go to sleep and leaving it alone to solve itself. Often the answer, the line, the scene, the sense or the key (see previous chapter for Janus symbols) is there when I wake. The magic of myth can give us a deeper truth.

Another method of access is via 'light hypnosis', as Brande describes. It is well known that trance-states, rhythms and the enchanting of singing and music have this effect, of bringing us into what you might call 'ritual space'. Repetitive activity suspends the mind and allows the fluency to work. Walking, as mentioned in the previous chapter, is also a good cure for writing problems, and can work well for 'incubation', as Brande calls it.

In chapter seventeen, she describes how, to hold the mind still, one stills the body, or suspends it in some rhythm. To get the real depth of the mind, we must likewise hold the mind still. These techniques of refreshing the mind by stillness or rhythm are well known to those who meditate. In this, her last chapter, she gives us the idea that, having been on the deep journey, we can shape our works for the world. This is where the editor-self takes over. 'Read all the technical books' about 'writing you can find. You are at last in a position to have them do you some good.'   ←

We know already, the truth, the depth, may not always be welcome. Bob Dylan's song 'The Wicked Messenger', from *John Wesley Harding* (1968), is about this. In Greek tragedy <u>the messenger plays a crucial role</u> in reporting *Narrator* <u>the key moments of the drama</u>, and Dylan has something fittingly ambiguous to say. On the surface it seems to be a lyric against telling the bad, but true, news and one that also accuses the messenger of inner falsity.

The messenger in the song is associated with Eli, who, in the Bible, was God's priest, but his sons were corrupt, but then, when old, he comes to recognise that the servant boy Samuel is God's chosen prophet. So, if the messenger in Dylan's song came from Eli, he could be Samuel, or he could be one of the corrupt sons. Whichever way, it is an ambiguous role he has, in an ambiguous time. The prophet/ messenger in the song tells bad news in an exaggerated manner. But by the third and last verse we get a sense that his words were not so inaccurate, as his prophesies come true, but the messenger also decides to be more positive in his message, in a final ambiguity. The song then seems to be about a balance of <u>what people can or will hear,</u> or their <u>unwillingness to hear</u> of the inevitable decay of life. Even God, in 1 Samuel 3, says, scarily, 'I will do a thing . . . at which both the ears of every one that heareth it shall tingle' (xi). The truth is not always welcome, but it gets our ears tingling, like Dylan does.

In Greek myth, the Cassandra story is the ultimate one of the unacceptable truth, as she is cursed to tell it, but never to be believed. When truth is painful and against popular imaginative constructs, or conventional 'wisdom', then the disbelief of the naked cry seems only too inevitable. Cassandra was loved by the top god Apollo, who promised her any gift, if she would allow him to make love to her. She asked to know the future, which seems like a good deal. Even asking for this, though, is maybe to know too much, to be like a god. If we knew the future, the uncertainty which makes life valuable, which provides the grist to our trying to live properly with the contingent, would disappear. The world would become flat. The writer must risk seeming to know too much, to be as brave as Cassandra and not be surprised if our words challenge.

Cassandra, smart and beautiful, was not even prepared to be content with this, though. She also thought she could get away with the gift without fulfilling her side of the bargain. She tried to better a god.

Apollo then, according to Lempriere's *Dictionary* (1864), 'wetted her lips with his tongue, and by this action affected that no credit or reliance should ever be put on her predictions, however true or faithful they might be'. Later, 'Cassandra was looked on by the Trojans as insane, and was even confined, so that her predictions were universally disregarded. Her beauty, however, procured her many admirers . . .' She became a soldier's mad whore in the Trojan Wars and became part of the spoils for the Greek, Agamemnon. He took her and married her, although he was already married, to Clytemnestra. Despite marrying her, he also never believed her warnings of what would happen when he returned to his first wife, who murdered them both.

Aeschylus' *Agamemnon* is the best source of Cassandra's stories and the speeches have 'the shrill declamation of prophesy', as the Philip Vellacott translation describes it in a stage direction (*The Oresteian Trilogy*, 1959).

Cruel Apollo! Why
Why have you led me here?
Only that I may share
The death that he must die!
CHORUS: She is insane, poor girl, or god-possessed,
And for herself alone makes this wail,
Unwearied in her tuneless song;
As the shrill nightingale
Unburdens her distracted breast . . . (lines discussed from 1140 onwards)

Cassandra's burden is all around her beauty, in a sense. The lie she told Apollo was taking her beauty as more powerful than the gods, then compounded by the lies told through the lust of her husband, whose first wife, seeming, from this view, the innocent party, has the same kind of lies and lusts and murder in her heart too. Beauty and the Trojan War seem to go together, as the war was said to be over another great beauty, Helen. But, if looked at mythically, or metaphorically, pride and weakness are what undoes the blessed, either by victory, beauty or love. We may not be as mad as Cassandra, or as cursed, or as beautiful, but the gift of insight is always a blessing, a given flash of inspiration. It can also be a curse, if we do not treat it with respect and if we try not to be surprised if it is unpalatable to some. This can be a sign that we are on to something. Mythic truth can be harsh and seem mad.

In the passage above, we get the tragic irony, for which trope Cassandra is a prime opportunity, of her talking complete sense, which is taken for the opposite. Her power is that she is cursed with the vision of the results of all human weakness, but is still beautiful. The cynical strength of the too well gifted is a powerful, forbidding force. We could see in her a future, feminist media-figure, seen as shrill, overlooked, but talking sense. The Chorus' response is telling, with tragic irony again showing in the phrase 'god-possessed'. They see her as selfish, shrill, 'tuneless'. As with Dylan's messenger, the news has to be told in a way which seems to have open-heartedness at its centre. A bit of modern irony is added here, as we see a view of the nightingale, that greatest singer among birds, as it was seen by some before the time of our sentiment about nature. We know now that the song is not a bewailing female, but a male seeking a mate. This again shows the ambiguity of what is true, what is musical even. All they hear is the shrillness of her cry, not knowing it is wholly appropriate to what is to come.

Cassandra, like a mad person, hears them and offers a different view of the bird:

> The lovely robe she wears
> Is feathered wings; and even
> The plaint she pours to heaven,
> Note answering note for tears,
> Rings sweet.

Even in her premonition of death, she answers and offers a sweet, temperate note, before the abrupt change, 'But I must feel/ The parting of the flesh/ Before the whetted steel'. She must have the experience before it happens. Even amid this, she is able to defend the sweetness of the sad song.

She is increasingly convincing to the audience, though not to any in the play, as she soon begins speaking in 'the quiet sadness of mourning', as Vellacott says. She is poetic in her attempt to change gear and persuade them:

Then listen. Now my prophecy shall no more peep
From under shy veils like a new-made bride, but blow
A bounding gale towards sunrise, on whose surge
A crime more fearful than my murder shall at once
Sweep into blazing light . . .

She then goes on to speak elegantly and persuasively of her gift, of her sin and her prophesy and almost convinces them by her eloquence, after telling them her story in full. Her knowledge of the corruption they live under also nearly convinces them. But this too is part of the curse of 'the God of Words', who is Apollo. Eventually, after earlier saying, 'To us your prophecies seem all too credible', the Chorus, the voice of the people, say, 'Silence, you wretched outcast – or speak wholesome words!', reminiscent of Dylan's reformed messenger. Dylan knew the self-irony of his words, just as Cassandra knows she cannot avoid the feeling of her death before it happens. There is something of the existential curse of knowing we will die here, knowing our words will not save us, even if they tell us a truth: as William Burroughs says, in the opening pages of *Nova Express* (1961), 'to speak is to lie, to live is to collaborate'. The truth 'rings sweet' but may 'blow/ A bounding gale', as it does in another song from *John Wesley Harding*, 'All Along the Watchtower'.

Cassandra's eloquence is given so brilliantly and so absolutely in vain. She speaks plain truth, in epic-style simile, in absolute self-knowledge. Yet nothing will persuade the Chorus, as the curse dictates. 'Scorned, jeered at like some gipsy quack, by enemies/ And friends alike . . .', she says, while she accepts her death: 'O gates of the dark world, I greet you as I come!' The possibilities for *writing* here are huge, the opportunity is for a tour-de-force, and Aeschylus does not disappoint. She ends with philosophy: 'Man's happiest hours/ Are pictures drawn in shadow . . . And grief itself's hardly more pitiable than joy.' The voice of truth can shine in her dark fate.

Just as Cassandra greets the darkness, the other great Greek prophet is the blind seer Tiresias, who appears in *Oedipus*, *The Bacchae* and *The Odyssey*. One of the stories of how he became blind is perhaps more baffling than the cause of Cassandra's curse, but is equally to do with sex and with knowing. In Ovid's *Metamorphoses*, Book III, we hear that he had once been turned into a woman for seven years, after hitting copulating snakes with his stick. Here snakes represent a changeability, a god-like quality, due to their metamorphic form and ability to shed skin. He changes back, after hitting the snakes again. As he is then already knowing about sex, the queen and king gods Juno and Jove ask him to say who gets the most pleasure from it, Jove saying that women do. Tiresias cannot win, obviously, but he sides with Jove. Juno then strikes him blind. The important thing here is that each god wants to give the other the less controlled role. The judgement is immaterial, but the knowingness, about sex and in being too near to the gods, of Tiresias is both his curse and his blessing, as Jove gives him the gift of prophecy to balance the curse of Juno.

Tiresias is a know-all, we might say and know-alls have blind spots. Or, Tiresias has insight, as his outer world is invisible to him. The connection with the knowingness of the unconscious is undeniable and brought to life in Cassandra and Tiresias, who negotiate the ground between the known and the invisible.

We live perhaps in a fact-obsessed world, where such dualities are, as we know they might be from the old tales, overlooked or misinterpreted. Fiction is often presented as fact, to sell it. From the Ossian stories to the Hitler diaries, we are keen to believe in facts, if that is the only way we can get the depth of myth, having lost the way to think of a double kind of truth. As psychologist James Hillman says, in part six of chapter two of *Healing Fiction* (1983), called 'Active Imagination: the Healing Art', we have 'fallen into the disease of literalism' and seek the healing of this through the myth-making process. The mythic writer can often reconnect the deeper truths to 'the facts'.

All good fiction, all good writing has its demand of truth, of honesty and courage and in that it is mythic. A poem like Allen Ginsberg's 'America', from *Howl and Other Poems* (1956) has at least this and one other mythic aspect. Addressing the nation is an element of epic, public poetry, nowadays hard to pull off, but achieved here by refusing to be one-dimensional about it. The ironic tone is unmistakeable, from the first line where he mocks his poverty, to the last, where he vows to work hard. Bloggers and whistle-blowers, in industrial and financial corruption cases, have the same kind of mythic power. My friend Nigel Burch, of London band Nigel Burch and the Flea Pit Orchestra, has a song which gives an honest alternative view of the contemporary world:

> We're soft as shit – not hard as nails
> We're frightened freaks and failures
> We're entertained by fairy tales
> And exposed genitalia
>
> *It's horrible – it's horrible*
> *It's horrible but true*

Note the knowingness, sexual as well as wider, which curses as well as blesses the knower, the writer and the listener.

John Osborne's *Damn You England* (1994) takes its title from 'A Letter to My Fellow Countrymen', which was printed originally in the *Tribune* (18 August 1961) and is against nuclear weapons. The angry energy is palpable, as is the way it enters the mythic: high-flown rhetoric, dealing with an apocalyptic situation, with a taboo, death, with disbelief and credibility, on the part of the writer and the intended audience. The letter is theatrical in the Greek, Tiresian, Cassandrian sense: 'This is a letter of hate,' he begins. 'You are MY object, I am not yours. You are my vessel, you are MY hatred.' This is a curse and still bracing to read, but full of the usual danger of not being taken seriously, while retaining its defiance. Osborne is famous for being angry perhaps, but that might be better than being famous for being scared to enter into the area of real, subtle, challenging truth, which is the mythic kind.

Poet Stevie Smith, in 'Poets on Poetry', from *An Anthology from X* (Wright, 1988) has no doubts about the demands of the Muse, these personifications of the demands of the mythic realm of writing. 'It is not the Muse who is weak, but the poet. She makes a strong communication. Poetry is like a strong explosion in the sky.' Later she says, 'Poetry is like the goddess Thetis who turned herself into a crab with silver feet, that Peleus sought for and held. Then in his hands she became first a fire, then a serpent, then a suf-focating stench. But Peleus put sand on his hands and wrapped his body in sodden sacking and so held her through all her changes, till she became Thetis again, and so he married her, and an unhappy marriage it was. Poetry is very strong and never has any kindness at all.'

Writing mythically is then both healing and powerful, as it must deal with that which is hidden, that which is changeable and that which is full of dark, even angry, strength. This is the nature of true truth, a deeper truth than we normally aspire towards. One of Jesus' few witticisms, shown in the epigraph above this chapter, shows how much power belief and disbelief have, how much power the imagination has and our tendency not to be able to hear the truth of the inner world, of the mythic world. Even the son of God, in this story, is affected by his own neighbours' capacity for literalism. A prophet, 'not without honour, save in his own country' reminds us of Cassandra, Tiresias, Ginsberg and John Osborne. We look to writers to enter the depths of truth, however 'unspeakable' it is, as Roth says in the other epigraph. The writer works towards hidden truths which lie beyond our normal perception of the world of fact, so we can get a glimpse of it. To paraphrase Conrad in his preface to *The Nigger of the 'Narcissus'* (1897), this kind of truth is the kind that we are inclined to forget. It is the job of the prophet, the seer, the fool and the writer to remind us.

Writing

Write Cassandra's story in the first person, placing it in the contemporary world, using the setting of a blog, or a whistle-blower's diary, or a therapy session, kiss-and-tell, etc.

Is irony the lie that tells the truth? Write of a 'true word spoken in jest' incident.

Write a fictional 'horrible but true' confession.

Write a half-affectionate, half-ironic, half-angry poem to your country, your workplace, your town, your street etc.

Cassandra Song (by A.M.)

As soon as your lips are wet you lie
but the truth may be hidden there by and by
Love made you say the intemperate thing
but it also inspired the truth you sing

When you placed your hand upon her hip
and she turned to you and kissed your lip
it was as if you were turned inside-out
and it made you sob and it made you shout.

Write about falling in love with someone who makes you lie, and tell an unwilling truth (as above).

Write a version of Aesop's 'The Boy Who Cried Wolf', reversing the moral, 'no one believes a liar, even when the liar tells the truth', to 'people only believe lies'.

Create a character, using the Cassandra myth, where there is a trigger of some unfair treatment, when the character is young, innocent or naïve (as Apollo's treatment of Cassandra), which results in a truth telling role, for good or ill.

The Truth Game: In a writing group or class, get everyone to write one lie and one truth about themself. Read them to the group, without revealing which is which. Then, perhaps later, going round again (best if the group do not know this third stage at first), ask each person to reveal which is the lie. Ask them what the lie reveals of their mythic, symbolic, metaphoric or psychological truth. Write, using the lie or the truth, or both as a starting point.

Reading

Aeschylus, *Agamemnon*, in *The Oresteian Trilogy* (old): Allen Ginsberg, 'America' (new): Dorothea Brande, *Becoming a Writer* (chapters 5, 12, 16, 17) (critical).

Chapter 4

◆

MYTHIC NAVIGATION DEVICES

Now that we have been to the depths and ambiguities of the inner world and allowed the mythic nature of creativity into our scope, it is time to take a step back. Myth can also provide patterns to aid understanding of this inner creativity. This, in turn, can give us patterns of narrative which can help us create stories and movements through our writing. These can give contemporary work added resonance. Myths show us maps of creativity and maps for creativity. Myths connect our inner worlds, and can help towards connecting our writing, towards the outer world. This is the world that seeks shape, meaning and depth in common experience.

We tend to ignore the inner world, which may be a tendency of all humankind, or, as some would say, a particular feature of our age and culture. It has been the job of the writer, the artist, to address this problem of our time, where once it might have been the job of religion or of a shared belief in a narrative of life's changes and contingency. Materialistic, rational individual achievement, as the direction we follow might be described, keeps us from thinking in anything but a literalistic way about ourselves. But all these viewpoints, ours and older ones we wonder towards, are the myths we live through, whether we think it is myth or not. We are mythic creatures and we can easily fail to tell the good stories. The good stories are those that add depth to our lives, help us to see the ambiguities and repressed truths described in the last chapter.

When we talk about myth, we are talking about what we have in common, about shared feelings, as well as experiences. Religion, art, psychology and stories, symbols and metaphors all move from the individual towards the communal. This process, of going out towards greater understanding, is both an inner and an outer journey and myths tend to describe, or provide a map of the journey.

'We think we are so civilised, so highly educated . . . It is farcical', writes D.H. Lawrence in 'The Novel and the Feelings' (*Phoenix*, 1936). This is because 'our knowledge . . . never gets there. It leaves us feeling lonesome inside'. In fiction, he says, we have to listen, but 'not listen to the didactic statements of the author, but to the low, calling cries of the characters, as they wander in the dark woods of their destiny'.

The first step to thinking mythically, that is symbolically and metaphoric- ally, is to learn to see beyond the surface to a more multi-dimensional world. Ralph Metzner says that, in his work, symbol

> is more likely to be an object or a thing; whereas *metaphor* stands for a process that extends through time. Thus, the tree is a symbol of the human being, standing vertically between heaven and earth, linking the upper world of Spirit with the lower worlds of Nature. On the other hand, the growth of a tree from seed to flowering maturity is a metaphor for the growth of the individual, the unfolding of the human life from seed-conception to full creative expression. The path, or road, is a symbol of development of consciousness; travelling on the road is a metaphor for the process of expanding the horizons of awareness.

While this quotation, from the introduction to *Opening to Inner Light* (1986), has a 'new age' style, for the writer it does drive home the idea that all is mythic, that the world can be seen in symbolic and metaphorical terms and that these terms describe thought that links the inner world with the outer. Further, it tells us that the symbolic and metaphorical language of myth can be a knowable map of the 'dark woods of . . . destiny' which Lawrence says we need to listen to. Even in the basic fertility symbol, which is one strong root of the natural world lending the mind a pattern, Metzner uses the words 'creative expression'. Writing, creativity and this most natural, primal metaphorical process already go together.

Ted Hughes, in his influential essay 'Myth and Education' (*Writers, Critics and Children*, ed. Fox, 1976; *Winter Pollen*, 1987), takes the reader through these stages of thought in a convincing and inspiring way.

> A child takes possession of a story as what might be called a unit of imagination. A story which engages, say, earth and the underworld is a unit correspondingly flexible. It contains not merely the space and in some form or other the contents of those two places; it reconciles their contradictions in a workable fashion and holds open the way between them. The child can re-enter the story at will . . . In attending to the world of such a story there is the beginning of imaginative and mental control.

Note how similar the dimensional aspect Hughes reaches for, in 'earth and underworld' corresponds both to Metzner's 'upper' and 'lower' worlds and how the mythic thinking is enabled by seeing below the surface in process, just as the images of fertility enable us to do. A hint is given here too by Hughes of the healing power of the process of insight, of the opening of possibilities, where 'contradictions' are 'workable' and 'the way between them' is 'open'.

Hughes goes on to describe how one word can open the whole story, like a switch. He gives the example of the story of Christ, as this is a story, a myth, that we know, where all that we know about it is triggered by the one word. 'The voltage and inner brightness of the whole story is instantly there . . . just as you need to touch a power-line with only the tip of your finger.' He emphasises here how much these mythic connections are 'a kind of wealth' and, for me, proves that we understand the world in stories, in these shared tropes, more than we realise. There is an episode of *Star Trek*, where an alien tribe communicate only by reference to their myths. Like all good fantastic writing, the premise contains a truth about our own world that we tend to overlook. 'Behind' that simple word like 'Christ', which might trigger a known story, 'stands not just the crowded breadth of the world, but all the depths and intensities of it too.' Hughes is not teaching us a religious lesson, but rather a lesson of how powerful the stories we live through can be for us.

The key thing for us here is that the mythic stories can act as a connection both between the individual and the wider world, but also within the individual mind as a way of reflection and openness to meaning. 'Stories think for themselves, once we know them. They not only . . . light up everything relevant in our own experience, they are also in continual private meditation, as it were, on their own implications', he says.

The strangeness of the inner world, both in itself and in its strangeness to us, shows how we neglect the imagination. Mythic devices, like dreams, stories, symbols, religion, metaphorical patterns and patterns of nature give us a visual guide to the invisible world we inhabit along with the outer world. We can think about this 'inner world', but 'only in a detached way', but 'the eye of the objective mind is blind' to it. We tend 'to solve the problem by never looking inward'. This, Hughes says is 'the modern ideal', but 'the more rigorously the ideal is achieved, the more likely it is to be disastrous'.

Towards the end of Hughes' wide-ranging essay, essential reading for those interested in these subjects, he makes his claim for myth:

> The myths and legends . . . can be seen as large-scale accounts of negotiations between the powers of the inner world and the stubborn conditions of the outer world, under which ordinary men and women have to live. They are immense and at

the same time highly detailed sketches for the possibilities of understanding and reconciling the two. They are, in other words, an archive of draft plans for the kind of imagination we have been discussing.

Their accuracy and usefulness, in this sense, depend on the fact that they were originally the genuine projections of genuine understanding. They were tribal dreams of the highest order of inspiration and truth, at their best. They gave a true account of what really happens in that inner region where the two worlds collide. This has been attested over and over again by the way in which the imaginative men of every subsequent age have had recourse to their basic patterns and images.

Here Hughes means the Greek myths, but myths 'all over the world' are 'uncannily similar'.

With Hughes' essay, the single most important, accessible text for understanding the concept of mythic patterns is Joseph Campbell's *The Hero with a Thousand Faces* (1949), where he traces the way all myths relate to one heroic story and one basic pattern. A version of Campbell's structure specifically for writers, though mainly aimed towards screenwriting, can be found in Christopher Vogler's *The Writer's Journey* (1992; revised 1996), which will be looked at in the next chapter.

Campbell's thesis is that there is only one story in the world, albeit with some nineteen stages, reduced by Vogler to twelve. Christopher Booker has produced a book called *The Seven Basic Plots* (2004). I have a book from an earlier era called *The Thirty-Six Dramatic Situations*, by Georges Polti (1921). If we look at the old tragedy/comedy axis, we could say there are only two basic stories. Either way, we begin to get a sense of absurdity. Like any threshold, to use Campbell's own methods to defend him, these reductions, or patterns can be a key to open us up, or a stick to beat us away or to beat ourselves up with, inasmuch as they hold the gateway to the use of myth as a map of the inner world. The map can be used for good or ill and there are many maps to choose from, and many realities in the inner world.

Campbell mentions three basic stages of inner journey: 'separation-initiation-return' (Prologue: The Monomyth, 3). Ralph Metzner talks of 'stages of the mystic path' in the introduction to *Opening to Inner Light*, which could be used as another framework for writing, using well-known stages of understanding or growth as a basis. 'In Christian mysticism the stages are (1) awakening; (2) purification; (3) illumination, visions; (4) "the dark night of the soul"; and (5) union with the divine.' He also gives us a three-stage version, from the Gnostics: 'awakening', 'revelation' and 'recollection'. He describes these as examples of 'developmental sequence'. I have used a three-stage story structure in writing exercises, based on the words Conflict, Crisis and

Change. All these formulas, and I am sure you can find some others, can work as merely formulaic or as useful, basic maps which bring the invisible inner world into visible and vivid focus. The potential for seriousness is great, as this mythic work connects us as individuals both to ourselves, but also to what we have deeply in common with the rest of human life. Like most truly serious matters, as we discovered in the last chapter, it is easy to get it wrong, but all the ways work if animated with creative respect. Putting these patterns under contemporary writing can give them extraordinary hidden power and their patterns can be used to create a narrative, or shape, around a basic idea.

It may be that any number between one and thirty-six, say the twenty-two cards of the Tarot major arcana, will do, but the important point is that patterns reveal connections, processes and archetypes. The map is useful, but it is the journey itself that really counts.

Perhaps the most obvious correlation we find in the outer world that seems to map the inner is that seen in nature. The pastoral mode of poetry, where nature is the metaphor for such things as innocence, love and the alternative to the city, is a long tradition. Likewise the Romantics rediscovered the wild, natural world as their route to the sublime. Animism is the word for a religious belief in the life-force as non-material, in the world itself being alive, while ecology has brought us to the idea of Gaia, which represents the alive-ness of the earth itself. Jonathan Bate's *The Song of the Earth* (2000) is an example of what is called 'eco-criticism', writing on literature where nature is seen in balance with culture. Our inner world, in this way, is seen as part of nature, in that it lacks self-consciousness and contains a wild law of its own, which we try to trace, so we can learn about ourselves. Just as we talk of darkness and light in understanding, so we see the simple parallel in day and night. Here we are thinking in mythic images of Nature and Culture, of Chaos and Cosmos, or what we control and what we cannot control.

Negotiations in these two parallel worlds of Inner/Outer, Nature/Culture, Chaos/Cosmos or Mythic/Literalistic is a tricky one, as we can see from the dangers of the formulaic. The narrow pride of the human mind resists the process and goes for the quick formula, without the true meaning. Where should we look but to myth itself to show a map of this at work? The story of Actaeon is a mysterious and cruel-seeming story. Actaeon, briefly, is a hunter who comes by accident upon the goddess Artemis, or Diana in Roman myth, who is bathing. She turns him into a stag and he is hunted down and killed by his own hounds.

Ovid's version, in Book III of *Metamorphoses*, struggles with why Actaeon was punished. Actaeon

> Sprouted outlandish antlers and the hounds,
> His hounds, were sated with their master's blood.
> Though, if you ponder wisely, you will find
> The fault was fortune's and not guilt that day,
> For what guilt can it be to lose one's way?

A.D. Melville's translation (1986), our main text here, suggests an ambiguity in the last line quoted here. Ted Hughes' modern take, from his *Tales from Ovid* (1997) starts with this point, 'It is no crime/ To lose your way in a dark wood'. The dark wood motif is a reference to Dante's *Inferno* (part of *The Divine Comedy*), but here the ambiguity still stands, as this is the dark, lost place of sin for the Christian pilgrim in Dante's epic.

Actaeon's story seems mad and unfair at first glance. But if we look at the link to the balance of nature, the connection to the proper approach to the mythic and to the threshold which can be a trap or a doorway to a deeper understanding, we might get a bit closer to what this myth-map could have for guidance.

Diana is also a hunter and her attitude to hunting is in contrast with that of Actaeon, from the start of the tale. He sounds like a businessman, when we first meet him in Ovid, at the end of a successful day: 'Come, friends, our nets are wet, our javelins/ Drip with our quarries' blood; today has brought/ Success enough . . .' There is a song by Leonard Cohen which has a businessman portrayed as a hunter in the city, in a kind of reversed pastoral, but equally primal, reduced world of money ('Hunter's Lullaby', *Various Positions*, 1984). Both have a sense of greed, of material possessiveness, which is hardly in tune with the natural world, in Actaeon's 'success' and abundance of 'blood'. Cohen's commentary on the mythic hunt is apt, where something is irredeemably lost to the hunter, or to his blindness. Actaeon has lost his sense of respect for nature, but the natural world has a surprise for him, and proves itself stronger. The story begins to seem less mad, less unfair.

Looking at the next scene, where we meet Diana, the contrast could not be greater. 'There was a valley clothed in hanging woods/ . . . / Sacred to chaste Diana, huntress queen.' Diana is 'chaste', in other words, she has the innocence of nature still upon her. She lives in harmony with the natural world, being a 'huntress', but within the world of nature. The inner and outer world are balanced. 'Deep in its furthest combe, framed by the woods,/ A cave lay hid, not fashioned by man's art.' The sexual symbolism here is obvious and this is a tale of the rapacious, of experience which leads to arrogance, versus innocence and harmony. Here, the female could stand for the inner world of nature and innocence and the masculine for the world which seeks rational control of the delicate balances of nature. The balanced unconsciousness of innocence is confronted by the hunter in an unrealised fault, a seeming guilt-lessness, an ignorance of the inner world, which leads to his doom.

While mad and unfair might be the first reading, Cohen's song lyric might give us a clue to the kind of inevitable feel of most mythic tales. Here, no one can prevent the loss of self, which arises from this hunter's need for possession.

The dark wood of the story, as well as in connection to Dante's allegorical meaning in the first line of *The Inferno*, is the place of change, of fear, but also of transformation. The transformation can go either way. If Actaeon is seeking the natural, he does it in an unnatural, or too cultural way. His con-scious pride and control seek to dominate the place where these rules do not apply, but where only the mythic can help.

Diana is bathing in a spring, another symbol of renewal and fluent har-mony with nature, and here Ovid reminds us that she is also called Titania, the Queen of the fairies, as in Shakespeare's *A Midsummer Night's Dream*. Actaeon is lost, but for once 'wandering idly', but his way of thinking is not ready for the place of change and chance. He sees her, she throws water in his face. Water is the element of change, of movement, of fluency. Actaeon seeks nature, but he has also sought to dominate it. When nature then comes to him, he gets more than he can handle. It is not his intention to be in the wrong, but his attitude has not prepared him for the power of what is in tune with nature, with the mythic.

This is emphasised even more by the change into a stag, where, inside, he is the same man: 'All changed except his mind', Ovid tells us. Here, the bal-ance between the inner world and the outer is disrupted and distorted. He is beastly without natural grace, he is intelligent, a great hunter, without a sense of respect for what he cannot control. He is us, the normal person in the world, unversed in the mythic dualities that might have saved or transformed him into something worth being. The fact that this mad story, or story of ordinary madness, makes us feel he is hard done by is one of its great strengths.

'"I am Actaeon, look, I am your master!"' he attempts to shout, but, as a stag, he has no voice, making the obvious writerly connection for us. His violent death follows, with one last death cry, 'Not human, yet a sound no stag could voice', as if in his dying he finds one moment of voiced balance.

Ovid's tale ends as ambiguously, as teasingly as it began: 'some believed/ Diana's violence unjust; some praised it,/ / Both sides found reason for their point of view.' But we know the story is not about reason, but what reason cannot address, which is the negotiation between the mythic and the logic, the unconscious and the conscious.

Ted Hughes version, 'Actaeon' (*Tales from Ovid*, 1997) offers a vivid, sexualised version, but Hughes offers too the picture of the inarticulate, unbalanced man. 'His only voice was a groan // From the grief of a mind that was still human.' Is it a stretch to see Actaeon as a personification of writer's block? Not if we understand that writing needs the depth of the unconscious to nourish it into voice.

Hilary Llewellyn-Williams' version of the story in *Scintilla* (2002) brings it brilliantly into the world of writing.

Actaeon

The Hunter enters the forest
alone and on foot, so sure is he of the ground
and its beaten paths
where he slips his hounds, all under his command

skilled and well-equipped
with a quiver full of arrows, a well-sprung bow
never afraid to venture into the thickets

He is here to start an idea –
to pursue images, to run them down,
to harry them from the bushes and bramble-clumps
transfixing them as they bolt for the canopy
sunlight netting their wings

His hounds retrieve the ragged feather bundles
he strings them together as trophies and drags them home

Sometimes his triumph is greater:
he'll capture a larger beast, a black boar
with wicked tusks, a hind with velvet ears
her liquid eyes rolled back
as the dogs snatch at her throat

Women fall for this Hunter

Perhaps it's the sweat from the chase
the forest musk
or it might be the lingering spoor of blood
that draws them clustering hoping to touch him

But of course he must run freely among the trees –
this is my place he says *my right place*
and he wants to name every single thing
he sees, and lay claim to it

Nothing shall be forbidden
because he is a great artist
nothing escapes him, it's all fair game

If only he had gone as a gatherer
grateful for what the glades and dingles offer
rootling around on the forest floor
and listening to the creatures

he might not have blundered on the pool
of shadows and believed what he saw there:
the image of a woman bathing naked
the image of his desire

He imagines he is shielded
crouched behind the hedge of his intellect

He should have noticed the bearskin spread on a rock

What a shock when he feels those claws rip
at his human shape, letting the stag out!

None of his metaphors can save him now

His four legs stagger, his muzzled antlered head
is filled with the baying of hounds

The arrogance of this writer, depicted in the poem, is palpable, as the poet offers a version where he gets what he deserves. The phrase 'letting the stag out' gives a picture of the repressed victim, the repressed innocence, in the knowing man. Here, Actaeon's coldness is shown, rather than that of the seemingly too-pure Diana. This poem is a good example of how a mythic thread can be taken and unravelled to make a thoroughly modern poem. The resonance could work without knowing the myth, but some of its depth derives from the story behind it.

If we have both Diana, the balanced, and Actaeon, the unbalanced inside us, then the obvious contemporary connection with Diana, Princess of Wales would be that she is both the pure, in the public mind, and the worldly hunter of fame turned hunted and hounded, so the story is combined or reversed. Either way, it seems to be a version of the same kinds of problem.

Actaeon sees what he should not see, behind the veil, for which he is not truly prepared. Just as the key can also be a stick, if the entrance is not approached correctly, so we can go wrong if we seek to force our creative worlds to conform. As Mark Hedsel says, in chapter one of *The Zealtor* (1998), 'the secret knowledge is protected ... the seven veils of Isis were protected by seven magical seals. At each stage, a magical name must be pronounced to protect the one who dares such sacrilege.' In chapter two of Metzner's *Opening to Inner Light*, he tells us that 'it is an ancient notion that the world perceived in our everyday consciousness is a shadow play of appearances, illusory and evanescent, and that the transformation of consciousness involves transcending or dissolving this web of images'. Metzner also quotes William Blake as his epigraph here: 'If the doors of perception were cleansed everything would appear to man as it is – infinite' (*The Marriage of Heaven and Hell*, [Plate 14]), to which we could add the next line, 'For man has closed himself up, till he sees all things thro' narrow chinks of his cavern.'

The shock and the change of Actaeon, as he sees the harmony of the world and the wild, being unprepared for it, brings us a vision of ourselves as we use or misuse our mythic navigation devices. We confront the balances of the demands of writing in a human world just as unbalanced, or perhaps more so, or unbalanced in our society's own particular way. The easy harmony, the easy and potent power of the goddess Diana, who is also the goddess of the moon, of the symbol of the darker light, is the one we must cultivate, where we bathe in the waters that flow freshly at every turn. We live in a world as full of shock: flood, fire, famine, war, pollution, apocalyptic and financial destruction. But the world is equally full of hard-to-look-at, hard-to-find visions of renewal and true harmony. Dealing with the shocks of change by understanding the patterns of change is what the mythic navigation devices help us to do. We name the right names as we find the truth beneath the veil of conscious illusions, as the patterns of mythic structure, in an echo of how Gestalt psychology works, seek to resolve themselves into a state of creative equilibrium.

In the last few pages, with a poet's help, we have explored a myth for its meaning and its relation to creative and mythic balances. What is useful to us, as writers, is that these myths and their patterns respond to being taken seriously. If we chose, say, the story of Odysseus' son Telemachus, from *The Odyssey*, we could have seen how his story too, as he sets out to find his lost father, has many writerly echoes. We writers go in search of stories, of motifs, which give us the aid we need, just as Telemachus finds help in a goddess, disguised as a Mentor. Find the myth, and the patterns will be our maps and the truth will deepen with what we bring from our own world to them.

Writing

Rewrite Actaeon's story sympathetically, depicting him as a writer. He writes wildly one night, thinking he is at last inspired. In the morning, he sees that what he has written is inarticulate nonsense. He is one 'who scribbled all night rocking and rolling over lofty incantations which in the yellow morning were stanzas of meaningless gibberish', as Allen Ginsberg has it ('Howl' I, *Howl and Other Poems*, 1956).

Write a tale called: Lovely Nature bites you in the ass.

Find a mythic narrative structure, or part of one, from the ideas or books mentioned above, or analyse one from a favourite myth/ story/ poem. Choose the stages and use them to create a new work. Example: Conflict, Crisis, Change.

Write about a shock or change created by being 'in the wrong place at the wrong time'.

Write about hunting, nudity, Princess Di, the gift of speech being taken away, trespass, an encounter with a goddess or god or becoming your obsession by losing real connection with it.

Is hunting a good thing? Or does it depend on how you do it? Write a tale that makes the point.

Write about contemporary hunting as a sacred act, for food or sacrifice, gone wrong.

Use Ralph Metzner's 'tree' or 'road' symbols to describe a person, or a journey.

Reading

'Diana and Actaeon', in Ovid's *Metamorphosis*, Book III: 131-265 (old); 'Actaeon' by Ted Hughes and 'Actaeon' by Hilary Llewellyn-Williams (new); Ted Hughes' 'Myth and Education', from *Winter Pollen*, 1987 (critical).

Chapter 5

◆

DARK MATTER

THE DARK-TO-LIGHT (by A.M.)

I was in my first job, which seemed like a prison to me, working for the summer in a coal-yard. The job was dirty and the humour of the other men working there was dark and limited. I felt like a boy, vulnerable and narrowed. My tired hands were getting hard and black and I couldn't play my guitar.

One evening I went to see my girlfriend, and she was unkind about my hands. My tiredness seemed to lead to an argument that went on late into the night.

I had missed the last bus by hours, so I had to walk the six miles back home in the dark. I had always been a bit afraid of the dark, but at first I welcomed its feel. I felt like everything had been stripped away and I enjoyed being free of society in the empty, grey road. I tried to hitch-hike, but the last few cars passed without stopping.

The night began to get darker and I began to feel light-headed. I kept walking but I didn't really know exactly where I was anymore. I must be somewhere in the forest, I thought, but still on the road that runs through it. But the road seemed to be turning into a track. I kept going, afraid to go back, or compelled to go on. My own sense of purpose had gone, but some purpose carried me on.

I was on a bumpy path and the dark was getting darker and darker.

I felt I was dissolved, consumed, vulnerable, threatened, but the purpose carried me. There must have been fog, or mist, as well as dark, and I couldn't see my hands. My feet felt like they might fall anywhere, into an endless, leg-breaking hole, for instance. I was in motion, carried forward, but the purpose was dark.

Then, a shock. Ahead, I could make out a line of men, lit by blue points of light that shone, eye-like, from either side of dark helmets. They were still and silent, dressed in dark Army clothes, and there were five or six of them. They were pointing large, black guns at me.

I stopped moving, feeling foolish as well as insubstantial and speechless. Then, and I can't explain why, I just walked past them, breathless with fear, stumbling, shambling around their stillness. A few steps on into the dark, I heard them moving away.

Just as suddenly, the fog seemed to clear and a huge moon appeared. I was beside the old main road through the forest. I felt dizzy and feeble, as the fog lifted.

Then, as if in a mirror, I saw myself walking towards me, from the opposite direction. This felt uncanny, although it did not seem to shock me.

I was a dark, heavy being, carrying a weight of dark with me. I thought of my father. I felt like I might fall down.

I heard a car coming from behind me and turned away from myself. Foolishly, I stuck out my thumb. The car stopped. It was a neighbour, an older woman I recognised but did not know personally. She addressed me by my name, as if she knew me well, and opened the passenger door for me. The other self had vanished.

Inside the green car, she had some loud, rhythmical, modern classical music playing, that I now think might have been Stravinsky's *Rake's Progress*. She didn't speak again till she dropped me by her tall house, about a half-mile from my Dad's place.

Then she said, 'Now you're nearly home, you're newly home', and laughed.

***

This story is another dark tale, like that in the previous chapters, like that of Actaeon and of Cassandra, where an encounter is connected with darkness, with a kind of death, or death-in-life. But the story of creativity via myth is essentially one of 'Dark-to-light', begun by darkness, but entering a new lightness. To think about Actaeon is to think about Diana, whose name comes first in the Ovid version, who is also Artemis, the goddess of the light-in-dark, the Moon. She is the wild protector of innocence, who runs with the beasts, and who demands a high sacrifice. Her central aspect as a goddess could be seen as working through initiation.

Initiation is another mythic rite, the essential rite of passage, from the ordinary world into that of the mythic, from the profane to the sacred, from the veiled to the world of symbol and metaphor. It is death and rebirth, the old year giving way to the new, the dark to the light. The stages of initiation could also be seen as another version of mythic structure.

We are everywhere surrounded by versions of initiation, just as mythic thinking lurks often behind the veil of the everyday. An initiation is a bringing-in. Education is an obvious example, with 'big school', university and degree ceremonies in robes to make the graduate feel newly part of society. Births, marriages, deaths, funerals, hen and stag nights, gang ordeals, comings-of-age and 'proms' are all initiatory rites, as is all education.

The story above is mostly about the first stages of initiation, as they are spoken of by the world of magic and of myth. The first is a loss of self, a separation from the world. The second is a descent to find the opposite, and the third is a sense of union. These three stages sit well beside the Crisis, Conflict, Change pattern, or Campbell's 'separation-initiation-return'. The story is straightforward, contemporary in tone and incident, but infused with myth nonetheless.

As in the stories of Cassandra and Actaeon, there is an element of sexual initiation always present, as an encounter with the opposite. There is also the threatened sense of loss of the past self, which may be an actual threat, ceremonially, or the element of the myth which has the potential to be dangerous, because it has the potential for change. Childhood and youth are initiations towards maturity.

One element of the story is about the finding of the opposite or twin self, or of seeing the self anew. In chapter eight of Robert Graves' *The White Goddess* (1961), Hercules has 'his spear-armed twin, who is his *tanist*, or deputy', who later 'succeeds him and reigns for the remainder of the year, when he is [also] killed by a new Hercules'. This is the renewal of the self.

The element of a union of opposites is achieved in the third stage of initiation rites. The opposite for the initiate is a goddess of light-in-dark, played in the story by the woman who gives the lift and says '*nearly* home' and '*newly* home'.

The hero of Campbell's monomyth is also, of course the initiate, the writer, always, when on a new journey of writing, starting afresh, entering dark matter. Self-renewing, the initiate is the heroic archetype for writing. This beginner, and writers are always beginning, is well illustrated by card one of the Tarot's major arcana. 'The Magician' represents the creativity of the youthful adventurer/ hero in this archetypal character. He is part conjurer, part chancer and above all he is game, 'up for it'. He is the writer about to create, the hero about to set off on a symbolic journey.

This is a more positive view of the protagonist than that of Cassandra or Actaeon, one that gives us creativity in all its serious energy, without which nothing fresh happens. In John Sampson's *Gipsy Folk Tales* (1933), the 'Jak', the storyteller, was often a smart hero of his own stories. This is Sampson, quoted in the foreword:

> Always the youngest brother and generally despised as a fool, he is cunning and fortunate rather than wise and deserving and, while possessed of courage, somewhat of a braggart and a liar. His virtues are reverence for his mother, generosity in sharing food with strangers and helpfulness to men or animals in distress. In love affairs, in spite of his uncouth manners and slovenly appearance he is always successful over his rivals . . .

This is the mythic adventurer, the writer, with his tricksy role and his bohemian atmosphere, seemingly a more traditional figure, rather than merely an invention of Romanticism.

In the first story of the book, 'The Fiery Dragon', 'Jack' kills a giant who is stealing cows, by using help from a dwarf, who is generous with advice after Jack shares his food with him. The 'mentor' figure of the dwarf, the courage and the proper generosity make sure the hero wins the battle with the antagonist, or villain, the giant.

Fairytales and folktales often have these questing heroes who match the positive view of the creative force. The negative force of the antagonist is the evil twin with whom the self-renewing adventurer/ writer must engage. In James Hillman's *Healing Fiction* (1983), the beginning of section three gives us another positive story of encounters with the darker, negative side. A patient 'dreamt of an unknown young man in white shirt and green cap who was in prison'. This man was 'scruffy and moved jerkily like a mime or an acrobat or "someone who is crazy"'. The patient had the desire to release him. After being told to try to talk to him, the patient reported resistance and her own anger with him, but she persisted.

After observing each other in silence, he puts his head in her lap and she asks him non-judgemental questions about how he is, while realising that what he wants is to be comforted only, to be accepted. Eventually he speaks, saying, '"Thank you. I have been alone so long. I won't go crazy now."' She has accepted an aspect of herself.

This conversing with the imagination, with the inner and opposite self, where the 'Jack' of the tale is the occult one, rather than the writer/ speaker, is an example of how writers can balance their adventures. Mythic and personal depth can be found, via the archetypal encounter with the opposite.

Campbell's stages of the mythic adventure, or creative journey also include these Jungian archetypes, one type of which, the 'threshold guardian', we have already met. Christopher Vogler, in *The Writer's Journey* (1996 edition) gives a list of the 'most common' archetypes to be met on the Campbell-mapped journey, in the 'Archetypes' section of Book One. These are The Hero, The Mentor, Threshold Guardian, Shapeshifter, Shadow and Trickster. Jung himself says, in 'The Shadow', from *Aion* (1959; 1968) that

> the archetypes most clearly characterised . . . are those which have the most frequent and the most disturbing influence on the ego. These are the *Shadow*, the *anima* and the *animus*. The most accessible of these, and the easiest to experience, is the Shadow, for its nature can in large measure be inferred from the contents of the unconscious . . . The Shadow is a moral problem that challenges the whole ego-personality . . . To become conscious of it involves recognising the dark aspects of the personality as present and real. This act is the essential condition for any kind of self-knowledge . . .

This Shadow could be the giant met in battle, the inner writer waiting to be let out, and the Shadow has 'an *emotional* nature' and 'a kind of autonomy', as Jung says in the same passage. The Shadow has much in common with the monster, inasmuch as the monster is a creature of the unconscious, showing what is repressed, or, more creatively, what is trying to be said.

For the writer, the monster is the figure on which all that cannot be said can be projected, just as it is for the audience. Monsters have power because they cannot conform to anything but their monstrosity. They are the larger-than-life aspect that insists that life must be larger than our conscious control allows. Monsters can seem one-dimensional, but these manifestations of Shadow are not so simple.

Take the monster with many limbs or heads, for example. As Tom Chetwynd points out,

> 'mythical monsters with many heads such as the Hydra, Scylla, or Ladon [are] . . . one force [that] has many appearances or projections in the outside world. For every head that is cut off, two more appear: symbolism points to the mistake of trying to tackle dark Shadow problems in the outside world without coming to grips with them inside first. However hard you try to eliminate a problem . . . it will occur later in another form, possibly worse'.
>
> (*A Dictionary of Symbols*, 1982)

This illustrates the adaptability of the monster/Shadow to give body to what is hidden and also, for a writer, the immense power of the imagination.

Projections of the imagination tend to work with size as an additional metaphor and the shadow can also be a twin, uncannily alike to us, or a huge thing, or, of course, a tiny thing, like an imp. Small creatures of the imagination are often powerful and their size can represent something which seeks its full form, or full expression. The unconsidered, telling detail of the small creatures shows us secrets we might easily overlook. The dwarf, in the Gipsy story 'Feiry Dragon', holds a key secret to overcoming the giant, who is the monstrous projection of greed, amongst other things.

Tennyson's poem 'The Kraken' (1830) gives a fabulous picture of a sea-monster. The sea is often used to represent the unconscious, so, for the poet, this huge vehicle of repression becomes very powerful in a mere fifteen lines, like a slightly monstrous sonnet.

> Below the thunders of the upper deep;
> Far, far beneath in the abysmal sea,
> His ancient, dreamless, uninvaded sleep
> The Kraken sleepeth: faintest sunlights flee
> About his shadowy sides: above him swell
> Huge sponges of millennial growth and height;
> And far away into the sickly light,
> From many a wondrous grot and secret cell
> Unnumber'd and enormous polypi
> Winnow with giant arms the slumbering green.
> There hath he lain for ages and will lie
> Battening upon huge seaworms in his sleep,
> Until the latter fire shall heat the deep;
> Then once by man and angels to be seen,
> In roaring he shall rise and on the surface die.

I wonder if someone has used *The Latter Fire* as an apocalyptic title of a world ended by global warming or by nuclear holocaust. Feel free to try it. The size of the Kraken, 'huge', 'enormous', 'giant', gives no hint of his harmlessness. All he does at the end of his life, and ours seemingly, is roar and die. He seems to have more to do with the timeless, the 'ancient', 'millennial', 'ages' which define him. Here the poem seems to have something in common with Shelley's 'Ozymandias', where the 'antique land' holds things 'which yet survive' and messages of how the past has been betrayed by the present. Both these poems are about the present being haunted by the Shadow of the greatness of the past, and somehow betraying it. They are poems of anxiety about what the world is coming to, while it ignores the strength of what it suppresses. This is why these poems, in the proper mythic way, still seem relevant in their messages, as well as their monstrosity.

As Christopher Vogler says, in his section on 'Shadow', in *The Writer's Journey* (1992; revised 1996), such shadows 'represent the energy of the dark side, the unexpressed, unrealised, or rejected'. He quotes the publicity for the film *Ghost of Frankenstein* as his epigraph: 'You can't keep a good monster down!' Aspects of the self or the story that 'we have renounced or tried to root out', but that will not go away, are balanced by the notion that 'the Shadow can also shelter positive qualities that are in hiding or that we have rejected'. These aspects are given to 'villains, antagonists, or enemies' and, likewise, these can be out for the hero's destruction, or, in the case of 'antagonists', sometimes on the same course but moving in a different direction. What is interesting for the writer is how closely the Shadow is linked to the hero and how the opposites speak of each other and therefore are closer than a simplistic reading (or writing) might assume.

Vogler links the Shadow to other archetypes. 'If the Threshold Guardians represent neuroses, then the Shadow archetype stands for psychoses that not only hamper us, but threaten to destroy us.' It may also represent our own inner struggles, but always has the potential for damage, for violence. 'Many Shadow figures are also shapeshifters, such as vampires and warewolves', he adds here.

Dramatically, the Shadow offers 'a challenge' and a 'worthy opponent' for a writer to use. It also acts as a test for the hero, in an extreme, or potentially destructive situation. 'A story is only as good as its villain' is another old true truism called on, to give the 'good', especially for the writer, view of the Shadow, again. The Shadow has 'challenging energy'. It need not merely reside in one character, but can manifest itself, like the multi-headed Hydra, in any of the characters in a story, such as in the hero's internal conflict. The Shadow can also be 'doubts or guilt', selfishness, self-destruction and the 'death wish', or pride and abuse of power.

Any character can become the Shadow half of the hero and this is especially true of love relationships. Dark heroes, like Heathcliff, or what Vogler calls 'shady ladies', can represent the repressed side of the hero, the destructive force that repels but attracts in its opposition. Seduction can be an attractive evil that leads to danger. Georges Bataille's *Literature and Evil* (1957) is the book to read here, for the thirst of all human life for evil, as this manifests itself in writing.

An example of a shadow figure who combines another archetype could be a Threshold Guardian who represents an accumulation of past difficulties, which, in turn, present a problem to be confronted. 'The "Facing of the Shadow" implies the realisation of the reality of the subconscious mind and the acceptance of material often at variance with that of the conscious mind', as Dion Fortune says in the 'Esoteric Glossary' of *Applied Magic* (1987). 'The "Dweller on the Threshold"', she goes on, 'represents the *entire* past of the individual . . . it is therefore the aggregate of *all* his Shadows. The "Facing of the Dweller on the Threshold" is the confrontation.' Here the Shadow is shown as a metaphor for time, which prevents the protagonist living in the present. It is one's 'own averse character rising out . . . into seemingly independent life'.

This is a good example of how the mythic functions, not, as some suspect, to make us live in the past, but to help us live in the present and to cope with changes that make this possible – to be 'newly home'.

'Shadows need not be totally evil or wicked', either, Vogler reminds us. They need, for the purposes of depth of character, to be given redeeming features. They can be attractive, as in the dark men and dark women of lustful projection, or they might have a hidden weakness or kindness, as well as the possibility of beauty. What they always do have is a kind of power, an energy that can transform a piece of writing. They might also be 'vulnerable', or even 'frail', vessels of difficult 'moral choice', as Vogler says. Shadows think of themselves as heroes: 'from his point of view, a villain is the hero of his own myth'. Men who think of themselves as being right, and Vogler points to Hitler here, are just as 'sincere' as the hero, often perhaps too serious, too convinced of their rightness, like a hubristic tragic hero.

The Shadow may be destroyed in battle, but can also be 'redeemed and turned into positive forces'. Vogler adds, 'the Shadow shelters the healthy, natural feelings we believe we're not supposed to show', such as 'healthy anger or grief'. It can also represent 'unexplored potential' and the path we did not take.

In 'The Dark-to-Light' the Shadow is also a darkness, an experience as well as a self, so the process becomes a metaphor for the archetypal. The Shadow can be shown in a place, a thing, a feeling, if that element challenges the identity of the protagonist towards facing a dark side, or a change.

These days, as Karen Armstrong says in 'Look on the dark side of life' (*Guardian*, 21.2.04) there is a cultural imperative to 'think positive', as people say. We tend to ignore the darker aspects of life. There is a tendency to view faith as a consolation. In our own time, negative aspects of the world have been suppressed and have come back to us in terrorism. She concludes that we should acknowledge darker things or they will return to us in monstrous shapes. It is worth reminding ourselves that the musical form of the blues is a cathartic form, one that gets us outside of our troubles, giving them an external form. This is again confronting the Shadow.

The dark matter of the Shadow calls for a symbolic death of initiation. The writer, seeking renewal, grapples with this dark, both in writing and in subject. The writer must descend to find the opposite, and the union with what is suppressed brings new energy to the writing and to the world, through the interplay of these archetypes.

To the one-dimensional mind, the dark matter or monstrosity is to be feared, but writers nurse their monsters, as the best *fiends* might prove best *friends* in the writing. The writer sees the monstrous in the 'good' and the good in the 'monstrous', and understands that this is the initiation into new strength. The job of renewal is then one of re-visioning, in both the work and the process of creation.

Writing

Think of someone who is your opposite – who hates what you love, for example – and write in their voice and in the first person, about yourself.

Write about a positive, smiley, sunny TV-style person who has a hidden Shadow side.

Write about a Shadow as a place, time, thing, journey or atmosphere.

Write about the renewed time after confronting the Shadow, when all looks fresh (see the poem 'Life' by George Herbert, for a positive view of living, confronting temporality in a positive way).

Write about an apparently evil, or monstrous person who brings, or initiates a positive good.

Reading

The speeches of Satan in Milton's *Paradise Lost* (old); Mary Shelley's *Frankenstein* (1818) or a film version (new); *The Writer's Journey* by Christopher Vogler (critical).

Chapter 6

◆

LATE HEROES

If we think of a 'Guitar Hero', we might well picture a preening, pretentious posturer who thinks himself possessed by loud genius. Meanwhile, the rest of us snigger quietly to ourselves. On the other hand, we know, from popular entertainment, that people seem to have a need for some kind of hero. The hero could be a joke, but it is a joke people cannot quite stop taking seriously. It may seem to us too late for a mythic hero, like Odysseus, with all the heroic virtues, including that of being superhuman. But behind the unexplored and easily dismissed term there is some truth waiting to be uncovered. As with so many mythic ideas, the heroic lurks under the surface and has much resonance for writers, as it remains something to do with the struggle to lead a good life.

In literary terms, of course, the meaning of the word has been reduced to indicating a principal character in a work. In the public sphere, heroes are what you get in comic books, movies and figures of fantasy. With 'superheroes' in ludicrous costumes, they are not to be taken unironically. We no longer believe in such one-dimensional characters in real life. So, reduced and ridiculous on all fronts, where is the heroic to be found? This is our subject.

One answer is in the journey of the writer, as we have already been discovering. This may not be the hero as man of action, but there is a precedent for seeing the writer, undertaking a quest for truth, to be the bringer-back of the boon that will renew the world. In the proper mythic way, this also brings back the word 'hero' to its Greek roots, as being closest in meaning to 'protector', as Eric Partridge suggests (*Origins*, 1966). Myths protect the human world from its tendency towards barrenness.

Like the good monster you cannot keep down, the hero is a mythic archetype which is hard-wired into human beings. Because of our trouble with the concept, this does not mean the hero is a redundant, passé figure, but rather that trouble itself gives us a clue of a mythic slipperiness of meaning the writer can explore.

Let's turn to the hero of many myth-smith writers and writers on current energy in myth, Joseph Campbell. In *The Hero with a Thousand Faces* (1949), he gives us some old heroics that we can still use, and some clues as to why it is not too late.

In part three of 'The Monomyth', called 'The Hero and the God', Campbell gives us the basic formula of the hero myth, 'separation–initiation–return: which might be named the nuclear unit of the monomyth'. As indicated in previous chapters, this is an initiation, but one into the heroic. He explains this further: 'A hero ventures forth from the world of common day into a region of supernatural wonder: fabulous forces are there encountered and a decisive victory is won: the hero comes back from this mysterious adventure with the power to bestow boons on his fellow man.' He gives examples from Prometheus and Jason, but the epic example he gives comes from *The Aeneid*, where Aeneas goes into the underworld, at great risk and through great danger, where 'all things were unfolded to him'. This epic heroic journey must have also appealed to Dante the poet, hero of his own epic, where the journey through hell becomes the journey of the poet, as much as that of the pilgrim.

Also illuminating is Campbell's use of the story of Buddha. Important here is the element of humility, as Buddha 'moved as a beggar through the world'. This is not the hero as joke or cartoon. It is opposite to how many might see the outdated believer in the heroic, which might be a military-type, a war-monger or possible fascist. One of the aspects of the warrior hero in epic poetry is, like Odysseus, the ability to go in disguise. The writer can be the hero in disguise of symbol and metaphor, just as the heroic element of the writing may hide itself in a small illumination, a point of light in the dark. The late hero always, you might say, must move 'like a beggar through the world' in the clothes of the mocked, the shadowed, the disbelieved. Buddha triumphs towards enlightenment through contemplation and meditation, not through literal battles.

Doubt, we might say, then, is an element of the heroic too. Buddha 'doubted whether his message could be communicated', but 'was persuaded to proclaim the path', as Campbell reports. What he communicates, as emphasised in a footnote, is the '*way*'. The 'way' can be told, but the goal can only be achieved by taking the journey. This is important for writers because it explains why the creative process is the path to mythic truth. The doubt and humility are again emphasised by Campbell, when he says that 'the really creative acts are represented as those deriving from some sort of dying to the world; and what happens in the interval of the hero's nonentity'. This is so that the return is made, having been 'reborn . . . and filled with creative power'.

The final test for Campbell's hero is the returning phase, which is often the hardest and trickiest. 'If the hero . . . like Prometheus [who stole fire from the gods], simply darted to his goal (by violence, quick device, or luck) and plucked the boon . . . then the powers that he has unbalanced may react so sharply that he will be blasted from within and without – crucified, like Prometheus, on the rock of his own violated unconscious.' Prometheus was famously condemned to be chained up and have his liver eaten by an eagle every day, the liver being regenerated, and eaten again. This is the heroism of contemporary celebrity, for example.

The stages of the return are a mythic pattern, quickly outlined here by Campbell and worth quoting as another structural pattern. '(1) "Refusal of the Return," or the world denied; (2) "The Magic Flight," or the escape of Prometheus; (3) "Rescue from Without"; (4) "The Crossing of the Return Threshold," or the return to the world of common day; (5) "Master of the Two Worlds"; and (6) "Freedom to Live," the nature and function of the ultimate boon.' We need, but do not want to hear, what we repress. But the writer/ adventurer brings a needed message of renewal, despite all odds.

The old mythic stories and the popular stories of today's entertainment 'represent the action as physical', as Campbell says, while 'higher religions show the deed to be moral'. Just as it is a path and not a goal, Campbell tells us to remember it is not 'attainment but reattainment, not discovery but rediscovery'. We are on the journey of self-rediscovery: 'the godly powers sought and dangerously won are revealed to have been within the heart of the hero all the time. He is "the king's son" who has come to know who he is and therewith has entered into the exercise of his proper power . . . From this point of view the hero is symbolical of that divine creative and redemptive image which is hidden within us all, only waiting to be known and rendered into life.'

Now we have been to where we feel the presence and importance of the hero, we can begin to examine some of the aspects of the heroic in a useful way. What is a hero like? What is a hero for? Who are our heroes anyway? All these are good writing assignments. Campbell has already answered some of this by implication in what a hero does, but the etymological and literary history of the term reveals other patterns.

The word, like the literary role, starts with 'superhuman strength, courage, or ability, favoured by the gods', as the *OED* tells us. The second meaning is one of war: 'martial achievements' and 'noble deeds; an illustrious warrior'. Subsequent meanings diminish through 'greatness of soul' and achievements, 'subject of an epic', or 'chief . . . personage' in a literary work. It is worth noting that the *OED* ends its entry with the American phrase 'hero-to-zero', which is 'a sudden decline'.

Likewise the literary history of the term charts a decline. Lorna Sage, in an entry from *A Dictionary of Modern Critical Terms* (edited by Roger Fowler, 1987) talks of the problem of the hero being seen as separate from 'dramatic context' and tells us that 'getting rid of the "the Hero" seemed a critical necessity', where one-dimensional greatness upstaged understanding of literary structures. However, she identifies 'a continuing ambivalence', where 'the concept seems inescapable despite its extra- or anti-literary overtones'. As she says at the beginning of her incisive, short essay, 'the hero is not easily demoted from his mythic status'.

The story of the hero in literature is then one of decline, just as it is in the meaning of the word itself. The epic hero gives way to the tragic hero, to mock epic, then to the anti-hero. This decline is a decline in faith, a decline in belief, where the mythic element is the nagging reminder of some, seemingly, older strength, yearned for, yet not trusted anymore. The absence of the hero in 'realist' fiction is an example of both its strength and its weakness, as it struggles to be itself a heroic form.

The old heroic virtues of courage, adventurousness, moral strength, persistence, being close to the gods and hence to nature (as opposed to culture) can then, for the writer, be linked to being disbelieved (as Cassandra), troubled and clever (as Odysseus), but being possessed by a kind of simplicity which can overcome decline (as in the term's history).

Here we are getting closer to what a hero is like, which is human, but on a big scale, where the human struggles with how to be virtuous, which may not be obvious, but may well be simple. What is a hero for? To remind us of the possibility of the simple and the good, which has to be earned by experience of the mythic journey.

If we then ask ourselves who our heroes are now, we might be a bit stumped, if we are being serious. We might say Nelson Mandela perhaps, but, for the most part, our current version of heroic decline is in the absence of a public sphere in which to believe or take seriously. My own heroes are writers, naturally, and there is, in the literary history of the hero, a precedent for this.

Dante was the hero of his own epic, *The Commedia*. While some critics say *Paradise Lost* has no hero unless it is Satan, or Christ and Epic poetry must have one, perhaps the hero is the author, John Milton. The 'grand style' and the writing of an epic at all has the smack of the heroic about it. The writer, as mythic hero-adventurer, shares in the heroic and seeks to rescue the term from its tendency to decline. The oldest written Epic we have, that of Gilgamesh, has him lamenting in verse over the death of the Shadow figure Enkidu, when 'with the first light of dawn he raised his voice' to lament (N.K. Sandars' translation, 1964). If a hero can be a writer, then a hero must be someone who can bring us an earned reminder of a nourishing truth, however small or unlikely that truth or character might appear.

There is a current band called The Mock Heroic (I know one of their Mums), which I always think is a great name. What mocks the heroic, like Pope's Mock-Epic *The Rape of the Lock* (1712), calls us to examine where it really lies, as in questioning guitar-hero status, for example. The Mock Heroic's Ralph Simmonds is a very good player, by the way. These are just two examples of how the hero has continued to be a big theme and how its critique has called forth its lack. In examining how writers have played on this, we can see the usefulness of this central mythic concern. Here is Tennyson:

Ulysses

It little profits that an idle king,
By this still hearth, among these barren crags,
Match'd with an aged wife, I mete and dole
Unequal laws unto a savage race,
That hoard, and sleep, and feed, and know not me.
I cannot rest from travel; I will drink
Life to the lees. All times I have enjoy'd
Greatly, have suffer'd greatly, both with those
That loved me, and alone; on shore, and when
Thro' scudding drifts the rainy Hyades
Vext the dim sea. I am become a name;
For always roaming with a hungry heart
Much have I seen and known; cities of men
And manners, climates, councils, governments,
Myself not least, but honour'd of them all;
And drunk delight of battle with my peers,
Far on the ringing plains of windy Troy.

I am a part of all that I have met;
Yet all experience is an arch wherethro'
Gleams that untravell'd world whose margin fades
For ever and for ever when I move.
How dull it is to pause, to make an end,
To rust unburnish'd, not to shine in use!
As tho' to breathe were life! Life piled on life
Were all too little, and of one to me
Little remains; but every hour is saved
From that eternal silence, something more,
A bringer of new things; and vile it were
For some three suns to store and hoard myself,
And this gray spirit yearning in desire
To follow knowledge like a sinking star,
Beyond the utmost bound of human thought.
This is my son, mine own Telemachus,
to whom I leave the sceptre and the isle –
Well-loved of me, discerning to fulfil
This labour, by slow prudence to make mild
A rugged people, and thro' soft degrees
Subdue them to the useful and the good.
Most blameless is he, centred in the sphere
Of common duties, decent not to fail
In offices of tenderness, and pay
Meet adoration to my household gods,
When I am gone. He works his work, I mine.
There lies the port; the vessel puffs her sail:
There gloom the dark, broad seas. My mariners,
Souls that have toil'd, and wrought, and thought with me –
That ever with a frolic welcome took
The thunder and the sunshine, and opposed
Free hearts, free foreheads – you and I are old;
Old age hath yet his honour and his toil.
Death closes all; but something ere the end,
Some work of noble note, may yet be done,
Not unbecoming men that strove with Gods.
The lights begin to twinkle from the rocks;
The long day wanes; the slow moon climbs; the deep
Moans round with many voices. Come, my friends.
'Tis not too late to seek a newer world.
Push off, and sitting well in order smite
The sounding furrows; for my purpose holds
To sail beyond the sunset, and the baths
Of all the western stars, until I die.
It may be that the gulfs will wash us down;

It may be we shall touch the Happy Isles,
And see the great Achilles, whom we knew.
Tho' much is taken, much abides; and tho'
We are not now that strength which in old days
Moved earth and heaven, that which we are, we are;
One equal temper of heroic hearts,
Made weak by time and fate, but strong in will
To strive, to seek, to find, and not to yield.

Tennyson's 'Ulysses' (1842) takes a small incident from the twenty-sixth canto of Dante's *Inferno*, where Odysseus (Ulysses is the Roman form of the Greek name), sets out on a last journey as an old man, long after his epic journey home, as portrayed in *The Odyssey*. On the surface this is just one of the poet's works 'on classical subjects', but Tennyson makes the hero address the deficiencies of his own time. At the centre of the heroic is the balance between the individual and the communal. While, in *The Odyssey*, the hero's personal qualities suit his adventurous quest, in peacetime the cunning and ruthless champion has no role. This alone tells us something about the modern world Tennyson was observing, where science and progress ruled. The individualism that Ulysses possesses, which served the world so well in the past, now seems destined for redundancy at best. The question the poet asks is, where is the place for the heroic in the modern world?

'How dull it is to pause, to make an end', he says, and it is the end of the heroic which makes life dull. Most telling is his portrait of his son, who is the leader of the peacetime: 'Most blameless is he, centred in the sphere/ Of common duties' and while 'He works his work,/ I mine'. The denial of the heroic is to deny part of the self: 'that which we are, we are'. The conflict between the two halves of human nature, one being neglected, is something the mythic is used to addressing. While Ulysses avoids, studiously, criticising his son, he really accuses him of dullness and the heroic part of the human mind must have its way. Though 'the long day wanes', even so, '"Tis not too late to seek a newer world'.

We can share with the Victorian reader a need of the heroic, even while living in a 'civilised' world. But we know we can feel too safe. The poem still works, as we have not accommodated the heroic into our own safe world. For us, it might seem to return in a corrupted form, that of rampant individualism and all the violent negativity which modern youth is heir to, we might say. The heroic is stolen from us by mere terrorism, perhaps. Understanding that the heroic impulse is an old one and towards a source of true strength, in our own writing we can address our version of the problem.

Another Victorian poem grapples with what we seem to have become:

Dover Beach

The sea is calm to-night.
The tide is full, the moon lies fair
Upon the straits; on the French coast the light
Gleams and is gone; the cliffs of England stand;
Glimmering and vast, out in the tranquil bay.
Come to the window, sweet is the night-air!
Only, from the long line of spray
Where the sea meets the moon-blanched land,
Listen! you hear the grating roar
Of pebbles which the waves draw back, and fling,
At their return, up the high strand,
Begin, and cease, and then again begin,
With tremulous cadence slow, and bring
The eternal note of sadness in.
Sophocles long ago
Heard it on the Aegaean, and it brought
Into his mind the turbid ebb and flow
Of human misery; we
Find also in the sound a thought,
Hearing it by this distant northern sea.

The Sea of Faith
Was once, too, at the full, and round earth's shore
Lay like the folds of a bright girdle furled.
But now I only hear
Its melancholy, long, withdrawing roar,
Retreating, to the breath
Of the night-wind, down the vast edges drear
And naked shingles of the world.

Ah, love, let us be true
To one another! for the world, which seems
To lie before us like a land of dreams,
So various, so beautiful, so new,
Hath really neither joy, nor love, nor light,
Nor certitude, nor peace, nor help for pain;
And we are here as on a darkling plain
Swept with confused alarms of struggle and flight,
Where ignorant armies clash by night.

'Dover Beach' (1867) by Matthew Arnold is an even more elegiac evocation of the sense of lost strengths, but the poem finds its heroic spark, like so many must do now, in love, which seems sometimes the last realm of the heroic, or even of the mythic. Here we have a return of the mythic, but in a negative sense of its dark confusion, where the heroic age is long forgotten, like 'faith', with 'Its melancholy, long, withdrawing roar'. The world promises much, but has no true strength to offer and the lovers can only find the heroic in their particular love, when they find they 'are here as on a darkling plain/ Swept with confused alarms of struggle and flight/ Where ignorant armies clash by night'. Even the realm of war has made its return in monstrous form and the heroic is only available in the personal realm.

These two Victorian works of loss amid the gains of 'civilisation' still speak to us of the loss of the heroic, of the tendency of the heroic to become lost, to become corrupted. They address the loss with a heroic effort of mind, to gain some element of strength from addressing the problem.

Ted Hughes' 'Famous Poet', from his first collection, *The Hawk in the Rain* (1957) deals very directly with the writer as a hero, or seeker of the heroic. His magic is gone, he seems like a trapped animal, and as dumb as a novice, proto-hero writer, like a questing being, as embodied in the Tarot card of the Magician. He created something once, but he cannot do it any more. His youth had brought him to a heroic pitch, yet now he is as one in ruins, because he cannot do this trick again, despite his fame. This poem seems then to be a direct descendant of Tennyson and Arnold, inasmuch as it seeks the heroic in an unheroic time, where the hero is lost to the world.

Again, like most of the mythic themes we are exploring, once you begin to see it, you see it all around. Just as sci-fi is a realm which deals with the epic and the mythic, so another genre which examines a less-safe past, the Western, has a habit of exploring the heroic. A favourite of mine from this genre is *Lonely Are the Brave* (Miller, 1962), based on the novel *The Brave Cowboy* by Edward Abbey (1956), with a screenplay by Dalton Trumbo. Kirk Douglas plays a heroic cowboy of the old school, trying to live the old way in the trivial and rule-bound modern world. He is told by his friend's wife that his world is unreal and that he cannot hope to survive.

He is unable to believe in the reality of the contemporary world, which is depicted as absurd, trivial and destructive, just as in the other post-heroic texts above. His relationship with his nervous horse shows his attachment to the spirit of a kind of humane freedom, denied by the brutal or narrow laws of men. When his horse is killed, as he crosses the road to make his escape to the freer world of Mexico, we have a last glimpse of him being carried into an ambulance. The driver who hit him asks the ambulance man if the cowboy is about to die, to which comes a reply about filling in forms about the accident, which is a last glimpse of how empty the world has become. The last thing we see is his abandoned cowboy hat on the rain-swept highway.

Earlier in the film, Jenny, his past love and friend's wife, tells him that men cannot get beyond their foolishness. By this she means they have not been able to face up to the post-heroic world. This is one example of how the concern with the heroic was to became a central question and focus of both the women's and men's movements and in recent discussions of gender. Vogler, in *The Writer's Journey* (1992; revised 1996), is at pains to emphasise that 'as used here, the word [hero], like "doctor" or "poet," may refer to a woman or a man'. Books like *Women Who Run with the Wolves* (1992) by Clarissa Pinkola Estes can supply the writer with a reconnection to the heroic via a holistic and ecological view of the world.

Robert Bly's *Iron John* (1990) gives an especially mythological view of the lack of true initiation and positive elements of the heroic in men. He uses the Grimm's tale 'Iron Hans' (tale 136) to structure the process of initiation. The book has been mocked and criticised, especially by intellectuals, but offers to the writer a redefining and poetically suggestful reading of the way men are in the contemporary world. 'The images of adult manhood given by the popular culture are worn out', as he says in the first sentence of his preface. This is an invitation for him and for any writer to offer an alternative view, which Bly then does, to compelling effect.

We tend to believe we are in a post-heroic age and, in writing, the anti-heroic has been in the ascendant, since, at least, *Notes from Underground* (1864), Dostoyevsky's persuasive depiction of the hero as dissenter from the modern, rational world. This, of course, is still heroic, just a version of heroism in a guise that makes sense in the contemporary world, against the grain, which is how the heroic works anyway. The unnamed 'underground man' is the hero of protest, who is stuck in the deep, dark part of the hero's quest. His irrationalism is a protest against the bland materialism of his time, bringing back the fertility of ruthless, cunning honesty to a climate where that is neglected. The anti-hero is a comic hero, celebratory where there is no true celebration, showing the bitterness inherent in the hero-less world.

From the beginning of the text there is a kind of taking on of the world's madness. 'I am a sick man . . . I am an angry man. I am an unattractive man . . . if I don't have treatment, it is out of spite' (trans. Jessie Coulson, 1972). This is comically depressing, but the subtext is heroic. In an age that values the rational, he argues for the leavening of irrationality to prove life is not mechanical. In chapter one, section eight, he says, 'What does reason know? Reason knows only what it has succeeded in finding out . . . while man's nature acts as one whole . . . consciously or unconsciously . . . and though it is nonsensical, yet it lives.' Our clinging, whether we like it or not, to the irrational, he characterises in a definition of mankind, which says man is 'a creature that has two legs and no sense of gratitude'. By the end of the book, he claims the heroic outright, when he says, to his invisible audience, 'Perhaps I turn out to be more alive than you'. Three paragraphs earlier he explains that 'A novel needs a hero, and here all the features of the anti-hero . . . have been collected', but this is justified because 'we have all got out of the habit of living'. This is anti-hero as hero, or, put another way, hero as Shadow, or hero in the underworld or underground. One archetype appears in the guise of another, as appropriate to the time.

Songwriter Jim Eldon's song against the idea of the 'superhero', the repository of the ego-heroic, sees the heroic in the everyday. 'There isn't any Superman' (*Golden Arrows*, 1991) begins:

> There isn't any Superman
> For you to be less super than
> The world is run by Joyce and Stan
> We stand or fall by little men

Later, he says:

> There isn't even greater men
> Who rate above the rest of men
> Kings and Queens are Joyce and Stan
> There isn't any superman

If the hero is the individual who expresses an individual point of view, but for the benefit of all, then Jim Eldon's assertion of the anti-heroic is a kind of modest heroism.

For the writer, defining the truly heroic is a heroic quest in itself. In a time when individualism, for the West, is, apparently, the prime focus of desire, the role of the heroic seems set against itself. The true individualist would never accept individual wealth and apparent, material freedom as being any kind of heroic freedom. The public world, if you do not know your neighbours and if the streets are full of people ignoring each other, while each talk into their machine of private matters, is a place where the heroic is appropriated for the purpose of selling.

So, in a sense, the sphere of negotiation which Tennyson wrote about, where the adventurous had to leave the dull but worthy public sphere, is no longer so clear-cut. The heroic has been falsely, commercially appropriated by the public sphere, so that neither seems to exist, except as images to be sold, where crime and celebrity seem versions of the same bad myth.

The above paragraph sounds like a depressing picture of the post-heroic, but the point is that the appearance of infertility is just the situation with which the mythical hero has always had to struggle. The heroic is the bringing back of life to the lifeless world. The ecological model, the eco-hero might be a sphere where this is possible for writing. The writer then is someone who deals with these mythic journeys back towards creative life.

The heroic path is the most difficult, but this is again always the case. The two- (or multi-) dimensional hides behind the veil of the one-dimensional, as in Jim Eldon's song. The hero acts when the world is 'on the point of ruin', as Campbell says, in 'The Hero and the God', from *The Hero with a Thousand Faces* (1949). The anti-hero is the hero inasmuch as he is the debunker of the one-dimensional, or the fake-heroic. The antihero leaves it possible for the truly heroic to emerge. The hero as an archetype is always in danger of idealisation, trivialisation and utopianism. We mistrust, rightly, the fascistic tendencies in ourselves, but we tend to replace the heroic with nothing or with vanity. When we reject this, we get the hero as scapegoat in a rejected leader, who, after all, has only reflected our own vanity. The one-dimensional, negative aspects of the heroic illustrate no more than a lack of creative imagination and a lack of a sense of the possibility of goodness.

Despite the valid criticisms of 'hero worship', as in the love of the great, rather than of the actions of the great, Thomas Carlyle, in *On Heroes and Hero-Worship* (1840), is aware of the dangers of the one-dimensional hero. 'These days' heroism is seen as 'finally ceased'. If you 'show our critics a great man', they will 'bring him out to be a little kind of man', as he says in the first of the lectures that make up the book. But it is 'difficult to do well in any age. Indeed the heart of the whole business of the age, one might say, is to do it well' (Lecture II). He takes on Mme Cornuel, who said that no man is a hero to his valet, by saying that it takes a heroic attitude to see a hero (Lecture V). We know, via P.G. Wodehouse's Jeeves, that a valet may easily also be a hero. Writers need to find the heroic against the odds.

So it always seems to be too late for a hero, but when it is too late is exactly when the hero is needed, is due, is called for. You could say it is never too late for a hero. The time of the hero is the post-heroic time, by definition. Just as the idea of the hero has been called too 'simple' for today, so the need for true simplicity is called for. The heroic is only available to the community capable of recognising the heroic. The stage of the journey where the hero must be able to overcome resistance to the boon is the hardest one. We live in a time when 'those great co-ordinating mythologies . . . are now known as lies', as Campbell says during the final chapter of *The Hero with a Thousand Faces*, in 'The Hero Today'. At the end of this chapter, he says, in challenge to the writer, 'it is not society that is to guide and save the creative hero, but precisely the reverse'. The moral quest of the hero and of the mythic writer is for the god-like aspect of us all, the liveliness of life. This struggle is also about the simple moral worth of the human world, so the heroic, as religions and Greek tragedies have often suggested, is paradoxically, close to humility.

Writing

Using the 'separation, initiation, return' motif, write a work, or an idea for a work, about a hero of today. Start by describing the place of separation where the heroic quest reveals itself to the potential hero.

Describe a most unexpected hero, one that suits an especially non-heroic, or fake-heroic aspect of our time and who fights for a wider view of virtue.

'Heroic deeds upon a puny scale', is a phrase with which Virgil describes the lives of bees in his *Georgics*, Book IV. Write about a small act of heroism, such as one beginning, for example, 'Armed with a dozen eggs and a bottle of Irish whiskey, she returned to the party on her bicycle, and completely revivified it . . .'.

Create a hero who moves from a Shadow figure into a more heroic stage.

Write about an anachronistic heroic type, adrift in a world that cannot understand such an attitude.

Describe a hero (for example, a celebrity) who is abandoned in the one-dimensional view of the heroic, who moves towards the truly heroic, via an ordeal.

Reading

The Odyssey (old); *The Brave Cowboy*, by Edward Abbey (new); *The Hero with a Thousand Faces*, by Joseph Campbell, especially 'The Hero and the God' (critical).

Chapter 7

◆

HAPPINESS WRITES

Practical Comedy for writers in an age of Tragedy

'The Things that Make us Happy/ Make us Wise' (end of Chapter 1, John Crowley, *Little, Big*, 1981).

If the heroic is possible in this seemingly dark time for myth, then we must move from the world of shadow and unheard prophets, from abandoned heroes and ordeals into that other sphere of the mythic, which is the other side of tragedy and the other side of darkness. This is the world of light, of enlightening and the world of comedy, of the festive, of the happy end. Knowing the darkness is to recognise the seed of light. The Greek root of the word 'comedy' means, at essence, a celebration, a party, a festival. This making happy is the mythic route we will follow in this chapter. Greek comedy was originally connected with Dionysus and with fertility. This comedy is serious mythic stuff. The happiness or the happy ending is then the defining element of comedy, including Shakespearean comedy.

Have we been brainwashed by literature and, heaven forbid, by Creative Writing courses into thinking that you cannot write about happiness? Happy families are all the same, only miserable is interesting, says the Russian propaganda, by old *War and Peace* himself, Tolstoy, in *Anna Karenina*'s (1876) first line. This was writing your own excuse for miserablism up front, so assertively as to brazen out or exclude any questions. It *sounds* irrefutable, but it is, with a bit of thought, as banal in its overconfidence, as saying the opposite, which, on consideration, is probably more true. Misery is dull and tends to be all the same. That could be one way of starting to write happy perhaps, but why does it still feel taboo to us to try?

Why we cannot do happy is to do with why we cannot do a happy ending. We can do comedy, but not so convincingly the festive kind that ends in a wedding, such as we see in Shakespeare, except in an obviously escapist way. If we do not do comedy in that sense, if we do not do happy, what do we do? We do tragic comedy, which laughs at folly. We do gloomy without redemption, where the truly tragic, which involves heroic greatness, is only half-done at best. And the rest, even at its best, we think of as showbiz. We say the heroic and the happy are for escapism only, or for an ending that is not really the end, in truth. We feel this in the air and we want to be honest as writers, as if the last heroic act is telling the awful truth. Can we go beyond that? Can we dare think that this kind of thought just might be the reverse side of sentimentality, merely cynicism?

Nietzsche's own 'Attempt at self criticism' about his *The Birth of Tragedy* (1872) asks some big questions: 'Is pessimism *inevitably* a sign of decline?' and again, 'Is there a pessimism of *strength*?' Perhaps we feel both of these are true. Our strength in the West is all in the abstract, in the material, or in Nietzsche's Apollonian sphere. Our decline is in our sense of ourselves as valuable beyond the material, our lack of spirit, of joy for life in an alienating, mechanical world, along with a suppression of the Dionysian sense of abandoning of the self to something greater in nature. How can we explain or expand from here?

Joseph Campbell, in *The Hero with a Thousand Faces* (1949) (chapter two, 'Tragedy and Comedy') gives us a clue. 'The happy ending', he writes, 'is justly scorned as a misrepresentation; for the world . . . as we have seen it, yields but one ending.' But we have missed the point of tragedy too, which is the purification in Aristotle's sense of catharsis and an acknowledgement of the 'principle of continuous life' that survives death, in a kind of 'redeeming ecstasy'. Our literal view from our materialist strength sees only the material death of the body. 'The fairytale of happiness . . . cannot be taken seriously', as in 'the ancient world', he says, when comedies 'were regarded as of a higher rank than tragedy'. He explains the old balance thus: 'Tragedy is the shattering of the forms and of our attachment to the forms; comedy, the wild and careless, inexhaustible joy of life invincible. The two are the terms of a single mythological theme.' Here he quotes Ovid: 'All things are changing; nothing dies'. Myth should help us to get 'from tragedy to comedy'. In myth we can see the dark in the light, but also vice versa.

Art that starts to look for fun in the darkness, like much recent gothic-style dark humour in film, as in the work say of Tim Burton, is working towards this. When we try to write happy we should be feeling perhaps that we are like a natural offspring of positive ancestors, if we have a sense of life as being a renewing process, rather than a destructive end of progress. To personify our problem, we might then be confronting an evil, rich friend of our grandparents who has discovered how to live forever, but this living comes with a catch. This forever is living on, but miserably, like those sad souls who cannot die, but wish to do so, in *Gulliver's Travels*. Comedy should not be how to abandon darkness, but how best to acknowledge it and the life that survives it somehow. Comedy is growth versus stasis.

The best and most generous commentator on this problem for writers is not a heavyweight academic critic but someone wrongly, I think, thought of as only a 'middlebrow' writer. At his best, J.B. Priestley is considerably more than that. In light of what he says, maybe it is the 'middlebrow', though, in a kind of mediation, who can heal the gap. Priestley wrote, in the conclusion of *Literature and Western Man* (1960), that we are both 'at the mercy of . . . unconscious drives and . . . beginning to lose individuality . . . in the power of huge political and social collectives'. Writers are 'farther removed from the centre than ever before' but try to respond. The problem is that we have also 'become one-sided' and 'over-introverted', only appealing to others who feel the same. We need to try to bring the inner world and the outer world near again, to find 'the right healing symbols for the inner world', where 'the whole of man should' be 'touchingly reflected', as in Shakespeare's Forest of Arden, where life is like 'a flower'; where life also flourishes.

Our pessimism as writers then looks like a form of loneliness and our sensationalism, our reversed sentimentality of violence and our taboo on tenderness becomes something that sells itself as a kind of escapism into the self. The pessimism of half-baked tragedy sells, just as the 'light' comedy of fantasy love does, though neither are satisfactory redress, to use a word Seamus Heaney has applied to the purpose of poetry. The difference is that 'tragedy lite' is taken seriously.

It is the job of us mythic writers to confront what is taboo. A taboo is something different and something special, as well as something forbidden. What is it about the forbidden, the unspoken, which disturbs us? If it gets under our skin, it wants us to reveal something mythic. Cynicism is a safe position which denies its own power. A hero, or a mythic writer, needs to bring the fertility back into focus.

But surely a hero cannot be comic? Heroes are serious, aren't they? As we know, the hero may come in disguise, however, and what better disguise to don than that of an idiot? This reversed hero, our fool, confronts the taboo and mocks it. Cynicism takes itself seriously, even in its shrill laughter. The character we are creating has, at essence, the heroic boon, the positive fertility, but smuggles it in under a funny hat. 'Poor Yorrick', in *Hamlet*, is only a skull in a graveyard, but he reminds the Prince of happiness. Our fool represents the hero reborn in a changeable, hence renewable form. This is our character's heroic essence. He is our internal struggle for our hero made manifest.

The struggle of comedy is a good one and a serious one, paradoxically. Comedy, as in the happy and the fertile, can and must have a tough essence. As Joseph Campbell says, 'where the moralist would be filled with indignation and the tragic poet with pity and terror, mythology breaks the whole of life into a vast, horrendous Divine Comedy. Its Olympian laugh is not escapist in the least, but hard . . . mythology . . . makes the tragic attitude seem hysterical' (*The Hero with a Thousand Faces*, 'The Monomyth', Part 4).

Writing happy may be unfashionable, like the hero, but an achieved optimism is what we still look to writers to provide somehow, especially now. We need an alternative view, an alternative space, a place from which to bring back a fresh view of the world. 'The cataclysm has happened, we are among the ruins, we start to build . . . We've got to live, no matter how many skies have fallen', D.H. Lawrence says at the beginning of *Lady Chatterley's Lover* (1928), a novel as much about hope as about anything else.

But what about conflict, though? Isn't *War and Peace* about conflict? Does happiness not 'write white', as French writer Maurice Maeterlinck reputedly said? The Creative Writing teacher urges us to reveal the conflict, start the argument, get the drama going. The blues rules, in our confessional first efforts and in our considered gritty dramas about contemporary issues. The conventional feeling dictates that comedy is just for wimps, unless it is black comedy. Again this is a kind of reversed sentimentalisation, one of assumed, fake authenticity in the tragic.

How do we deal with this in the narrative, the drama of our writing? A start is to take all this culture of pessimism with a pinch of salt. Tension might be a better goal than conflict, but perhaps the more even-handed notion of contrast is the better thing. You do not have to spell out your writing in ABC Creative Writing teaching style. There is a place for flatness, for peace as well as war, as even old Unhappy Families himself knew. And isn't happiness put into contrast by the normal, dull unhappy world? That's how Wordsworth does it, up near Tintern Abbey, away from 'the din/ Of town and cities'.

So keep the contrast and take us somewhere else, perhaps. Freud called such dreams 'wish fulfilment', but we are wishing creatures, seeking what is better for us. If wishes can beguile our dreams, why not our writing? We just need to get the beguilement right. Writing happy then can be a small grain of unease about the culture of pessimism, a subtly done contrast and all the more effective for that. But you still have to write the happy bit. And as in most ideas about writing, you can explore the opposite, too. Write miserable, then a glimpse of happy. But you need the happy. Even Beckett, the gov'nor of doom does so, in the humour of course. Same goes with Kafka, or with Dostoevsky in *Notes from Underground*.

We are so reassured by our smug feeling of a lack of sentiment somehow, but this could be fake and fatuous. We perhaps feel we need to keep our sentiment secret, our shameful happiness likewise, in somewhere like the soap-style romance of our secret mind. But, also, perhaps our problem with happiness is our last taboo about death. Death does not fit our materialist world-view, except as a spoiling, or a confirmation of pessimism, which is at best unmentionable. We don't quite believe in material happiness, so we make a fetish of violence and death, to remind us to enjoy our money. But could you write a happy death? Aldous Huxley tried it in his answer to his own dystopian *Brave New World* (1932), the little-read novel called *Island* (1962). This neglected work is definitely serious and not an entirely unhappy attempt.

Imagining Utopia, meaning a 'no-place', which can be a good place, is part of our literary job and perhaps the oldest instinct. The Fall would never have worked without the Garden of Eden, which still haunts us and we still compare ourselves with it. We need writers to create Edens, so we have something with which to compare ourselves. An Eden is a womb of renewed life, a place which gives fertility. This is, then, not a static place, but a place where innocence can be regained. Mythically, a return to Eden can be a return to the inner world of the imagination, of the creative essence. This is serious comedy and no mere escape or return to safety fantasy. If the world needs to be fertile, it needs to be renewed by writers who can visit their mythic, creative Eden. Many things can symbolise an Eden, or a means of renewal, in our writing. This does not make us dumb optimists, but in contact with the hidden, real news.

'Bad news travels fast', as John D. Loudermilk, the American songwriter who also wrote 'Tobacco Road' and 'Abeline', wrote in a song for Johnny Cash. We have what Ian D. Suttie called a 'tenderness taboo' in his *Origins of Love and Hate* (1935). We find happy a bit scary to contemplate, in case it vanishes in the acknowledgement. Bad news gets the headlines and we think in terms of social and political alienation. Writers tend to think they have to do the conflict, to go towards the fight and wave their arms about, like a bad television reporter.

Is a writer's job to just say what people expect? I think rather that it is to contradict the norm, or to present the individual against the stereotype or the typical, which are the realm of journalism and science. We have a problem with any celebration that we can really take seriously. There seems to be little to celebrate and the celebration we see is of the corny, applaud-anything Hollywood kind.

As a songwriter myself, I see the desire for happiness revealed in how people relate to songs. Songs tend to get straight to the emotions and the singer feels from the audience the need to be uplifted. If twentieth-century literature is dominated by the darkness of despair at history, then the demand for celebration retreats into popular, or folk, arts. We need a happy song. But where do we find the literary models?

Well, the best can do happy *and* sad. Dickens and Shakespeare teach you to enjoy as well as endure life, to follow Dr Johnson's words. We may need to narrow down as writers, to get into a corner, or do a small thing well, but we must also look at how rich the world is, if we can. The great fools of drama and fiction have their serious messages.

The writing section below is longer and more detailed than in other chapters, as we might all need a bit more help in getting positive writing started. True mythic writing must be able to do this. Writing, then, must not exclude anything, even our sentimental joys, our small hopes and puny celebrations, our tentative flowerings of happiness and the resilience, even in the face of death, of what is quick, what is alive.

Writing

Happy calls out the cliché. That is one of the practical problems that has to be addressed. Sadness calls them out too, but we are more adept at dealing with the minutiae of despair perhaps, and perhaps less embarrassed in our therapy culture. Addressing this cliché problem is the first, then, of some practical ways of writing happy, which start here. Clichés are revealing, mythically, as they show us something we feel we have in common, like an old story. To get the essence from them, though, they need renewal and re-examination.

Re-cast the cliché. Try this writing exercise. First describe a happy event, using the most clichés you can muster. A holiday might be a good start, even writing the postcard home. Then re-cast the clichés, by examining the detail of memory. If you were 'having a lovely time', in what way, in what detail, thing or dramatic event could that 'lovely time' be revealed'? Was it the quality of the air? The fish and chips in the rain? A tiny, comic detail can do happy best, as can the old trick of using the senses. Did your time smell lovely, taste lovely, feel lovely, sound lovely? Corniness can then be avoided and humour tapped into and we will know it for real. This is rewriting, really, but it also trains the mind to look for the tiny symbol of the bigger truth. Twisting the cliché round is also worth a try: 'Having a lovely here . . .'. Or, try opposites: 'Not having a horrible time . . .'.

Tap in to your creative exuberance. Writing is a buzz, or it should be. If you feel that it is a chore, stop writing and write something that is not. Get high on writing something outrageous, something that tells the truth, something that reveals you. Tune in to that feeling of elation, of having written something cathartic and explore it for positive material. As Blake said, 'Exuberance is beauty'. Tuning in to this raw energy has a mythic charge and myths are all about feeling the strength of the renewing stories through you, to help you write heroically.

Change the world. Imagine that you have won the lottery and write about how it would change your life for the better. Imagine being happy without any money. Earnest conversation is often called 'putting the world to rights'. Think of a wise character having a late-night discussion with you, where you do this. As someone said to me and an old pal I was chatting to in the street the other day, 'Putting the world to rights? Someone needs to . . .'. Write a manifesto for your writing or for a political party, resistance movement or pressure group. Write your party or group an anthem, a song to sing, a rousing speech to recite. Here I refer you back to Chapter 1, Starting Creation to help you make a new world.

Describe something good. Think of someone you admire and get into the subtle detail of their qualities. Animals are a good option to write about for getting outside the self, suggested by Rilke, in his *Letters to a Young Poet* (translated 1934). Write about what is, not what something is like. Happy is immediacy, something happening, like a celebration. The tiny gesture of comfort says more about love than any platitude or generalisation (see the 'cliché' bit above). God is in the detail, as well as the devil. The tiny, bright element of a mythic celebration is where the festive comes alive, like a new growth showing through dry soil.

Celebrate something. 'It was . . . a blonde to make a Bishop kick a hole in a stained-glass window,' wrote Raymond Chandler (chapter thirteen, *Farewell, My Lovely* (1940)), showing the untoward exuberance of comedy, celebrating the keenness of desire. Comedies, in the happy-ending sense, often meant that the story had a wedding at the end. The comic speech at the wedding is still a living tradition. Celebration is as necessary for us as the keening of despair. The festive ritual is a powerful uplift.

Throw off self-consciousness. You can do this by drafting freely, in the heat of remembered, or even actual, happiness. Then use your craft to sharpen the vision and the expression. Writing is not irredeemably self-conscious, it reveals, at its best, an emotional truth. It is what rings true in this way that stays with you, both in reading and in writing. The ringing true of the emotional self comes sometimes despite us. Inspiration can feel like this and can be intensely exhilarating. Writing, of even the doomiest dirge, is an affirmation in some sense. See Chapters 2 and 3 for delving into the positive force of the dark inner world.

Try being silly. Humans like to become dignified, so try being mature enough to enjoy being immature, creatively. Spend time with kids, who put few fetters on their daft or deft imaginations and enjoy verbal play, as do we all, underneath our assumed adulthood. 'The Ying Tong Song' may not be great poetry, but it lifts the spirit, as Spike Milligan and The Goons knew. A parody of something over-serious can be a route to silliness. Musicians, playing 'Stranger In Paradise' for the umpteenth time, used to refer to it as 'Strange Looking Parasite', just to keep sane. I often, academically acciden-tally-on-purpose, say 'sewage outfall' instead of 'learning outcome', which may not be that great or funny, but you get the idea and it does tend to annoy those who are over-serious about education. Silliness restores proportion to the deadly serious world we live in. When someone moans a lot, someone saying, 'It's being so cheerful that keeps you going' is silly, but it breaks the ice. The buffoon who reveals the surprising truth is a mythic staple.

Achieve the positive. The mythic hero is one who finally brings back the festive with the fertile. If you work through the pain, work out the tension through writing, you can often get to the plateau of calm and reflective peace. Writing about a hard-won optimism has a moral as well as a merely 'happy' force about it.

Try nature. See 'Describe something good' above, on animals, but nature has been the great subject of myth. 'Pastoral' writing goes back to Greek times.

There's nothing wrong with the refreshing shower or the suddenly seen flower, the sweep of the tide coming in, flowing, or ebbing away. I'm not the only Essex writer who has written an ode to the rich mud of the estuaries and coasts, which has its own, unexpected kind of glory. Nature is our big, nearby, myth. It is an obvious world of cyclic truth and symbol.

Lerve, Lerve, Lerve. The oldest and best happy subject *can* be done without cliché (see **Re-cast the cliché**, above). Robert Graves, in his poem 'Not to Sleep' (*Poems Selected by Himself*, 1957) describes happily staying awake overnight, as he waits for a lover to arrive – or is it dawn? Or is it life itself? He feels like he could take off and fly, if he chose to do so, as he is so exuberant in anticipation. Stories of love are stories of mythic initiation and transformation.

If all else fails . . . Do mock-happy. Ivor Cutler, the great eccentric Scots songwriter, has a song which repeats the line, 'I'm happy, I'm happy, and I'll punch the man who says I'm not' four times, before the verse concludes, 'I'm happy. Punch.' Real cheesy, sick-making happy can also be very funny. 'Have a really sincerely nice day.' Here, you are playing the Trickster in challenging expectations, to create a change of view and something new. If you're really desperate the other alternative is to do mock-unhappy, of course, and make people laugh at least by the over-the-top doom of your gloom from the womb to the tomb . . .

Reading

Part 3 of *The Birth of Tragedy* (1872), Nietzsche (old); 'Not To Sleep' by Robert Graves (new); Joseph Campbell, 'Tragedy and Comedy' in *The Hero with a Thousand Faces*, and Ian D. Suttie's *Origins of Love and Hate* (critical).

Chapter 8

◆

MYTH MADNESS

As we have already discovered (in Chapter 3), myth challenges our idea of what is true and 'rational', in a useful way for writers. Now, having looked at the happy side of comedy, it is time to look at the positive mad humour of myth, epitomised in the Lord of Misrule and in the god Dionysus. Much writing is about the tension between order and wildness, or stasis and energy, as represented by Apollo, the god of order and light, opposite Dionysus, the god of dark fertility and wildness. This dynamic is vital for the mythic writer and the energy in your writing and it is also a source of narrative and of structure generally, where these forces contend with each other. We must seek to harness the irrational by realising, in our processes and in our texts, how close it is to the spark of the creative. Mythic madness knows the link between absurdity and creativity, as seen in the Trickster and the Fool. There is mythic method in our wild ideas.

Laughter is, you could say, unnecessary or irrational. On the other hand, the cliché goes that laughter is the best medicine. Laughter is then the irrational brought into useful being. Or, we could say that myth is the irrational brought into useful being. All this glad talk about the irrational and myth is a joke itself, because if we talk of the irrational, or the unconscious especially, we do not know what we are talking about. There is a madness here, but the madness must be respected and allowed within the ritual space of the mythic sphere, where it is safe, or, at least a safety valve for destructive madness to let off its anarchistic steam.

When we talk about these balances of seemingly opposed factors – the madness and the medicine – we know we are in the zone of myth and that the mythsmiths may well find some useful tools there for their crafty craft. But laughter, the mythic madness of comedy, is also a physical response and to do with the body as much as the mind. The mind and the body, in laughter, are dancing to a different dance from one we learn. This basic and timeless aspect of ourselves, where the rawness of life is embodied, again gives us a clue that we are on to something mythic, something primal and worthy of attention.

In *The Act of Creation* (1964), that essential work on the mysteries of creativity, Arthur Koestler starts with laughter as the root of all creativity, or as the traceable source of being able to think of two things at once, which he calls 'bisociation'. 'The creative act . . .', he says in chapter one, 'The Logic of Laughter', 'always operates on more than one plane'. In laughter he locates a kind of dynamic between thought and feeling, which is 'unstable', but which gives way to 'creative instability'. This reminds me of my favourite definition of comedy, reputedly from the twentieth-century English comedian Joyce Grenfell (1910–1979), 'distortion to restore proportion'. There is something of the convulsive, rebellious, mind-with-body feel of all creativity in this phrase, when it comes right, when it feels like good madness.

Elvis Costello, in a song called 'Harry Worth', describes the close connection between crying and laughter (*Momofuku*, 2008). Koestler's frontispiece is a diagram illustrating just such movement, but tracing also the source of the creative in its width.

> Each horizontal line across the triptych stands for a pattern of creative activity . . . for instance: comic comparison – objective analogy – poetic image. The first is intended to make us laugh; the second to make us understand; the third to make us marvel. The logical pattern of the creative process is the same in all three cases; it consists in the discovery of hidden similarities. But the emotional climate is different in all three panels: the comic simile has a touch of aggressiveness; the scientist's reasoning by analogy is emotionally detached, i.e. neutral; the poetic image is sympathetic or admiring, inspired by a positive kind of emotion.

The 'short cut' Elvis Costello indicates is seen on this diagram as from 'bathos' to 'pathos'. Thus the creative spark which sees a monstrosity or a diminution, which projects, you could say, from the unconscious a manifestation which triggers a response gives a sense of the 'yeast-like, universal ferment' of laughter. Its anarchistic tendency to bridge the gap between reflex and thought gives us a clue as to the reversal of Costello's line, which echoes the old 'sublime to the ridiculous' idea, where positive 'gains . . . could result from the reversal'.

Laughter like myth accommodates the possibility of change and is a reminder of the depths and heights of which we are capable. Laughter is also 'universal' and an aspect of communication, and of community. The sharing of the common response to the absurd, or the seeing of the absurd in the apparently serious is a model for the 'bisociation' which makes communication possible. 'Tension is suddenly relieved and exploded in laughter', as Koestler says, as the comic sees the connection in what is normally seen as 'habitually incompatible'. Humour 'deepens the primary comic disparity between what we would like to be and what we are, between what we aspire to make and what we are made of', as Howard Jacobson says in *Seriously Funny* (1997). The bringing down to earth function is, naturally for us myth-smiths here, an elemental and mythic way of coping with change and with vanity. Writers then can explore and explode the highs and lows of life in their works and in the characters they create.

Myth, by those who only see its surface, can be seen as a kind of fantasy which elevates the ordinary to some kind of unearned quality of the sublime, but here we see the opposite being true. Myth, with its roots in earth, in elements is, for us here especially, often a reminder of what we cannot elevate, what we cannot deal with in ordinary ways. The half-submerged aspects of ourselves, which somehow know more about us than our reason, want to turn the world upside-down, to gain a rebalanced perspective. Much of what remains of our mythic or ritual activity seeks to remind us of our need to bear change. Myth confronts the mad things that really happen, as writers must.

Christmas is a well-worn ritual which bears examination in this way. The old pagan winter festival obviously bears the seed, at the darkest time, towards the light. Christmas is there to remind us, in festivity and with symbols of the evergreen, that spring will come eventually. The old year dies and the new one is born. It is a festival, whatever else it is, of on-goingness. It might surprise some that the anarchic comic reversal, the mythical madness of Christmas, its life and death enacted in earthy fashion were once embodied in an official English folkloric figure.

The 'Lord of Misrule' section in my copy of Chambers *Book of Days* (1864) covers two full columns, for the entry of 24 December. This book is one of my top ten mythsmith source books and is still available, albeit in a short, selected form. It is full of extraordinary scholarship and stories, ready to be adapted and full of mythic energy.

Under the heading about the Lord of Misrule, the entry begins, 'The functionary with the above whimsical title played an important part in the festivities of Christmas in olden time.' You already get the feeling that they are playing it down, despite the cute, Stephen Fry-like tone. The Lord is someone whose job it is to put the world into comic reverse and let the madness loose. This old, primal part of ourselves will, like all things mythic, not really let us go – or, put another way, will let us really let go. The Lord of Misrule keeps breaking out, bidden or not. And he's still around, demanding we honour his power. Writers do this most often.

On the surface the Lord of Misrule was just somebody to organise leisure, to be 'the Master of Merry Disports', through the Christmas holiday period. However, the mock-royal appointment always had more symbolic and chaotic functions attached to it. With the Lord of Misrule, it can go either way. In the time of Charles I, one such Lord was knighted, but on the other hand the Lord was once given 'power and authority . . . to break up all locks, bolts, bars, doors, and latches, and to fling up all doors out of hinges, to come at those who presume to disobey his lordship's commands'. Is this just a holiday camp leader, a cheer-leading game-show host? In a way, yes, and part of his job was also to 'absolve' people 'of their wisdom', so that they were 'just wise enough to make fools of themselves'. As *The Book of Days* points out, some of this spirit has been kept in UK Christmas pantomime.

On the other hand 'scandalous abuses often resulted from the exuberant licence assumed by the Lord', as the puritans came along to 'denounce' the role. The puritan source is quoted as making the link with 'Bacchanalian festivals', which meant pagan, non-Christian and therefore all bad. For us, of course, this is a good clue to the root of controlled madness. The same puritan says, in an orgy of words, that the Lord's rule involved 'revelling, epicurisme, wantonesse, idlenesse, dancing, drinking, stage-plays, masques, and carnall pompe'. Sounds like a good party.

Another, more recent book, *Everyman's Book of Ancient Customs* (Chaundler, 1968) goes further in condemnation.

> 'By the time Henry the Eighth came to the throne the whole affair had got quite out of hand. The rioters would even invade the churches while services were in progress, blowing trumpets and making discordant noises, setting up booths in the churchyard for drinking and dancing, and forcing worshippers to hand over to them the alms intended for church offertories. That the custom was at last put an end to, and never revived, is something no one need regret.'
>
> Spoilsport

The source of the trouble, so rightly pointed out in Chambers', is the god Bacchus, which is the Roman term for the Greek god Dionysus. Euripides' play *The Bacchae* is the Greek tragedy which tells of the new/ old god coming to town and driving the women mad. They are sensible enough to join him on the hillsides and celebrate the animal freedom humans suppress in their desire to avoid what seems undignified. The uptight King, Pentheus, will not sanction the worship and drunkenness and he ends up destroyed by his own controlling, suppressed nature. A telling moment occurs near the beginning of the play, when two old men decide to go to the wild worship.

Cadmus, ex-King and grandfather to the current one, along with Tiresias, the 'blind Seer', as he is perfectly described in translator Philip Vellacott's version (1972) say they will 'go to dance/ And take our stand with the others, tossing our grey heads'. The old men contain the wisdom which realises the power of the older, primal power of spring, of celebration and balancing the wild with the world. In other words, they understand the creative duality of freedom and control. As Tiresias says, 'We see things clearly, all others are perverse.' It is perverse, then, *not* to let the wild in. As Cadmus says, 'I don't despise religion. I'm a mortal man', meaning that to understand the cycles of balance, of life and death, it is right to celebrate in the seemingly crude way of the properly celebratory. Tiresias confirms this view with his statement against any 'subtleties' of control: 'The beliefs we have inherited, as old as time,/ Cannot be overthrown by any argument.' He knows that 'It will be said, I lack the dignity of my age . . . Not so; the god draws no distinction between young/ And old . . . no one is exempt.' Rock on.

It strikes me as strange, but not unexpected, how the texts and characters I quote on the god of madness and drunkenness get more radical the older they get, just like the wise old fools in *The Bacchae* (the title means the women who are Dionysus' followers and dancers). Dionysus is also the god of fertility, of life and regrowth. His arrival in the depths of winter is the reminder of the joys of spring, of new life, just when the human spirit is about to close down into itself. In a way, the writing and celebrating of madness act, as I have heard Dudley Young say, as a kind of inoculation against what happens if you suppress these things. A pinch of good release can guard against bad madness.

A good example of the happy upheaval of life, put into use by a writer, is Richard Thompson's song 'God Loves a Drunk', recorded by Norma Waterson and also by the composer, on his *Rumour and Sigh* album (1991). Here, even a drunk's freedom is a kind of religious experience, described in religious language. Elsewhere in the song he questions the merely conventional and safe, sober world, asking if that is equally valid in the face of some kind of breakthrough to freedom, such as the one the drunk finds.

The writer's use of the comic reversal hero is strongly connected to the figure from Native American Indian culture, called the Trickster, which is an accepted archetype of the controlled use of madness. Jung, in 'On the Psychology of the Trickster Figure', in *Four Archetypes* (1970), noticed the connection to 'the carnival in the medieval Church, with its reversal of the hierarchic order', which would include the Lord of Misrule. The buffoon who has the wisdom, as he says, is also a figure found in fairytales and folklore generally. This function, of the idiot who brings the truth, also contains an element of sacrifice. The returning to the animal side is a returning to the earth, to nourish the seed. Followers of Dionysus' sacrifices tear the victim to pieces. They are then back in the fertile cycle. This Jung calls an 'approximation to the figure of a saviour'. The Trickster is known for 'sly jokes and malicious pranks . . . powers as a shape-shifter' and a 'dual nature, half animal, half divine'. The bringing down to earth is a strong element of the Trickster, as is the quality of cutting 'big egos down to size', as Christopher Vogler puts it, in his section on the Trickster in *The Writer's Journey*.

The silliness of the Trickster, the animal crudity is part of the picture, part of the trick. Jung explains this by the strong element of the unconscious in the primal and prankish figure, who 'points back to a very much earlier stage of consciousness'. The Trickster is 'God, man and animal at once . . . both human and superhuman, a bestial and divine being, whose chief and most alarming characteristic is his unconsciousness'. When we let the fool out, he is our unconscious come to life, to remind us of what we tend to forget.

If we gave an example of the kind of 'bisociation' of humour Koestler discusses, in the 'comic simile' mode, we can come to the same view. If a man impersonates a dog, sniffing a lamppost and raising his leg as if to urinate, he is doing two things. First he is saying that humans are like dogs, in that they are animal, but he is also proving a cleverness about the analogy, which, at the same time, says he is knowing about this. Thus a kind of inferiority and superiority are accepted and asserted and a kind of balance is achieved. Lewis Hyde, in *Trickster Makes This World* (1998) connects this kind of function to hunting and to mankind making his steps away from nature to culture, to cleverness. This god of change is the one who is linked with the transitional, with journeys, with boundaries and with crossing them. This trick of clever movement is the creative mind and the clever mind, in tune with both sides of its nature, its animal and its trickery. It is notable that the Coyote is the figure in most Native American Indian Trickster stories. Animals as other selves are important tools for writers.

The magic and the trick of the magic are also one in the Trickster figure. The artist, including writers, as Tricksters often feel, like Ted Hughes' 'Famous Poet' (see previous chapter), that their trick cannot be easily captured, that it might even be a fraud, but this is the Trickster again working through them. The psychologist Rollo May (no relation), who has written on myths, discusses this in 'The Search for Oneself', in *The Art of Counselling*

(1989). 'While an artist is intensely engrossed . . . the creative process seems to grasp and carry him or her along.' But when the work 'is finished', there are 'two emotions: one is satisfaction and the sense of psychological catharsis which all creative effort brings, the other is the guilt feeling', which is 'a realisation that something great has taken place which the artist did not merit. Great artists have this curious realisation that they are dealing with something dangerous.' This feeling of trickery is the negotiation between the unconscious and the conscious, the gap between 'what we aspire to make and what we are made of', as Howard Jacobson, quoted above, put it. Writing is a trick that must have some of the magic in it.

D.H. Lawrence's poem 'A Sane Revolution' (1929) is an example of the positive view of the madness of change and trickery, of a kind of openness to adventure. The revolution in the poem is to turn even revolution on its head. 'If you make a revolution, make it for fun,/ don't make it in ghastly seriousness/ don't do it in deadly earnest', the poem begins. Later Lawrence calls on the animal whose name means fool to us: the ass. He asks for a revolution where we can all 'kick our heels like jolly escaped asses'. In Shakespeare's *A Midsummer Night's Dream*, Bottom is famously loved by the beautiful Queen of the Fairies, Titania, while he has the head of an ass. The extremity of the foolishness calls forth the extremity of change.

Love is, of course, one of our last areas of irrational belief. Our irrational love especially is our remaining refuge for mad and revolutionary behaviour – for mythic behaviour. You cannot, either, divorce the madness of love from the sexual element of the festive. Howard Jacobson traces the links with the second chapter of *Seriously Funny* (1997), 'Where There's a Fool There's a Phallus'. The comedy, the playfulness and its balance with the animalistic, with a kind of over-serious passion that might tip over any minute into absurdity which sexuality has, among other things, make it, especially for the writer, a ripe playground of the comic reversal. But we even tend to take sex too seriously, even though we know it looks absurd to the uninvolved eye. Greek drama knew the source of comedy was the proud fertility of sex and the obvious bursting of the bubble of human vanity was to be found in the comedy of genitalia.

The comedy of earth is the comedy of sex, of dirt and piss and shit. It is also, of course, the comedy of death, but, by mythic extension, of life too and of the cycles of fertility. The anarchic comedy gives us a dose of reality, but enables us to see that laughter is a way of seeing the world in balance between the basic, the shit, balanced with the clever 'shit' of insight and expression. Where our great foolishness is, there is what we really are, what we really think and it is there we move into the mythic. Literature is full of useful idiots and none are more idiotic than the writer, attuned to the subtle which is revealed in the unsubtle stumble.

Creativity is a kind of sane madness and the creative process of self-renewal needs the surprise of misrule to goad it into the trick of creative suddenness. It is both the magic and the trick. If the artist is mad, it is a madness that seeks sanity in its startling revelations. To create is to go sane, to paraphrase psychologist Adam Phillips.

The twelfth card of the major arcana of the Tarot is called The Hanged Man. There is already a joke on us if we think of hanging as being about death. The card is already a tease, a card-trick. If you look at the picture the man is hanging upside-down by his ankle and does not look in distress in any way. With this unexpected feeling, we are already approaching the meaning of the symbol. The Hanged Man is the world turned upside-down, the revolutionary card where the reverse is true and where the truth is unexpected.

Jung identifies 'the civilising process' of the figure of misrule, or Trickster ('On the Psychology of the Trickster Figure', in *Four Archetypes* (1970)). The need to be reminded of our own chance, luck and ability to be creative works against the negative aspects of 'civilisation', which tends to overlook our 'hidden and apparently harmless shadow', which 'has qualities whose dangerousness exceeds his wildest dreams'. We cannot understand with the 'head alone'. The awareness of the redeeming madness is a double, or tricky, creative state. 'Two contrary tendencies are at work: the desire on the one hand to get out of the earlier [animal-like] condition and on the other hand not to forget it', Jung says.

The Lord of the Trick, the Revolutionary Revolver, the Shape-Shifter and the new view of the Upside-down Man are all personifications, for the myth-smith, of myth itself. Myth is the ever-changing, constant reminder of what and who we really are, at our highest and lowest levels. We writers are the Changelings who create.

Like all mythic energies, the figure has its own inbuilt tendency to hide, like any hero, in the one-dimensional. But myth madness will break out to a new view. Lewis Hyde says the Trickster is the boundary crosser and also the boundary creator, dealing with 'the great distance between heaven and earth'. He warns, again in his introduction to *Trickster Makes This World*, that now when 'everyone travels, the result is not the apotheosis of Trickster but another form of his demise'. Later, he says, 'most of the travellers, liars and thieves, and shameless personalities' of our own time 'are not Tricksters at all ... Their disruptions are not subtle enough'. If the Trickster 'lies and steals, it isn't so much to get away with something or get rich as to disturb the established categories of truth and property . . . and open the road to possible new worlds'. Creativity and energy are available in the useful madness, the sane disruption that offers itself in writing from mythic depth and from mythic height.

Writing

Write about a current or returned Lord of Misrule. Some ideas/ titles for this might be:

> The Lord of Misrule Returns
> The Lord of Misrule Goes Christmas Shopping
> The Lord of Misrule Gives a Lecture
> The Lord of Misrule and the Queen's Speech/ President's Address
> The Lord of Misrule and The World Leader
> The Lord of Misrule and The World Leader's Wife/ Husband
> The Lord of Misrule on Reality TV
> Lord of Misrule, Style Guru
> The Lord of Misrule at the Office Party
> The Lord of Misrule Drunk Drives
> The Lord of Misrule Wrote My Essay
> The Lord of Misrule Ate My Pot-bellied Pig
> The Lord of Misrule Resigns
> The Pantomime Clown Takes Over

On 11 December 2006, the *Daily Telegraph* reported an incident concerning the Bishop of Southwark and member of the House of Lords, the Rt Rev Tom Butler. The Bishop took a service with a black eye and said he had been mugged, having his briefcase, mobile phone and crucifix stolen. But sources said he had been at a drinks party at the Irish Embassy with the head of M15 and David Trimble, the Northern Irish Protestant politician. They say he ended up in Crucifix Lane, SE1, where he climbed into a stranger's car and began tossing toys out of the windows. The car alarm was going off and the owner came to ask what he was doing. As widely reported, the Bishop replied: 'I'm the Bishop of Southwark, it's what I do.' He staggered off. Later, one of his church congregation refused to condemn him for drinking.

Write a fictionalised version (perhaps with extra research) of this story as a case of the Lord of Misrule taking over.

Write about an unexpected encounter with an animal that brings a character down to earth.

Research a coyote/ Trickster story and turn into a contemporary piece of writing.

Find a foolish tale from folklore or fairytales and update.

Write about a great weakness of character giving strength.

Write about inappropriate love.

Reading

The Bacchae by Euripides (old); 'A Sane Revolution' by D.H. Lawrence (new); *Trickster Makes This World* by Lewis Hyde (critical).

Chapter 9

◆

MODERNISING MYTHS

Until now, the adventuring writer has been taken through chapters attempting to develop the courage and understanding of mythic processes. Myth has been seen to be inextricably bound to the creative process, in its echoing of the depth and revelation of insight all writers seek to achieve. We will now move towards encountering mythic materials from scratch and working directly with myth towards writing.

The creative resonance of the mythic has showed us that there are many routes we can find into using myth in our writing. Myth will, as we have also seen, adapt itself to *every* type of serious attention, so all that is said below is, once more, conditional and merely some approaches to method. You will, as a mythsmith, make your own way, or make the way your own.

That said, there are two things which I think are essential. The first is becoming a Myth-Browser and having a Myth-Browser's Library, as indicated in the key texts section of the Introduction. Having collections and dictionaries of myths is good, along perhaps with access to good websites, but developing a way of hanging-out with the weird old stuff is vital. As mentioned elsewhere, Ovid is a good place to start, for the sheer number of stories he uses, among other qualities. Browse *Metamorphosis* and see what jumps out at you. To see how various the uses of it might be, try some recent retellings in *Ovid Metamorphosed* (2001), edited by Philip Terry.

The second essential is telling the stories. Move away from the sources and tell yourself the stories – try them on tolerant friends, use them in conversation. Myths are stories, whatever else they are, and stories need telling aloud, to give them their scope and relevance. You can reconnect with the oral nature of story by seeking out a local storytelling club and go and see how they do it. With these caveats and essentials, we are ready to look at some specific ways of modernising myths.

After discussing what modernising means we will move through the stages of Beginning, via Self, Subject, Story and Symbol: then Growing, Developing and Writing.

There are as many ways of making mythic source material currently useful, which is what I mean by 'modernising' here, as there are any other ways of writing. Just as you might do in recreating your myth, I am making up some ways, indicating some tendencies, suggesting some starting and standing places. For example, 'modernising' might include making something old, if that is what is useful to you currently (see 'Developing' below). Likewise there are many examples, which you will know from your own reading, and from suggested readings in this book, from straight translations to wild re-imaginings.

UK woman poet Stevie Smith's 'The Frog Prince' (1966) does not change the fairytale, for example. Instead she goes into the subject of enchantment and asks if the frog might prefer being safe as he is, without risking being a prince, or being in love. She then manages to discuss the tale, the implications and the fear of change and risk. It is a re-focus, but a small one, making a timeless, contemporary poem that comments on the essence of myth, which is confronting change. The tale is not forced into the modern, merely nudged by close attention into revealing its depth.

What might inhibit you has been tackled in the Introduction, but seeing your writing as part of a history, or tradition of writing, or as a form of plagiarism on the body of literature need not be a blocking constraint. For a start, what you write will come out your own, so be bold and steal what you need. If you think of myth as a free sweet shop, rather than an exclusive club, that might help liberate you. You do not need to be an expert, just to have the courage that the mythic often, or always, points us towards. As we know, myth is always with us, creatively.

The old tales are a kind of free wealth, a gift from the past, which is never exhausted and always ready to respond to attention of any kind. When you know some old haunting or shocking tale, it will plant seeds in your mind, as it connects to your unconscious knowledge of life. Much has been written on this quality, but a word that sums it up is one directly connected to creativity, used by Robert M. Wallace in his translation of *Work on Myth* (1985) by Hans Blumenberg: 'pregnance'. If I wanted to suggest my own word, another neologism, I might try 'suggestful', meaning full of the inclination to 'cause idea[s] to present themselves', to adapt the *OED*'s definition of 'suggest'.

The mad quality, the extremity of many myths, their resistance to any one meaning, their tendency to hide, in meaning and in use by the whimsical or cynical – all these things make them challenging, as well as responsive, full of 'pregnance', 'suggestful', to personal feelings, or to becoming a map of how we feel. More importantly, they require us to go deeper into the difficulty, into its extremity. To get to the potentiality, you need this other quality, that of useful resistance. A famous example of the tough usefulness of myth is James Joyce's *Ulysses*, described by T.S. Eliot as heralding a new method of dealing with the difficulties of the modern world, which he called 'the mythical method'. Eliot's own *The Waste Land* is another example of this in action.

I decided to write this chapter by using childhood, with its potentiality, which is another adjective that would do too for the usefulness of myth, in-built. I feel resistance to the theme, but sometimes in writing I know that this feeling means there is something interesting for me there, something contentious enough for me to make a piece of writing worth it. The oldest, weirdest story about this makes me feel very uncomfortable indeed, but I know it will make me work better. It is the story of the child sacrifice of Iphigenia. My resistant fear of it might be the fear of death, or the fear of life, but my sense of excitement, of 'pregnance', 'suggestfulness' and potentiality, might be the sense of a parent contemplating the future of a longed-for child, of the writer contemplating a strong work that is full of life. Iphigenia reminds me also of the story of Abraham and Isaac in the Bible (Genesis 22). That story, too, has two possible outcomes.

But, before we go further, we must tell the tale:

Artemis, or Diana, the virgin Goddess of hunting, demands the sacrifice of Iphigenia for a wind to take the ships to the Trojan war. Her father Agamemnon, the warrior who needs the ships to go, once, like Actaeon, offended Artemis. He tricks his daughter to the altar by telling her she is to marry the other great warrior Achilles. In Aeschylus' version she dies, while in other versions she is replaced at the last second by a deer and is carried away by Artemis. She becomes Artemis' sacrificing Priestess, but rescues her brother Orestes and they escape. (Aeschylus, *Agamemnon*; two *Iphigenia* plays by Euripides; Ovid, *Metamorphosis* 12).

WAYS OF BEGINNING: SELF

Writing begins and ends here, with the self. Even if we start from somewhere else, we need to find the resonance within us. So, even if we do not begin here, we will return here to begin again, to grow, to develop and, finally, to write at all. Starting with mythic writing from the self, though, might involve the unconscious or the cultural world of the writer. A dream, a memory from childhood, a haunting experience, a random thought, a diary or free-writing exercise might be the impetus.

Using my example of childhood, a theme which held resistance, thereby showing some hidden, unconscious potential, I will go through some examples of ways in which this might start towards a creative reworking via myth.

Like resistance, feelings of fear and hauntings, what seems forbidden, taboo, special, or obsessive are direct links to the unconscious self and may reveal deep themes. On childhood, it occurs to me that we are all inhabited by another being, even haunted by them and that person is the child we once were and, of course, in some senses, still are.

In a similar way, dreams, writing journals, old diaries, memories, existential angst and the views, welcome or unwelcome, of close relatives and friends can also reveal useful unconscious resonances. I once had a dream of two children who were mine, a boy and a girl, both of whom had plump, healthy faces. I might be able to connect this image to myths of childhood. Also, there are photos of my family when I was a child which could give me some ideas, as well as family stories, which I might call family myths, about things said and done in childhood, by me and by others.

Free-writing (see discussion of Dorothea Brande in Chapters 2 and 3), free-associative thinking, experimental or 'automatic' writing, other art forms and any form of improvisation can help the unconscious mind to feed in to your ideas. My own playful, word-based habits of (childish?) thought make me ponder in an improvisational way, on the name Iphigenia. I'm sure the 'genia' bit is to do with generation, but the concept of something being 'Iffy', or questionable, in the modern idiom, interests me. Surely there is nothing more 'iffy' than being a child, being vulnerable, but full of hope, of potential. It also sounds to me like a name, so I might be able to use it. Does the whole name sound like 'pregnance'?

Another aspect of the self which can provide a link with the unconscious, is one's own behaviour. Misbehaving, behaving like a child, dancing, drunkenness and the hangover might reveal unconscious sides of our character. I believe that some writers take to drink and other drugs because writing can be a very self-conscious activity. The drink lets the dark in to feed the writing, as the unconscious needs to be working well. This extreme therapy might not be recommended, but it does remind us of some truths. The hangover is probably more influential on writing than actual drunkenness. In other words the recovery from getting out of your head, towards getting back in, is when writing is likely to occur and possibly to help. Extremity is the stuff of art, even if you believe, as Flaubert and Frank Zappa did, that you should save your madness for your art.

Indolence is a much maligned and neglected aspect of modern life. A writer is always working, in a sense, even when lying fallow, as a field recovers its ability to sustain a crop when it is left uncultivated. Most writers will know the benefits of solitude, of walking, of having time to let ideas come to you. Trying too hard does not always help. The dreaming child could find its way into my childhood theme. The sacrifice of a child seems to me to be about trying too hard, as in my story of Iphigenia, where she is to be killed to raise the wind to carry the ships to war.

Wherever else you start with your mythy writing, you must take it home to dream on it, subject it to not trying too hard and allowing it to enter your inner creative child.

WAYS OF BEGINNING: SUBJECT

Although I found more than one way of beginning happening at once, I did choose childhood as a theme, as a subject, first. The immediate danger here is starting to write in an abstract way, without the added depth of the restart, provoked by taking the subject back to the self. Researching via the subject remains a good way to start.

A theme or subject might be triggered off by the news, or by history, or might be given from outside. As with any creative, discursive, critical or other writing project, extensive research can do no harm. With the theme of child-hood, there is probably too much material, so I would look at anything I found which would give me a mythic or symbolic connection, or a narrative, mythic or otherwise. I consulted dictionaries of symbols, old ballads (remembering 'murder' ballads) and stories of lost children. Luckily, one of my favourite writers on myth, Marina Warner, has a section in her Reith Lectures book, *Managing Monsters* (1994), about childhood, which provided masses of information. The internet is obviously a good source of information, but the filter of one's writer's instincts, as under 'Self' above, must operate here.

Marina's 'Little Angels, Little Devils' led me to my classical dictionaries to look up the story of Iphigenia. Aware of the need for narrative to animate a subject, myths, tales and ballads help me think in terms of a tale, rather than a mere topic, even though any fact could be useful. For example, I know of someone writing a PhD on child soldiers, so I might request an interview and some guidance as to reading, if I wanted to follow that line. The involvement of children in death, with war, as with Iphigenia, seems like the horrible reality of war somehow being faced.

As well as the danger of being too abstract, other dangers include doing too much research, so that it becomes a way of not writing. Being overwhelmed by material or by contemporary events might result in a piece of writing that tries to do too much. Writing, like any other art, is about what you choose and therefore about what you leave out. If I get Britney Spears' problems with custody of her children (in the news as I write), child warriors, murders and myths and psychological research all in a messy, muddled poem, no one would care. No research is wasted, but selection will become part of the process, otherwise undigested material will make a mess of what I hope might come of my theme.

WAYS OF BEGINNING: STORY

Knowing and telling a mythic narrative is vital to moving towards your own version, even if you are not writing a pure narrative yourself. You will have noticed that, as soon as I chose childhood as a theme, I gave the story and this way of beginning might easily be first, before the subject and the self expand on it and bring it into your creative mind.

A problem for me with the tale of Iphigenia will be one of simply fixing on a narrative. It is in the nature of myth that the stories are unstable. Again, selecting a version of the myth which works for you might be a starting place for fixing your story. Choosing a version that suits your purposes, or offers psychological resonance, can take time to research. Euripides has two plays about Iphigenia, and whether she died or was rescued by the goddess at the last moment is an interesting and useful conundrum, which I would need to sort out. The options of life or death for her seem highly 'suggestful' to me and the moment of sacrifice is the crux of the tale.

Creating a story might also include combining two stories. For me, this could be Britney and Iphigenia. Finding a mythic tale from ancient myth, the Bible or from the news are not the only sources, either. Fairytales are often about children and any collection of urban myths will inevitably have material on childhood. Local and other folklore can provide both stories and settings.

For instance, to tune into the moment of sacrifice might be where we need some help from another tale. Agamemnon's heartlessness in the Greek tale, where he seems bullied by the goddess Artemis, might be made more real by using the tale of Abraham and Isaac in the Bible. Abraham, when told to sacrifice his son, seems to me to know that he is being tested and perhaps that all will be well. He trusts God, so his doubts would seem real, given his faith. Perhaps Agamemnon could also sense a test and hoped all might still be well. Genesis 22:12 has God say, at last 'Lay not thy hand upon the lad.' I could have Agamemnon thinking this will happen, imagining the goddess relenting and saying, 'Don't harm the girl', at the last minute. This would build up the tension as well as being a source of trust and doubt.

Again, starting from a story will lead you back to what resonates with you and to a process of development and reflection. The danger of the story alone, without connecting other ways of beginning, is that you end with a simple retelling, but the story must be part of you, so that the title or name of the character can call up all the associations you will gather to it. Remaking the bones of the narrative and telling them will bring it back towards life.

WAYS OF BEGINNING: SYMBOL

Symbol here can mean symbolic patterns, which you might also find in the mythic narrative above, but starting from a symbol or pattern already has a resonance and a connecting idea built-in. If I began as childhood as a symbol of creativity itself, my mind is already beginning to work in a useful, writerly way.

Using a heroic pattern from Joseph Campbell's *The Hero with a Thousand Faces* (1949), or finding another cyclic pattern could be another staring point (see Chapter 4, Mythic Navigation Devices). Time, in relation to childhood might lead me to the 'seven ages of man' via Shakespeare, or to seasonal time, exploring spring and growth. Symbolically, childhood is the stage of promise, potential and innocence. Looked at in relation to other stages of life, I would begin to ask what is retained of these qualities.

Dictionaries of symbols again might help, as might the mythic patterning and symbolism of such things as Tarot cards and the *I Ching*. The Tarot has a card in the major arcana which symbolises youth: number one, The Magician. The numeric order of these major cards suggests a pattern, or path of growth. The Tarot pack is like conventional playing cards to some extent, but with these archetypal, symbolic picture cards added. The meanings of them, both in themselves and as part of a sequence, are discussed in many books. One of my favourites, where the characters and archetypes address the reader, is Richard Gardner's *The Tarot Speaks* (1971). Likewise the *I Ching* can be read as a path or series of patterns and there are hexagrams on growth and youth and beginning, which may be helpful. Dream symbol dictionaries, of the psychological kind, may also suggest useful connections. The *I Ching* is based on images of nature applied to human life, with the 'as above, so below' psychological implication to the fore.

Books of Days, which give details of festivals and events associated with each day, provide seasonal relevance. For my childhood theme, I might have started in my lovely old Chambers *Book of Days* (1864) and found, perhaps, in the Christmas associations of childhood, the idea of the Boy Bishop. The child, who in a festive, symbolic and 'turning the world upside-down' way, was elected Bishop for a winter celebration, has all kinds of echoes of child-hood rites of passage towards adulthood, which is one of the great mythic patterns. Many folkloric books work on a seasonal structure and can be good starting points, with patterns and symbolic resonances built in. Once you begin to think symbolically, it becomes a writer's habit to find these con-nections. Part Two of this book, the Mythic Subject Dictionary, can also help get you started with symbol, subject and reference.

Seeing an object, hearing a word or looking at a building may set off a search for symbols and patterns in your mind, which can give shape to your thoughts. Being too allusive can be a fault of mythic writing, which could be a danger, if you were to get stuck with the symbol only. This type of beginning is very closely connected to both the 'Self' and to the 'Developing' of your material, but, from the simple metaphor to the elaborate system, symbol is an essential part of mythic work.

GROWING

Growing your idea begins after it has been chosen through one, or a com-bination of, or through a process of, the above ways of beginning – or any other way you begin. By growing here I mean a process of starting to 'get messages' from your source materials and from your thoughts, feelings and unconscious. I use the words 'get' or 'getting' as descriptive ones, meaning that once material has sunk in, you start to see connections and depths as you meditate on the subject, the story and the symbols and pattern, as they come to the self. If you 'get' the crux of your mythic project, then so will the reader. This is an organic process of absorbing, or of being absorbed by, the material.

To get the messages you need the same kind of techniques described in 'Self' above. Taking notes, seeking phrases and ideas, allowing the material to talk to you, combining disparate notions and free-association will all help. With childhood as a theme, seeing an abandoned doll might lead me to thinking about abandonment as a symbol in fairytale, for example. If I combined that with the Boy Bishop, I might think of a child who was lost in an adult role, or, perhaps, an adult who felt like a lost child.

Again, this process might take a while, but it is not a good idea to get stuck there. Living with an idea can make the 'getting messages' stage happen automatically, but the mind needs to relax at this point, before the greater effort of developing and doing. My mythic child begins to grow and begins a rite of passage.

DEVELOPING

Developing here means creating your own version of the story, adding and cutting, shaping it to your purpose.

Mythic stories' 'suggestfulness' includes a kind of adaptability to change, even to brutal reworkings, beyond recognition of any original source. So how you do it is open to your most extreme fancy. Perhaps the most radical thing might be to keep it the same. The terseness of Ovid's anthologising in *Metamorphosis* sometimes amounts to this. On the other hand, mythic material responds to extremity of treatment, as it is itself often extreme in its address of the taboo, the difficult, the special and forbidden. How you develop the material is perhaps the most crucial decision, but if you have prepared well for this fun part of the process, then your unique take will emerge. Among Shakespeare's multiple gifts, his skill at adaptation, or what we are calling developing here, is among the best. Developing your mythic material will make you aware, like Shakespeare was, that it is the way that you do it that counts.

So the first thing to consider is what could be called 'keeping it the same' to a large extent. Here you might translate, write a new version using other translations (as poet Christopher Logue, who could not read Greek himself, did with Homer's *Iliad* in *War Music*, 1981), expand a small section (as Ted Hughes with some of his longer *Tales from Ovid* poems) or retell in a straightforward or modern way.

Changing the mythic source might simply involve names of characters, for example. Greek names, especially, have meanings. I use the index of Robert Graves' *The Greek Myths* (1960) where he gives translations of Greek names, which are useful for extra insights into their characters. A quick check on the internet can help confirm the meaning. Iphigenia means 'mothering a strong race', which brings a whole new feeling to the character and speaks of either the efficacy of her sacrifice or of her subsequent life after being rescued by a goddess, where her ordeal might make her stronger. Already it is suggesting to me a tough, single mother and it works in opposition to the Iffy name idea I arrived at before. The possibilities of the name seem full of suggestion and the choice of name, old, modern and/ or nickname are always important in writing.

Characters can be changed to reflect strength where there is weakness, or be changed through gender switches, age or attitude. Angela Carter explores various aspects of character, among other things, in her retellings of fairy-tales, in *The Bloody Chamber* (1979). Just having a mute character speak can cast a whole new light on the story. The story of the hind that in some versions replaced Iphigenia at the sacrificial altar might make a good animal rights work about sacrifice, for example.

Changing the story radically can also work, if that is done to some pur-pose. Perhaps Iphigenia could return to prevent her mother Clytemnestra killing her father Agamemnon and thus fulfil her name's promise earlier. Or a female child could sacrifice her father to prevent war. Playing around with these kinds of reversals can reveal some unexpected possibilities.

The dangers of radical change are obvious, but worth mentioning. The psychological essence of a myth has a quality of survival built-in, so do not throw out the baby with the bathwater. On the other hand, in writing, some-times the bravest change can work best and be the best way of avoiding being whimsical, over allusive to too cynically trendy, which are the ever-present dangers of mythic writing, as well as perhaps of all other types of writing.

Combination of the old mythic material with new material can be the most fruitful. With this way of working, you get the benefit of double vision and the two-point triangulation effect of coming into focus from where you are. Stories within stories are meat and drink for the mythic writer, again from Shakespeare onwards. How you combine the new and the old may just be a simple modernisation, where the child sacrifice might take place among black magicians, or students of myth. Donna Tartt's *The Secret History* (1992) has some students of Greek myth enacting a Dionysian sacrifice. Another way is to have someone telling an old story within your new story. 'Piramus and Thisbe' as a comic play, within *A Midsummer Night's Dream* is an example of this. Using other writers' versions within your own is another option, as is combining more than one mythic story – Cinderella and Iphigenia comes to mind.

Generic development is another decision you may have to make. An essay on childhood seen through the idea of sacrifice might be an option, and I could even present my essay within a piece of fiction. The setting of a conference on childhood could have samples of two opposing views of the mythic in two opposing speakers, for example. Trying a different genre to your usual might be a way of gaining new possibilities of expression and construction. The most unobvious genre can work: maybe a fast rock song with a rap-like story of child sacrifice and war would work.

Playing with all these pieces of a pattern and bringing new elements together can be the fun part, the creative play part of the process. If you have followed some of these preparatory stages, or feel the necessary creative excitement which includes some of them, then the next stage will feel inevitable and eagerly anticipated. There are many ways, as many as we can imagine in myth, but finally we must make the decision, the choice, as to what will work for us individually.

THE WRITING

While some kind of rough plan, if only in your head, is inevitable, we know that allowing yourself the freedom to write is vital. If the material has integrated itself into you, been allowed to grow and been developed creatively in some way, then let the writer off the leash to run wild through the mythic chaos. Let some writing flow:

> We all kill the child which is ourselves
> sacrifice our softness for the adult business every day
> and yet the child sustains us, is us
> we kill ourselves to function
> and we don't mean it
> the child is snatched away
> to be used
> another day

This is too abstract maybe, but 'fell off my pen' in a first draft and has some possibilities for later use. No writing is useless, if it gets you towards the better stuff, and the feeling, expressed above, has an authentic sense of psychological truth which could underlie what is finally produced. The verse is a child of my theme and may need to go through several stages of writing before it emerges from the possibility of its sacrifice in editing.

When you have been living with your material, as we have been doing in this chapter, then probably, or eventually, a plan, pre or post writing, might be necessary or helpful. This would be the case if I were to combine my Boy Bishop with the Iphigenia story. He might be sacrificed, metaphorically, but might also read, or be told, the story of Iphigenia, via Aeschylus or Euripides.

Likewise, editing, or post-planning can be a vital stage. Obviously leaving a draft for some time, to give time for the preparatory work and the writing work to be integrated in your subconscious, will be useful. The fresh eye of the newly integrated, rational and self-reflective editor can sharpen and realign any loss of mythic intensity.

Of course, you could ignore this chapter's process entirely and do the writing first, or all the way through in a journal or work book, or ignore any of my suggestions. Your own adaptability, 'suggestfulness' and extremity will be strengthened by hanging out with the mythic and you can ignore the rules by being unruly, in the challenging myth style. This might bring chaos to the order, as well as order to the chaos, or negotiate between the two in a meaningful and useful way.

One final warning, mentioned in the Introduction, is worth repeating here: There is a danger in mythic writing of being tempted into a pseudo-archaic-epic, grandiose mythic style, which amounts to a pastiche of a nineteenth-century style. For example, I might have began this book thus: 'Oh Great Myth-Writers Who Embark Upon this Grand Voyage, Hark!', but you would have known, as would I, that this was nonsense and best avoided, except for parody, in serious writing.

For me, in my theme of childhood and sacrifice, staying true to the insights about human nature and about rites of passage myth offers seems vital, as is the sense of myth being an image of the way to adapt to change. This connects me to the 'suggestful' quality of myth itself, through any attempts at writing which might come from that rich source.

Reading

Again, *browsing through mythic materials is the most vital habit* a writer of the mythic persuasion needs, as mentioned at the beginning of this chapter. See the *key myth texts* bit of the Introduction, as well as some brief ideas below.

Old: any anthology, dictionary, sacred text, book of or on myth, fable, fairytale, folklore, symbol, etc. can be useful. Ovid's *Metamorphosis* is the great source-book in our literary history, but add other browsing places to your own list. Happen across the arcane in the secondhand book places, where secret tales hide.

Childhood: Euripides' *Iphigenia in Tauris*, and *Iphigenia in Aulis* (in *Oresres* and other plays), Aeschylus' *Agamemnon*, and classical dictionaries, plus the old border ballad 'The Cruel Mother'.

New: 'Ulysses', 'The Lotus Eaters' by Tennyson, *Ovid Metamorphosed* (2001, edited by Philip Terry), Angela Carter's tales. These are just a few examples of old tales (*The Bloody Chamber*, 1979) made new.

Critical: *Managing Monsters* (1994), by Marina Warner, T.S. Eliot on James Joyce (*The Dial*, 1923).

Writing

Write about a mythic researcher whose research comes to life in an alarming way.

Chapter 10

◆

THE DAILY
MYTHER

This chapter, with the previous one, is the second dealing with making your mythic writing current. If we understand how myth takes us through our creative process, we can start with what is happening in the world and connect it to ourselves in a mythic way. Here we have an imaginary newspaper called *The Daily Myther* so that we can start imagining how we would reinterpret the news for this journal, which will see the world in terms of myth. Myth, by now for us mythsmiths, has become a way of creatively interacting with the world. So it is proper to begin with a section on Writing, which has previously come near the end of chapters.

WRITING

The front-page headline of this weekend's UK *Guardian* is 'Day of war and peace' (9 August 2008). Russia and Georgia have a civil war, while the Olympic Games have their opening ceremony in China. The obvious mythic significances here are unexplored by the news agenda, but might easily be explored, by, for example, researching Mars, the god of war and exploring the war of the once joined (as Russia and Georgia were in the Soviet Union) as a war with the self, where the enemy is the archetypal Shadow. The Greek connection of the Games and the story of Atalanta occur to me as connections which could be researched. Peace itself is a whole other subject, where the pastoral, or rural, natural world could be evoked against the madness of war, or, perhaps, where ritual conflict might replace actual in a utopian fiction. War is the subject of epic and many mythic parallels can be found. Christopher

Logue's poems based on *The Illiad*, in *War Music* (1981) are a good example of the timeless games of war and peace. In trying to talk about peace, I have slipped into war, which itself is a hint to the way the mind finds peace hard to hold. The potential blindness of both states and their permanence in the history of humanity make them primal, difficult subjects, but there is no doubt of their mythic status or potential. War is the extreme revenge of the collective unconscious, a neglecting of the mythic depths which underlie relationships between peoples, some might say.

Pages 2 and 3 of the same newspaper have masses of detail to make a start from, while researching parallels could be an absorbing task. Page 4 presents the first domestic story, about the increase in home repossession. In Greek tragedy, banishment is seen as being on a par with death. We tend to think of travel as freedom, but the nesting, homing instinct is hard-wired into us and our identification with place, with home, is a primal aspect of our humanity. The balance between the world outside, the unknown and the safe world of home, the known, is as important as any mythic balance and it reflects our feelings about what we belong to, our sense of identity and safety. The hospitality of our culture is another strong mythic trope and it is a well-known thought that *The Odyssey* is about the way guests behave and are treated and about, specifically, homecoming. The wanderer seeking a home, a refuge, is one of the oldest human tales.

Again, there is much detail here, including an example of a single mother with two children who have been faced with the indifference of the world of money. Homelessness is an extreme state and the mythic elements are always strongly present where extremity happens. The tendency for the unfeeling, for the fixed and inflexible 'rational' world of man to override the natural need for shelter, for the allowing of human weakness, are not themes unknown to writers using mythic ways of tackling them. Kafka comes to mind, but so too does *The Bacchae*, with the ultra-rational Pentheus.

Page 5 has a story of a teenage, mountain climbing enthusiast who has died in a fall in the Alps. The climber, Ian Jackson, who was 19, says this: 'Climbing is my demon and also my cure.' If this is not a mythic pronouncement, then I do not know what is. Ian Jackson kept a blog, which may still be available to read, and he talks about climbing as a life-saver and as a meaning-giver. The obvious mythic story might be that of Icarus, but my own instinct would be to ignore using that in any obvious way, while keeping the story in mind. This story is one about the need for the mythic making his life heroic and his death a symbolic loss of that connection. Any early death of a promising young person is tragic. However, his search for a bigger meaning makes his life the thing worth celebrating, with its mythic connections explored.

So, we have only reached page 5 of a 40 page main news section and it seems we have had no trouble getting commissions for *The Daily Myther*, our imaginary mythic newspaper. A tabloid would do just as well and in some ways even better, as they often deal with tales of pride and fall, meat and drink to us, as well as to them. As discussed in the previous chapter, it is finding the one that gets to you and stays with you or nags at you that will turn into the most serious piece of writing. Any of the four themes would do for me: war, peace, home or youthful adventure. It is worth remembering, though, that the news deals with the particular in a general and detailed way, while the creative writer, especially the mythic writer must find the creative way in, where the vividness of the tale connects personally and with the powerful mythic subtext.

Realising the mythic possibilities of smaller stories might be harder, but, the depth of meaning is there in all human life, to paraphrase an old newspaper claim that 'all human life is here'. In Bob Dylan's autobiography *Chronicles, Volume I* (2004), the author claims to have spent much time reading old newspapers, where he finds the sources of the kinds of stories he was listening to in old ballads. Dylan, as a topical and political songwriter, especially in those early days, was finding the old/ new axis, where the new stories are the oldest too. These stories, for the mythsmith, are the presence of the mythic in the everyday.

ABOUT TIME

'All literary works are occasional in some sense; occasional verse differs in having not a private but a public or social occasion', as the entry on Occasional Verse begins in *The New Princeton Encyclopaedia of Poetry and Poetics* (Preminger and Brogan, 1993). I even think some of the lightweight feel of the term 'occasional' might be to do with it sounding as if the poet only writes now and then, which is not in fact any part of the meaning of the phrase. To write is to write about time and to write about time is to write mythically. To write about now is what we are doing and the mythic is now, in its presence. The mythsmith just has a better chance of making it good. The two-places-at-once element of writing about now, with some useful insight derived from myth, is a strength. Our mythic and creative insights can come into play.

Forms such as the elegy, the epithalamium (wedding song) and the ode offer straightforward examples of occasional writing and, as the entry on Occasional Verse points out, the old-style poetry feel of the term did not put off writers like Auden, Yeats, Pound and more recent, contemporary English poets, like Glyn Maxwell and Tony Harrison, from writing about specific, public events. In a sense, the best mythic writing can bring a public sense to a creative medium that seems sometimes to have lost touch with its public role. The wider, unifying context of the resonance that myth can bring to writing makes a move towards capturing an old strength in a new way.

Uncovering patterns in time is again a way to be timely. Being aware of the potential in the seasons (see the Lord of Misrule in Chapter 8, Myth Madness) and of their patterns and symbolic function are a good way in, as is discussing time itself. The unconscious feel of dawn and nightfall, or childhood and age, compared to the conscious feel of morning and afternoon, or of youth and maturity, are some examples of this kind of working.

Yet another definition of myth might be that which explores the timeless quality in time. We seek the timeless in myth itself, in literature, in escapism of all kinds, in love, in home-making and in connecting with time in a useful way, with our ancestors and children. Myths are stories about *timeliness* as well as *timelessness*. Fairytales begin, 'Once upon a time', which feels like a time out of time, if it is not 'in', but 'upon', as if time were a place, still available, as it is, actually, in a story. Much of literature is about escaping into the past or an ideal future, projecting our present woes and joys onto another world. We might yearn for Edens and places where there is no death.

Science Fiction, from *Gulliver's Travels* onward, often deals with immortality in positive or negative ways. Cryogenics seems the latest attempt of the rich to buy immortality, and might be a good writing theme.

The linear movement of time is thought about in images of movement, of rivers, clocks and their 'movements' and the movement of nature in change, growth and decay is never far away from our thoughts. Always it seems, to write is to write about time, if writing, especially for the mythsmith, is an attempted step sideways in time, to get an overview, or to slow or speed the narrative.

We seek the timeless through the timely. We might try fame or a face-lift, or critical superiority, we might feel we are in a circle of time, like a 'Groundhog day', or we feel we are 'in the wrong place at the wrong time'. The timely is the right moment, the moment of revelation or epiphany, the lucky chance or via the right placing of the stars. Ghosts are sometimes seen as those who cannot accept time and we see a fortune-teller or visit the underworld to consult what is outside time, so we can regain purpose in the ceaseless movement.

Tom Chetwynd, in his entry on time in *A Dictionary of Symbols* (1982), identifies three types of time, from the cosmic, or universal time, via evolutionary or historical time, to human time, of life and death. He also gives the picture of the past and present as consciousness, while present and future blend into the unconscious. The unity of time is seen as a circle, which might be an image of cosmic time, or of God as unbroken time, while in human time death is the break in time, the static.

Another powerful mythic view of time is through aging and decay and decline. Ovid outlines the four ages of man: gold, silver, bronze and iron. This pattern shows a decline into the mechanical and materialistic and still has a compelling weight to its imagery. The phrase 'as old as Methuselah' means as old as Noah's father. His name means 'the man of the javelin', or long throw and he lived 969 years and, since then, immortally as a popular personification of longevity. Our tendency to decline, versus the accumulation of wisdom in age represents another useful life/death duality, as does our desire to live fully within our limits, versus a view that sees time as a commodity.

For writers, time has always provided a rich source of stories and images. The edges of time in the longest day, which is the summer solstice, and in the shortest, the winter solstice, are powerful symbols of light and dark. The equinoxes too, when day and night are equal, in spring and autumn, are point of balance between the dark and light, when the world seems to pause.

The wonder at living in time is captured perfectly in Philip Larkin's short poem 'Days', (*The Whitsun Weddings* (in *Collected Poems*), 1964). Days repeat their time and provide us with meditations on life's possibilities. The final image of this short, lyrical poem invokes medicine and religion, which attend to such permanent, impenetrable, mythic things.

Shelley's 'Ozymandias' (1818) looks at historical time and compares it to a human perspective.

> I met a traveller from an antique land
> Who said: Two vast and trunkless legs of stone
> Stand in the desert. Near them on the sand,
> Half sunk, a shattered visage lies, whose frown
> And wrinkled lip and sneer of cold command
> Tell that its sculptor well those passions read
> Which yet survive, stamped on these lifeless things,
> The hand that mocked them and the heart that fed:
> And on the pedestal these words appear:
> 'My name is Ozymandias, King of Kings:
> Look on my works, ye mighty, and despair!'
> Nothing beside remains. Round the decay
> Of that colossal wreck, boundless and bare,
> The lone and level sands stretch far away.

The strangeness of time is evoked in this opening lines: 'I met a traveller from an antique land,/ Who said:' Already we are distanced and estranged into a wider knowledge, both in space via travel and in time, which is 'antique', both strange and possibly wonderful. The power and pride of the ancient king of the title are no match for the ravages of time, especially to our puny age. The gigantic statue is ruined and 'Round the decay/ Of that colossal wreck, boundless and bare/ The lone and level sands stretch far away.' So ends the poem, with an image of cosmic time's endlessness compared with historical time and that of human frailty and pride.

Yeats' 'The Second Coming' (1921) deals with prophecy, where current human 'mere anarchy' and confusion give birth to a return of something nightmarish, culminating in the last couplet: 'And what rough beast, its hour come round at last,/ Slouches towards Bethlehem to be born?' Like Shelley, it is through the contrast of human time with a deeper, longer sense of it that the effect of the poem's strength is achieved.

Feasts, festivals and customs can offer the cosmic to the everyday and contemporary poet Glyn Maxwell's poem 'Hometown Mystery Cycle' (published in *Guardian* 'Review', 29.12.07) offers a view of a local participant. Mystery plays are a medieval form of religious play, acted out by local people in the streets of the place the version belongs to. Maxwell's poem demonstrates the mix of the Biblical and the contemporary in vivid language. Tony Harrison is another contemporary poet who has worked with this material and his plays, staged at the National Theatre in London, collectively called *The Mysteries* (1985), were likewise a bringing down to earth of the religious.

Writers mix the cosmic with the historical and both with the human to provide the time out of time, which is the mythic effect. The creative process steps outside time, in order to reorder it, to gain perspective which helps define our feeling of being alive and of being located. The ritual space of writing is also ritual time, as time is reflected and suspended in the work. When H.G. Wells wrote his classic novel *The Time Machine* (1895), he was also describing the process writers go through and how the restless mind seeks to locate itself.

NEWS AND HISTORY, LIFETIMES AND BALLADS

Using history to write about now gives both a long view and a human view. We identify with the common humanity of historical happenings, while we feel the mythic tendency of a repeating pattern. The sense of discovery is thus tempered with a sense of rediscovery. If I know that Monday is a day sacred to the moon and that August is derived from 'Arn-monath', meaning 'barn month', when barns were filled, I might then have a grasp on the day I write this and even think of a harvest moon, around the later time of the autumn equinox, when there are usually evenings of bright moonlight, which light the getting in of the harvest. When the fertility of this knowledge is gathered, a day, as Larkin suggests, can be all we have to live in made wider and deeper. Riches of harvests are possible where the crops are gathered and the barn is ready.

Probably the best example of a historical view of human time is Shakespeare's passage from *As You Like It* (II, vii), which begins 'All the world's a stage'.

> All the world's a stage,
> And all the men and women merely players;
> They have their exits and their entrances;
> And one man in his time plays many parts,
> His acts being seven ages. At first the infant,
> Mewling and puking in the nurse's arms;
> And then the whining school-boy, with his satchel
> And shining morning face, creeping like snail
> Unwillingly to school. And then the lover,
> Sighing like furnace, with a woeful ballad
> Made to his mistress' eyebrow. Then a soldier,
> Full of strange oaths, and bearded like the pard,
> Jealous in honour, sudden and quick in quarrel,
> Seeking the bubble reputation
> Even in the cannon's mouth. And then the justice,
> In fair round belly with good capon lin'd,
> With eyes severe and beard of formal cut,
> Full of wise saws and modern instances;
> And so he plays his part. The sixth age shifts
> Into the lean and slipper'd pantaloon,
> With spectacles on nose and pouch on side;
> His youthful hose, well sav'd, a world too wide
> For his shrunk shank; and his big manly voice,
> Turning again toward childish treble, pipes
> And whistles in his sound. Last scene of all,
> That ends this strange eventful history,
> Is second childishness and mere oblivion;
> Sans teeth, sans eyes, sans taste, sans everything.

The absurdity of the 'seven ages' being played out echo archetypes of age. 'The lover,/ Sighing like a furnace, with a woeful ballad/ Made to his mistress' eyebrow' is still funny and the bleak, cynical ending, 'sans everything' paints loss at its cosmic and comic utmost.

Adrian Mitchell's 'To You' is a poem which uses a simple time structure in the first stanza to give the traumas of life a shape and the feel of a lesson in life's difficulties. 'One: we were swaddled, ugly-beautiful and drunk on milk', the poem begins. By 'Four: we were hit. Suddenly hit', we begin to feel the pain that time has made us inheritors to, where the refrain of the final lines of each stanza comes in: 'My love, they are trying to drive us mad.' Mitchell reports in his annotations (in *Out Loud*, annotated edition, 1976) that what he thought was a private poem to his wife became public when he realised that 'other people had passed through a very similar sequence of experiences', which made it a 'public poem' too. Time and the attention to the present feeling of pain has made the poem take the mythic step from the private world in to the communal, which is very much the journey that Mitchell's poems intend to make. Time offers cyclic structure that gives us a better view of where we are and makes the news more real than mere novelty.

Ballads are the great oral form of poetry which combine a traditional shape and structure often containing both history and news. The narrative immediacy of them and their continual use in poetry tell of their needing to have that combination which is an aspect of tradition at its most positive. This is the old frame which is self-renewing and built to contain nowness as a way of being built to last. The traditional ballads that often begin anthologies of English poetry offer some strong examples, while the literary ballad, from *The Ancient Mariner* to poems by Auden and Charles Causley, still flourishes. Glyn Maxwell's poem discussed above is not in a conventional ballad metre, but has several aspects of the ballad about it. The ballad was a song form, and perhaps, by derivation, a form that was connected to dance too ('ballet' is from the same root). Many modern songs, especially in country music, with its direct relation to folksong, are, intended or not, in ballad form.

The simple, four-beat iambic line, followed by one of three beats, then two more lines as above, with the second and forth rhyming, has its own laconic and on-going rhythm, which works well in English.

> As I went out one May morning
>> One bright morning in Spring
> I saw a woman on the hill
>> And she began to sing

This might make you wonder what she sang, but the rhythm and rhyme carry the narrative, the temporal, without lingering.

Often the stories of ballads were about scandal, about the kind of stories that people would tell each other, before writing. The form works well to help us talk in stories and the use of terse, sometimes repeating lines gives an urgency and toughness which poets still seek to balance with their contemporary ponderings, or allusiveness.

Ballads, like films, tend to work in scenes, which illustrate aspects of the narrative and speed and sharpen the telling. They often switch points of view, where speeches and persons might change to useful, multi-voiced effect. They often, as do newspapers, deal in tragic events and contain all the elements of a news story: violence, love, treachery, disguise, betrayal, posh people (Ladies and Lords in traditional ballads) and murders. They, like all mythic material, have the essential cosmic element of the supernatural. They are often strange stories, with shapeshifting, other worlds, ghosts, fairies, demon lovers and mythic encounters and ordeals. The stock phrases, like 'As I went out' are much in evidence, which are shortcuts and useful for the composer using a traditional form, to make the listeners feel comfortable and familiar, even though they might be presented with some new story. The simple, direct language is often stark and factual, wasting no time in its urgency to communicate.

Contemporary songwriter Nick Cave's *Murder Ballads* (1996) contains ballads that go back to the great collection of the Reverend Child, in the nineteenth century. A ballad like 'Thomas the Rhymer' (Child's *English and Scottish Popular Ballads*, 1882–98) tells of a writer's journey into the world of the imagination as an encounter with the Queen of Elfland. He kisses her and then must go with her to her world, where 'living land was left behind'. They wade through blood, which is 'all the blood that's shed on earth' and he is given an apple which makes him tell the truth, Cassandra like. He resists this at first, but comes back to the world, after seven years, inspired and dressed for poetry. This ballad poem describes the journey of the imagination and boasts the power of the same to see 'ferlies' or wonders and return with them to tell the tale. This old rhyme-story is a classic creative writing myth, describing the heroic journey this book seeks to explore, and is essential reading.

Auden's ballad 'As I Walked Out One Evening' (1937) gives a late and meditative feel to its subject by its subtle change from the normal 'morning' of the traditional form. The poem turns into a meditation on love and time's fleetingness. The ballad here is a 'live-while-you-can' time-work, like Marvell's 'To His Coy Mistress', which begins with the thought that 'Had we but world enough and time', it might be OK to be 'coy'. Auden affirms life finally, however broken or troublesome it may seem. This is a ballad which discusses the form in its immediacy and the difficulty of living in that immediate present. The form and the content, the imaginative journey and narrative of the poem work as one, via a vivid sketch of real life, of a walk in the real world.

Writing about the most current event with mythic depth is, in a sense, what myth, especially in its traditional manifestation, is for. So the view of myth as some kind of archaic nostalgia, or abstract pontificating can be properly dismissed, especially by the writer/ mythsmith. Myth is here, myth is now. This is the news and myth is the news.

Writing and reading about time

Philosophical: read T.S. Eliot's 'Burnt Norton' (1941), from *Four Quartets*, especially Part 5 and write a response to it.

Cosmic-Historical-Mysterious: write a parody of Shelley's 'Ozymandias'; 'I met a traveller from - - - -/ Who said: - - - .. .'. Write, alternatively, about an encounter with something ancient/timeless.

Wonder-Fear: Celebrate a season, a time of day, the weather, the stars, etc. See Larkin's 'Days'.

Prophecy: Write an alternative Second Coming, after reading Yeats' poem 'The Second Coming'.

Investigate local feasts, customs and festivals and visit/ describe.

Invent your own ages of mankind: e.g. typewriter, valve, transistor, chip.

Write about living forever: See 'The Struldbruggs' in Swift's *Gulliver's Travels*.

Write about now . . . and now . . . and now (investigate 'stream of conscious-ness' writing).

Writing and reading about history and news

Find a contemporary story in a local paper and find a historical or folkloric precedent. Write about one haunting the other.

Turn a news story into a ballad, using an old ballad as a source of phrases and narrative. Read anthologies of ballads and use some lines and constructions from the old ones.

Think of a strange but true story you know and write in ballad form.

Write, after reading Auden's 'As I Went Out One Evening', a ballad called 'As I Went Out At Midnight', describing the streets of your local town/ city, when the streets are full of the celebratory young.

Link the latest story with the oldest you can find. Practise reading the news mythically (see first part of this chapter and Part Two, A Mythic Subject Dictionary).

Chapter 11

◆

DOOMS AND DEAD ENDS

'Woe, woe, woe, to the inhabitors of the earth' (Revelation 8:13, *King James Bible*)

WHY WE DO DOOM

When all myths fail, a big death will do. A triumphant and total disaster, a death made massive, or an evil amplified to cosmos-destroying, explosive, annihilating power will come, bidden or not. When myths fail, a big mad myth will come to tell you its real, secret message, under whatever you might think about it. That message is that the myth is here, the myth will come, the myth will return. It is the quality of our myths to which we need to attend. The final two chapters of this section of the book now move towards a discussion of aspects of the mythic which seem currently most present in our Western world. These are the myths of fame and glory, and, at the other extreme, myths of universal doom.

Peter Cook's sketch 'The End of the World' from the album version of *Beyond the Fringe* (1961) does the story well. A few members of a millennial cult gather to await the end of the world, where only they will be saved. 'Now is the end/ Perish the world' they chant. When is does not happen, the leader ends the sketch by saying, 'Oh well, same time next week.'

But before taking the rise out of it, we must take it seriously, if we want to discover how pervasive, as well as how recent in some ways, this big myth of our time has arrived. From conspiracy theories to pollution, from invading aliens to nuclear holocausts, these myths persist in various convincing and unconvincing forms. The phenomenon of 'world wars', which Kurt Vonnegut called mankind's unsuccessful suicide attempts, haunts us. Our technological advances, and, perhaps, the failure of the world to perfect itself along with its machines may have led us to a kind of pessimism and confusion. The state is mythic, even if it looks post-mythic. When things look post-mythic is exactly the time when myth is the most useful tool. Myth contains the post-mythic without a struggle and will transcend it. That is what myth is for.

What are the sources of these apocalyptic myths, these doomsdays, millenniums, holocausts, Armageddons, which ask to be expressed only in the singular? The old flood stories of the Bible might provide a starting place and old prophesies of doom, but the move towards this extreme is surely more recent than the Old Testament and is brought to its pitch in the New Testament of the Christian Bible, in Revelations, as we shall see. Underlying all dooms are, of course, the older problem, that of evil. More recently still, we have the loss of faith, or the 'death of God' and the rise of science, with its own versions of revelatory doom, nuclear and environmental. Ends of the world without renewal seem to be an aspect of doom which has grown historically, through floods, which contain a new start, through to millennialism and finally to nuclear weapons. Our dooms have kept getting doomier.

EVIL AND DEATH

The problem of evil is the root of all our dooms. Evil arrives in the world with consciousness. Myth deals with innocence and experience, with the division between our states of being, which arrive in the world with creation. When there is day and night, there arrives in the world the thinking aspect and the unthinking. Nature seems good in its unthinking innocence and evil often comes as a reminder that our thinking cannot live without a reminder of nature, of the laws we cannot control. We are unable to live up to our conscious idea of good. The book of Genesis is a book of falling from the balance between nature and thought, or between God and man. The fall of Adam and Eve, the flood and the Tower of Babel follow this mythic pattern, as Edmund Leach tells us in *Genesis as Myth* (1969). *The Epic of Gilgamesh* tells the story of evil as a problem of civilisation, where a nature-boy, Enkidu, is created, to rebalance the city.

Evil is either caused by sin, or by the innate created dualism of the world. Adam and Eve's disobedience is seen as sin, or, on the other hand, the inevitable price paid for consciousness. When we are split from the divine, from God or from nature, or from the unconscious balance, evil is repressed into the shadows. It is behind the locked door, as in Orwell's *1984*. Evil and hell are with us in one form or another and dooms are their fulfilment, their ultimate form. We are drawn to evil, in its power to contain everything repressed, as Georges Bataille suggests in *Literature and Evil*. We are torn away from our animal other and seek to reunite with it via death, decadence and destruction. We desire to lose ourselves in the flux of the world, as we can never live up to our thoughts and dreams of perfection.

Along with the idea of evil is the idea of taboo. Taboos deal with the non-rational, the things we seek to avoid or repress, like death itself, or the loss of identity we seek in sex or drugs. Religion used to help with this, via ritual sacrifices and festivals. When something is destroyed, it returns to the divine, in its mythic state. To sacrifice is to make sacred.

After the Enlightenment and even now, we demand that God be explained to us as a rational concept. Literary writers have sought to redress this balance, in their tragedies and mythic work, as well as in the theoretical idea of 'defamiliarisation', of making the world strange again. The Devil asks us, via Faust or Christ, to make a pact. The Devil steals the show, as he did in *Paradise Lost*, and offers us the material world unbalanced by the myth of the divine. But the denial of evil brings back the apocalyptic fantasy. This is the return of the irrational: this is the end.

It might seem reductive, if mythically correct, to say that doom myths are to do with our inability to deal with death, cosmically, historically, as well as personally. An old English folksong, 'Death and the Lady' recounts meeting 'an old man by the way'. She asks him 'Of what strange place do you belong?' He replies, 'My name is death, cannot you see?/ Lords, Dukes and Ladies bow down to me . . . And you fair maid must come with me', as 'your time has come'. The strangeness of death, the inevitability and the dying of human pride are played out in the game with death, just as they are in Bergman's film *The Seventh Seal* (1957). In the song, the lady offers him all her wealth for 'a few years more', but death says, 'Put your jewels aside'. It is arguable that religion and science and even the cult movements towards myth and magic, from the 1960s onwards, have sought a way to overcome death. The revenge of these attempts at bargaining with the inevitable have given us the big, bad dream of the personal death as universal disaster.

WRITERS AND REVELATION

Yet, for writers, these big doom scenarios, these big booms, have been a big boon. From the Book of Revelation to *Notes from Underground* (Dostoyevsky,

1864) and *A Season in Hell* (Rimbaud, 1873; in *Collected Poems*), we have loved our big ends, with T.S. Eliot, wondering about 'the way the world ends', in 'The Hollow Men'. 'What does reason know?' asks the underground man, while Rimbaud's *A Season in Hell* (1873) presents us, in the opening section, with a comic decent into otherness. In Oliver Barnard's translation (1962), all human good seems idiotic and false: 'Charity is this key – this inspiration proves that I have been dreaming!' We all have our favourites, our versions of hellfire preaching and writing them is, paradoxically, fun and cathartic.

The word 'apocalypse' is often associated with The Revelation of St John the Divine, which is the last book of the New Testament and the last of the Bible. Much of our big doom comes from here. 'Apocalypse' and 'Revelation' both actually mean the same thing, an uncovering or something revealed, and in the Book of Revelation could be said to mean the revealing of what has often been called the End Times. The word 'end' appears in Revelation, but not 'end times', though the book does describe Judgement Day, when the world is destroyed and the saved are carried to heaven. In a strange way, the apocalypse, as an uncovering, has come to mean a kind of blind end, a slide downhill to destruction, without, or beyond any judgement. Doom without heaven is our own age's dark vision towards ultimate darkness.

Reading Revelation as a writer can reveal something of why this word has been so distorted. The book itself, the source of so much righteous madness, is, from a literary and from a writer's point of view, bonkers. When I asked a friend about it, she said, 'I wonder what he was on when he wrote it', and I have to agree. For a literal, evangelistic reader seeking comfort, this might not be a useful thought, but for a writer this side of the book is great. Its greatness is twofold. It is full of crazy stuff and memorable and mad images and phrases, but it is also the source book of much of our thinking about the end of the world, about good and evil, about the future and about much grandiose religious extremity, of the type we see so often now. If you want to write about any of this, any doom, St John the Divine is your man.

The confidence of the prophet is striking, especially at the beginning and the end of the book, and the book itself states that it is to do with beginnings and ends. This, we know from chapter one, already is a myth-alert. Chapter 1:8 gives a phrase often repeated in the book: 'I am the Alpha and Omega, the beginning and the ending.' This is God speaking through the writer, of course, but as the end book about 'end times', we know, has a greater significance. As a writer, John is saying, I am the ultimate. You will not read anything more far out, or final, than this. Not only is he the voice of God, but after him all writing is redundant. His is a rapper's big-up boast.

Read as a text about creativity, this sense that 'the time is at hand' (1:3) is a reminder that doom, like everything, is now, the ultimate present being the prospect of death. The whole text has this flavour and feels, underlying its influence, very modern in its egoistic, insistent urgency. When God 'cometh with clouds' and 'all shall wail because of him' (1:7), we have the kind of in-your-face God that people want, the showboating, death-metal God, a God of publicity, pizzazz and spectacle.

As a piece of writing too, the book is all *about* writing. 'I was in the Spirit . . . and heard behind me a great voice.' The voice says 'what thou seest, write in a book' (1:10–11). The whole of chapter one is about writing it down, a kind of manifesto of the writer's importance.

The promise of the beginning is matched by the threat of the end. This is in interesting opposition to the content. What he reveals is the end, followed by the saved, which is a beginning. The book is Omega and Alpha, as well as the other way round. However mad in content, the structure is tightly bound by assertions of confidence in its ultimate writer's strength. The writing, rather than the subject, offers another end, in the last chapter (22), with its ultimate threat:

> 18 For I testify unto every man that heareth the words of the prophecy of this book, If any man shall add unto these things, God shall add unto him the plagues that are written in this book.
>
> 19 And if any man shall take away from the words of the book of this prophecy, God shall take away his part out of the book of life, and out of the holy city, and from the things which are written in this book.

These kinds of threats were common in writing at the time of composition, which Biblical scholars and commentators have to admit, when they feel that this is not quite as holy in expression as they might wish it to be. For a doom-writer though, this kind of thing is meat and drink, if we think of the curse as a genre. The verses remind me of a curse-story by J.G. Ballard, called 'Now Zero' (*The Overloaded Man*, 1967), where what the author/ protagonist writes comes true. The story ends with a countdown, intending to kill the reader. The sci-fi potential of Revelation is endless, you might say.

It is hard for a writer to believe how seriously people have taken this book of the Bible. Seen as a work of allegory and imagination, it is baffling, bizarre and bonkers, but convincing in its extremity. The fact that it is food for extremists should not blind us to the fact that it is good too for writers who seek the truth (the revelation) through the extreme journey into the creative. The book within a book motif is strongly present throughout, alerting us to the discussion of the creative. The verse which goes, 'And I wept much, because no man was found worthy to open and to read the book, neither to look thereon' (5:4) is about making the message grander and more exclusive and about the importance of writing too. The writing is where the truth is and where the salvation is, therefore the salvation is in prophecy itself.

There even seems to be a little guilt showing in chapter 13:5, where we hear of 'a mouth speaking great things and blasphemies', but that is the others, of course, as 'no-one could learn the song but the ... redeemed' (14:3) or even open or see the book, as noted earlier. These boasts remind me again of rappers, as much as anything else. Often we get a hint at the visionary nature of the prophecy, in the sense that he imagines this stuff. Chapter 17:3 has John saying that the angel 'carried me away in spirit' and these insistences on the process of prophecy show, also, the sense of creative invention. Instances of words like 'book' and 'write' occur throughout and the whole could be read as a plea for the validity of the creative. Every insistence on the literal makes a hidden insistence on the writer's imagination. The wealth of great stories and phrases confirms this.

The writer takes part in creation and destruction and uses one to feed the other. One of the most telling chapters in Revelation is 10, where another repeat of the end and begin motif is enacted, on the theme of writing. The angel arrives as he is about to write and says 'write ... not' (4). Any 'mystery' (7) is to be done away with. If this is not a writer seeking truth through interaction with what is normally beyond rational knowledge, in the classic mythic way, then I should 'write ... not' myself. The angel bears 'a little book' (2) and commands, 'take it and eat it up; and it shall make thy belly bitter, but it shall be in thy mouth sweet as honey' (9). Then 'thou must prophesy again' (11). The bitter truth that sings well is another writing manifesto and another version of the creative working through the writer to reveal a curiously sensuous feeling of tasting the sweetness of the work. Eating the words and speaking the words is a process of intention, of seriousness and again, above all, about imaginative writing. Was he swallowing a drug, though? Well, maybe, but the drug is also a symbol of the truth arriving as if unbidden and the imagination working as if from elsewhere.

In *A Dictionary of Sacred Myth* (1986) Tom Chetwynd says, in the entry called 'Transforming', that the book is 'the most sustained mythological' narrative about transformation. 'It should be read with three eyes: one on the violent spasms of a dying Ego; another on the processes of corruption and decay that infest and infect the social collective ego ... ; and the third on the great roar of brute Energy ... devouring and destroying everything.' From here 'the potential of a new human society is born ... and a man is transformed and transfigured by the experience: John is turned into St John the Divine.' So the writer is transformed by the transforming mythological work and the song is learned and it is self-renewing.

Chetwynd also says that 'the overall pattern of the Bible conforms to the pattern of life itself' (*A Dictionary of Symbols* (1982), under 'Biblical Symbolism') and the book's insistent 'book of life' motif bears this out. Read symbolically, Revelation is quite a trip. Read literally it is quite a trap. If there was one piece of evidence to be given about not taking the messages of religion literally, this book is it. The riches of its verbal and imaginative power, especially in the King James version, are endless. If you want doom, nuclear heat-death, weird symbols, great whores and beasts, visitations and the damned city of Babylon, all human death is here, as well as salvation and the need and promise of 'all things new' (21:5).

DOOMS OF GOD

Even the other great force of doom and gloom, the 'death of God' seems to stem from Revelation, which is the source too of the antichrist, as in the great beast and the end of religion. The end has swallowed all ends and turned them to its tune. The millennial ideal of ends, often used by extremists, starts there, with direct references to one thousand year events, as does the religion of anti-religion. The ego-claim of this ultimate ego-book is all-pervasive. The 'death of God' is then a religious idea with its roots in the ideas of St John the Divine.

The whole, huge subject of the loss of faith, while also being the loss of myth too to some extent, is mostly beyond the scope of this book, while, like any post-faith activity, the book also grapples with and against the failure of myth, as much as its potential for success. The mythic age, you might say, ends with the Enlightenment. Later, the story goes, myth turns into psychology and the ego of the individual seems to be in the ascendant. Despite this, a desire for myth prevails and returns and myth here even seems like these are the very conditions it needs to work in, where the worlds needs renewal. Belief seems too literal for us now, but by understanding the symbolic, or mythic, we can approach belief in a more subtle or even more open-minded way. We might need to be more sceptical about absolute doom.

In a way, the 'death of God' became its own revelation of new possibilities, even for myth and hence for faith. Joseph Campbell says that 'the disintegration for the foundations of . . . faith . . . during the centuries of its own collapse, became (ironically!) one of the most influential, simultaneously constructive and destructive, forces in the history of mankind', in part four of 'The Death of "God"', in *Creative Mythology* (1968). The Devil, or the great beast of evil in Revelation is, after all, the god of material things, of temptation of Christ in the Gospels and of living 'deliciously' (18:7). Faustian pacts with the devil and the story of witchcraft are both huge examples of this creative and destructive energy at work.

Campbell points out also that our rational myth has resulted in 'new appreciation of the loveliness of this world and the arts of its celebration', in the same section of *Creative Mythology*, so the myth never stops returning, even when it is 'dead'. The arts of all kinds, writing not the least, have always concerned themselves with these mythical, or religious, matters and actually with the crises over them. Campbell's claims for mythology are 'awe, humility and respect', to render 'an image' of the processes of that wonder, to help the community and the individual make sense of the world. Myth, he argues in this chapter, still has its part to play. The balance between progress and now is also the balance of the imagination of who and what we are and how we belong to the world's story and the world's death.

The 'death of God' then is a modern myth, just as the nature worship of the environmental movement is. We move constantly and instinctively towards the thing from which we are disconnected. Nietzsche's own writing on the idea reads like sections of Revelation. Thomas Hardy's poem 'God's Funeral', written after the turn of the century and just before the First World War, is a revealing exploration of our mixed feelings about our brave nihilism, which, as Nietzsche pointed out, we are not quite ready for.

God's Funeral (1910)

I

I saw a slowly-stepping train –
Lined on the brows, scoop-eyed and bent and hoar –
Following in files across a twilit plain
A strange and mystic form the foremost bore.

II

And by contagious throbs of thought
Or latent knowledge that within me lay
And had already stirred me, I was wrought
To consciousness of sorrow even as they.

III

The fore-borne shape, to my blurred eyes,
At first seemed man-like, and anon to change

To an amorphous cloud of marvellous size,
At times endowed with wings of glorious range.

IV
And this phantasmal variousness
Ever possessed it as they drew along:
Yet throughout all it symboled none the less
Potency vast and loving-kindness strong.

V
Almost before I knew I bent
Towards the moving columns without a word;
They, growing in bulk and numbers as they went,
Struck out sick thoughts that could be overheard: –

VI
"O man-projected Figure, of late
Imaged as we, thy knell who shall survive?
Whence came it we were tempted to create
One whom we can no longer keep alive?

VII
"Framing him jealous, fierce, at first,
We gave him justice as the ages rolled,
Will to bless those by circumstance accurst,
And long-suffering, and mercies manifold.

VIII
"And, tricked by our own early dream
And need of solace, we grew self-deceived,
Our making soon our maker did we deem,
And what we had imagined we believed.

IX
"Till, in Time's stayless stealthy swing,
Uncompromising rude reality
Mangled the Monarch of our fashioning,
Who quavered, sank; and now has ceased to be.

X
"So, toward our myth's oblivion,
Darkling, and languid-lipped, we creep and grope
Sadlier than those who wept in Babylon,
Whose Zion was a still abiding hope.

XI
"How sweet it was in years far hied
To start the wheels of day with trustful prayer,

To lie down liegely at the eventide
And feel a blest assurance he was there!

XII

"And who or what shall fill his place?
Whither will wanderers turn distracted eyes
For some fixed star to stimulate their pace
Towards the goal of their enterprise?" . . .

XIII

Some in the background then I saw,
Sweet women, youths, men, all incredulous,
Who chimed: "This is a counterfeit of straw,
This requiem mockery! Still he lives to us!"

XIV

I could not buoy their faith: and yet
Many I had known: with all I sympathized;
And though struck speechless, I did not forget
That what was mourned for, I, too, long had prized.

XV

Still, how to bear such loss I deemed
The insistent question for each animate mind,
And gazing, to my growing sight there seemed
A pale yet positive gleam low down behind,

XVI

Whereof, to lift the general night,
A certain few who stood aloof had said,
"See you upon the horizon that small light –
Swelling somewhat?" Each mourner shook his head.

XVII

And they composed a crowd of whom
Some were right good, and many nigh the best . . .
Thus dazed and puzzled 'twixt the gleam and gloom
Mechanically I followed with the rest.

The poem describes a funeral procession of misery, 'scoop-eyed and bent and hoar', yet bearing 'a strange and mystic form'. Already the balance of belief and unbelief are shown with the tension between the ineffability of death and its material finality. The mystical feeling of this funeral procession is accented in the second stanza, as mass mind-reading happens towards 'consciousness of sorrow'. But the cry of stanza vi, 'O man-projected Figure' gives us again the doubt, summed up in the last lines of the stanza, where 'we were tempted to create/ One whom we can no longer keep alive'. We are left now with 'Uncompromising rude reality' and the question 'who or what shall fill his place?' (IX, XII), reminding us of Yeats' 'The Second Coming'. Towards the end some see a 'small light' and some deny it, but the ambivalence, which is also the ambivalence of myth, is summed up in the final lines: 'Thus dazed and puzzled 'twixt the gleam and gloom/ Mechanically I followed with the rest'. The overall feeling is one of human inadequacy here and the belief, or unbelief, of the time carrying us on.

From a writer's point of view the accepting of the strangeness of endings and of mechanical slides to destruction are the things worth noticing. If you want to do good ends, you must understand that ends cannot help but call to beginnings. 'The best', as Yeats' says, might 'lack all conviction', but to wield an end is not so banal as it seems. Myth thus describes the inexplicable with its emphasis on process, which deals with the 'Alpha and Omega' with every attempt.

To get in touch with old ideas of Doom, which means the Last Judgement, and liveliness of the threat and promise, the great medieval Doom paintings of English churches provide a series of images which take you through the process of hell and heaven. Once again, evil and destruction look powerful, especially via the common depiction of the 'hell's mouth' whale swallowing the naked sinners. The vividness of ending is always a refreshing one. The figures of the naked rising from their graves, especially in the Doom painting at Wenhaston in Suffolk, United Kingdom, are particularly touching in their humanity and even the rich approach heaven naked, except for their headgear. The gloom of the picture is extreme, but its vividness is the vividness of the book of life, to extend St John's symbol.

These old texts and visual works, where ends of worlds, especially last judgements, are so often depicted are an obvious contrast to how we think now and as such great for inspiring writing. When we have to confront the millennialism of our own time, the lack of distance sometimes makes it more difficult. Dudley Young says that science, sometimes seen as the enemy of myth, is 'calling us back to order', telling us 'that indeed there is a context of limitation in which the human story unfolds ... It's name is Mother Nature, and she is alive and not well', in *Origins of the Sacred* (1991), 'Perceiving the World', 1. In his introduction Young discusses the old word 'pollution' and its return: 'the worst of our pollutions [is] the nuclear bomb: the desire (disowned of course) to nuke the planet is but the tumorous extension of the old sacrilegious dream of making war on the gods, the desire "to become one of us", as Yahwe puts it in Genesis (3:22)'. With the possibility of ending the world, too, mankind has re-entered the mythic in the scientific age. If science can end the world with the press of a key, or by slower poison, then the myth needs renewing and we need to read about Faust and Frankenstein again.

DOOM NOW

Philosopher John Gray's book, *Black Mass* (2007), gives us a view of modern politics in terms of its millennial and hence mythic thinking. The book describes how our idea of progress is actually a utopian, apocalyptic belief, and mythic all the more despite or because of its avowed rationalism. The book begins with the bold sentence, 'Modern politics is a chapter in the history of religion'. In 'Post-Apocalypse', towards the end of the book, he says, 'Myths are not true or false in the way scientific theories are true or false, but they can be more or less truthful in reflecting the enduring realities of human life', while 'secular creeds are more unreasonable than any traditional faith, if only because they make a more elaborate show of being rational'. He also speaks here of 'The Utopias of the past two centuries' as 'deformed versions of the myths they denied'. For the writer, his chilling analysis of contemporary politics and how it is revealed in its 'deformed' Utopianism can provide an insight into how myth is now, in the least likely place we might expect it to be. His last few paragraphs spell it out: 'Apocalypse is . . . an anthropocentric myth.' And, 'ancient legends are better guides to the present than modern myths of progress and Utopia'. The final paragraph is worth quoting in full:

> The modern age has been a time of superstition no less than the medieval era, in some ways more so. Transcendental religions have many flaws and in the case of Christianity gave birth to savage violence, but at its best religion has been an attempt to deal with mystery rather than the hope that mystery will be unveiled. In the clash of fundamentalisms this civilising perception has been lost. Wars as ferocious as those of early modern times are being fought against a background of increased knowledge and power. Interacting with the struggle for natural resources, the violence of faith looks set to shape the coming century.

Given the part myth has to play at the centre of our current world and its 'woe, woe, woe', writing about the most pressing dooms is available and easy, while being the hardest thing to do well. We are in the midst of our own mad, revelation narratives, which, in their fabulous extremities of ego-blinded violence, seem to deny a cooler mythic approach. But for satire and for doom, the world, which may always be ready, is certainly ready now for mythic medicine and exploration.

DOOM-WRITE

Science fiction is the genre we are exploring indirectly here and the works of J.G. Ballard do ending particularly well, such as *The Drowned World* (1962). The important thing here is, however, that 'the time' really is 'at hand', to begin to write about the end. So ending here, then, are two works which do ending in contrasting contemporary styles.

'Always the Flood' is a response to the summer flooding in England, 2007, and is an example of a contemporary take on ending the world, which was, via Revelation and via nuclear science, said to be by fire rather than flood this time.

Always the Flood (by A.M.)

The fireman's pumping out the water.

It's always the flood,
though they said it was all going to end
with fire next time,
nuking us with fantastic, unnatural heat,
some heavy lightening,
civilisation cooked in its own oven.

But after all it's always the inundation,
it's what you need and what you're made of;
engulfed by being neglectful, out of balance.

It's elements and essences, not achievements;
Fire we play with: Water we are.

It's always after us, the deluge,
And what it means,
what it meant for Noah and Gilgamesh
and the Kraken waking,
is that you've made too much noise
and now you're on your own;

sinking, still after the impossible
arc of a rainbow.

And the fire brings the flood.
And the earth brings the flood.
And the air brings the flood.
And the flood brings the Flood.

(from *An Essex Attitude*, 2009)

Philip Terry's poem 'Dante: Inferno I' is hell translated into a modern university campus. It is not only a literary retake, but is a careful satire of extremity in dark vision and shows the possibilities of the formal taking on what seems the contemporary in all its apparent impossibility. All ends are about redemption, as all ends are mythical and therefore point to beginnings, even, or especially for writers, in their darkest visions.

DANTE: INFERNO I
by Philip Terry

Halfway through a bad trip
I found myself in this stinking car park,
Underground, miles from Amarillo.

Students in thongs stood there,
Eating junk food from skips,
    flagmen spewing e's,

Their breath of fetid
Myrrh and rat's bane,
    doners

And condemned chicken shin
    rose like
        distemper.

Then I retched on rising ground;
Rabbits without ears, faces eaten away
    by myxomatosis

Crawled towards a bleak lake
    to drink
        of leucotomy.

The stink would revive a
    sparrow, spreadeagled on
    a lectern.

It so horrified my heart
    I shat
        botox.

Here, by the toxic water,
    lay a spotted trout, its glow
    lighting paths for the VC.

And nigh the bins a giant rat,
Seediness oozing from her Flemish pores,
Pushed me backwards, bit by bit

Into Square 5,
> where the wind gnaws
> > and sunshine is spent.

By the cashpoint
> a bum asked for a light,
> hoarse from long silence, beaming.

When I saw him gyrate,
His teeth all wasted,
> > > natch,

His eyes
> long dead
> through speed and booze,

I cried out
> > "Take pity,
Whatever you are, man or ghost!"

"Not man, though formerly a man,"
> he says, "I hale from Providence,
> > Rhode Island, a Korean vet.

"Once I was a poet, I wrote
> > of bean spasms,
> > > was anthologised in *Fuck You.*"

"You're never Berrigan, that spring
Where all the river of style freezes?"
I ask, awe all over my facials.

"I'm an American
> Primitive," he says,
"I make up each verse as it comes,

"By putting things
> > > where they
> > have to go."

"O glory of every poet, have a light,
May my Zippo benefit me now,
And all my stripping of your *Sonnets.*

"You see this hairy she-rat
> > that stalks me like a pimp:
Get her   off my back,

· 136 ·

for every vein and pulse
Throughout my frame she hath
                            made quake."

"You must needs another way pursue,"
He says, winking while I shade my pin,
"If you wouldst 'scape this beast.

"Come, she lets none past her,
Save the VC, If she breathes on you,
                    you're teaching nights."

"This way, freshman, come,
If I'm not far wrong we can find
A bar, and talk it over with Ed and Tom."

(From *Oulipoems 2*, 2009)

Writing

A conversation with evil/ death/ otherness/ the devil.

A rant against 'goodness'; a stream of angry unselfconsciousness.

A turning away from the world's vanity; an adventure into the 'other', to run with the beasts.

Innocence versus experience.

Evil enters Eden.

Create a monster; monstrous or misunderstood.

My evil twin.

The university of hell.

Meeting someone who offers everything you want.

A banker is redeemed.

Write a threatening and promising end of the world letter.

Using chapter 9 of Revelation, write about a holocaust where the insects take over.

Using chapter 10 of Revelation, write about a contemporary prophet and how he might be made to tell the truth by technology.

Explore Prometheus as a source of nuclear fire.

Using chapter 11 of Revelation, write about a woman, 'clothed with the sun', who embodies the best spirit of the world, as it is ending.

Using chapter 13 of Revelation, create a contemporary 'great beast'.

Write a feminist take on chapter 13 of Revelation.

Using chapter 18, write about a new Babylon.

Describe a world renewed by the end of it, using chapters 21–22 of Revelation.

Write a modern writer's curse, based on Revelation 22:18–19.

Find a story in the news about pollution, climate change, nuclear power, or nuclear war and use archetypal characters, perhaps derived from actual characters, to create an ending/ saving scenario.

Choose an element (fire, water, earth, air) which will destroy/ recreate the world.

Describe someone who is changed by seeing a Last Judgement, or Doom, painting as the non-literal symbols of their life.

Reading

Revelation of St John the Divine (old); Thomas Hardy's 'God's Funeral' (new); John Gray, *Black Mass* (new and critical).

Chapter 12

◆

MYTHS OF FAME

After you have come to the end of a piece of writing, when the hero has returned, then comes one of the trickiest parts of the journey of the mythsmith. The piece of writing must then go on its own adventure into the world. Publication! Fame! Money! But we know it is not that easy, even if we understand that myth reconnects the self to the community and that, historically, the purpose of myth was to provide a useful story to a specific society.

Like all mythic journeys, though, this one begins long before its apparent beginning. To write using myth is to write with an intention of tuning in to a greater need than merely that of the writer's desire for fame. The creative journey into the self involves a depth of self not normally accessed and that journey too takes in a mythic connection between ourselves and what it means to be human. We are also part of a wider world, each a mixture of the known and the unknown, and our writings and renewals relate both inwards and outwards into the unknown.

To write with an awareness of myth is to be tuned in to connections and the world of connections will open itself to the humble mythsmith who has the right attitude. What is passed to us from our culture, from our family, from our friends, from our narratives and versions of narrative, from our jokes, loves and dooms, is our tradition. Tradition is where myth can live. Myth is a linking back to what we are already linked to. We are given a great richness of subtle and obvious gifts in both culture and nature. It is a cliché that we undervalue these things in an age of consumerism. But to think of it as merely cliché is another sales strategy to make us undervalue what riches we have for free. To be a traditional mythsmith is to be resistant to the idea that we are merely material, or monetary investments, as Bob Dylan says some seem to be, in his song 'It's Alright Ma (I'm Only Bleeding)' (*Bringing It All Back Home*, 1965).

How does this help us get published? If publication at its simplest level means 'making public', then writing with mythic intent is to make our writing public at a deeper level, but a more practical level might also be achieved from this attitude. If you examine the human connections you have, by, say, looking at your address book, or contacts list, or those you sent Christmas cards to, you can see that the real connections you have tend to operate on a tribal level. Most of us have roughly the same number of real friends and family, which adds up to the same size as a traditional tribe. If the old myths were for a specific tribe, then we are still operating on this level. We start from here.

Can myths be then both universal and local? The answer is yes and myth operates on just such a double dynamic. Just as in the self, a depth leads to finding a common link to the human condition, then so in a social group locality becomes a source of the universal. Joseph Campbell's *Primitive Mythology* (1969), in a paragraph from 'The Functioning of Myth', in the 'Conclusion', makes the point well:

> Functioning as a 'way,' mythology and ritual conduce to a transformation of the individual, disengaging him from his local, historical conditions and leading him towards some kind of ineffable experience. Functioning as an 'ethnic idea,' on the other hand, the image binds the individual to his family's system of historically conditioned sentiments, activities, and beliefs, as a functioning member of a sociological organism. This antinomy is fundamental to our subject, and every failure to recognise it leads not only to unnecessary argument, but also to a misunderstanding – one way or the other – of the force of the mythological symbol itself, which is, precisely, *to render an experience of the ineffable through the local and concrete* [my italics], and thus paradoxically, to amplify the force and appeal of the local forms even while carrying the mind beyond them. The distinctive challenge of mythology lies in its power to effect this dual end; and not to recognise this fact is to miss the whole point and mystery of our science.

Here Campbell, in his quest to find the universal language of myth, insists on the locality of the function, while highlighting the need for the 'antinomy', or paradoxical law.

For the writer, this is a liberating thought. To be a mythsmith, we do not have to be a classicist, quoting Greek in a superior way. We might be better quoting a joke we heard in the pub, some old family story or something from the news, local history or folklore. Likewise, in writing about these things, we are far more liable to be reminding our tribe of what it needs to be reminded of and also making an appeal towards the universal through our very individual locality.

Writing for your friends first, for your place and time and for something specific thus becomes the mythsmith's way and the self-renewing song has its communal setting and purpose. I heard the novelist Alan Sillitoe give a talk where he revealed how he came to write the novel which made him famous, *Saturday Night and Sunday Morning* (1958). This novel is set in the factories of his hometown, Nottingham. Sillitoe was visiting Robert Graves in Majorca, where the great mythographer was living at the time. Graves was a poet and classicist, living in exile and writing across cultures and places and times. However, when asked his advice, he told Sillitoe, who had already written several unsuccessful works, to write about his own tribal milieu. The surprising advice from seeming opposites, one a social-realist, the other a myth-poet, is a definition of Campbell's 'antinomy' in action.

Sillitoe's novel was quickly a success and has become a touchstone for fictions of the tough individualist resisting a grindingly dull, industrial job. Arthur Seaton is the mythic adventurer of his day, as tricky and cocky as Odysseus. Sillitoe's experience became his myth and connected him to all myth.

The practical application of this is the 'think global/ act local' ecological approach to publication, where a humble beginning is an advantage. Of all those studying creative writing, only a tiny percentage of us will become rich. Most writers are not rich and most writers do it for love. That is the mythic truth about it, so we had better learn to do it for love first. The internet drives us towards further universal links apparently, but it also works for the tribe, via how it has been used. Early use by scholars, who wanted to talk to their own tribe of experts on, for example, myth, even, proves its universal/ local dynamic. Publication there has a similar function.

The circulated satiric poem, in electronic or paper form, the chapbook, the play based on local folklore, the celebration of a local ugly or beauty spot place – all these kinds of publication are ways of starting to take the work into the world. It was the uncompromising locality of the Beatles that was a part of what made them successful. The same thing has happened recently with Arctic Monkeys, their northern song 'Mardy Bum' needing a translation for us soft UK southerners, but all the more appealing for that. Writing, for the true mythsmith, is a journey back to the self, to renew the self so that you can become more like yourself. Myth speaks in a local accent, while it loves diversity, including its own.

The point of using myth is not to be steeped in an alternative world of old stories. The old stories point is to make themselves new, so to be a mythsmith is to be steeped in new stories, or renewing stories.

Myths of fame are all around us and send their little tragedies and triumphs out endlessly. It does not take a master mythsmith to puncture their triviality. But the great literary tragedies also tell about people unable to live up to their image of themselves. Oedipus cannot be as great as he wants to be and becomes as blind and humble as the blind seer he mocks, the prophet Tiresias. His yearning for success has led him to ignore the warnings of the prophets. He has married his mother and killed his father. He did these things unknowingly, but symbolically he is married to himself, or to his pride. Narcissus famously falls in love with himself, which destroys him. As he gazes in the water, his image is the most beguiling thing he has seen. The temptations, which look so ludicrous from the outside, are overwhelming. In Ovid's version his parents are told that he will live a long life only if he does not know himself. The surface obsession and self-confidence are the paradox of knowingness and selfishness of a child, which destroys blindly, in these myths of fame and death. This is a social model of childishness, of the child archetype even, and a banal and addictive myth with which all can identify. The cure for this is just the kind of mythic locality we have been talking about. The truly heroic is at home and we are door-stepped by the greedy children of fame, who can never be satisfied.

Writers, as we have already seen, have often sought to define their role in relation to the world in essays, introductions and other works outside their normal genre. Joseph Conrad's 'Preface' to *The Nigger of the 'Narcissus'* (1897), from its first line, takes a serious and subtle approach to the writer's intention. 'A work that aspires, however humbly, to the condition of art should carry its justification in every line', he says. In other words, writing must be seen to be about honesty and truth. Writing must be credible and just throughout. This seriousness is not an obvious one, as we have to go through a process of discovery to find it: 'The artist descends within himself, and in that lonely region of stress and strife, if he be deserving and fortunate, he finds the terms of his appeal.' The process is mythical, as the artist goes 'to that part of our nature which, because of the warlike conditions of existence, is necessarily kept out of sight within the more resisting and hard qualities – like the vulnerable body within steel armour'.

Here Conrad seems to be describing the relationship of the unconscious to the conscious and the process in which our mythic writer moves.

> His appeal is less loud, more profound, less distinct, more stirring – and sooner forgotten. Yet its effect endures forever. The changing wisdom of successive generations discards ideas, questions facts, demolishes theories. But the artist appeals to that part of our being which is not dependent on wisdom; to that in us which is a gift and not

an acquisition – and, therefore, more permanently enduring. He speaks to our capacity for delight and wonder, to the sense of mystery surrounding our lives; to our sense of pity, and beauty, and pain; to the latent feeling of fellowship with all creation – and to the subtle but invincible conviction of solidarity that knits together the loneliness of innumerable hearts, to the solidarity in dreams, in joy, in sorrow, in aspirations, in illusions, in hope, in fear, which binds men to each other, which binds together all humanity – the dead to the living and the living to the unborn.

For writers thinking about publication, there are some key things here. The subtlety of what artists do, when addressing what is 'easily forgotten', is nevertheless 'more enduring', as it is 'a gift and not an acquisition'. This act of creativity is a sharing of the difficult insights that remain credible, although they are hard to grasp. The process of passing this gift on is then part of the creativity of reconnection with the wider world. Later, he says:

> The sincere endeavour to accomplish that creative task, to go as far on that road as his strength will carry him, to go undeterred by faltering, weariness or reproach, is the only valid justification for the worker in prose. And if his conscience is clear, his answer to those who in the fullness of a wisdom which looks for immediate profit, demand specifically to be edified, consoled, amused; who demand to be promptly improved, or encouraged, or frightened, or shocked, or charmed, must run thus: – My task which I am trying to achieve is, by the power of the written word to make you hear, to make you feel – it is, before all, to make you *see*. That – and no more, and it is everything. If I succeed, you shall find there according to your deserts: encouragement, consolation, fear, charm – all you demand – and, perhaps, also that glimpse of truth for which you have forgotten to ask.

'Immediate profit' is then not the goal, but the 'glimpse of truth' so easily 'forgotten'. Although Conrad's style is elevated and not the kind of thing a contemporary writer would produce, we can see that his understanding of the artistic process is close to our mythic one here.

Lewis Hyde quotes Conrad's essay in the epigraph to the introduction of his influential book on these views of art, *The Gift* (1983). Here he emphasises the importance of the idea that 'works of art exist simultaneously in two economies, a market economy and a gift economy'. He talks of several senses of the concept of the gift, one of which is the 'gifted' artist. We have already encountered this concept by another route, when the appreciation of the mythic journey is both a gift from the darker self and from the oldest, passed-on gifts of the mythic stories. This sense of hard-won depth is achieved by being open and honestly worthy and then it is given, to be passed on, in its return to the world. This is the 'gift economy', which must be passed on, as 'the gift that cannot be given away ceases to be a gift'. Later, he says, 'the only essential is this: *the gift must always move*'.

The sense of the artwork itself as a gift *to* the artist is also emphasised by Hyde. 'Usually, in fact, the artist does not find himself engaged or exhilarated by the work, nor does it seem authentic, until this gratuitous element has appeared.' Here he quotes D.H. Lawrence's poem 'Not I, Not I', where this gift of inspiration is 'the wind that blows through me', and here we note that inspiration means breathing in. Hyde emphasises that 'we should extend this way of speaking to . . . [the work of art's] outer life as well'. It is not how much we pay for a book that dictates its value to us.

Still with Hyde's introduction, he gives a story of 'an Englishman' visiting 'an Indian lodge'. They smoke a pipe of peace, which the Indians give 'to their guest when he leaves'. He intends to take the pipe back to 'the British Museum', but, when some other tribe call on him, they expect him to smoke the pipe with them and 'give them the pipe'. The gift must be passed on, and it is a symbol of generosity and sharing, more important in its symbolism than in its value as a commodity.

The spirit of the intention of the artwork must be carried on in its journey into the world. In Philip Pullman's essay 'Voluntary Service' (*Guardian* 'Review', 28.12.02), he talks about the responsibilities of the writer. 'Emotional honesty' means that 'we should never try to draw on emotional credit to which our story is not entitled', giving the example of a writer who tacks a 'Holocaust theme' on to a novel. The 'credit' which an artwork holds is debased if it does not hold its gifts honestly. Pullman does not deny the need to earn money, but the responsibilities 'to the medium' matter.

Pullman makes a point about humility, where the story, the work itself is the main thing and not the artist. 'We should keep a check on our self-importance. We who tell stories should be modest about the job, and not assume that because we've thought of an interesting story, we're interesting ourselves.' We do this by making the writing 'so interesting that the teller almost disappears'. He talks of the 'self-consciousness' of nervous teachers being transformed by telling good stories. Finding a way of not knowing the self too much reminds us again of Narcissus and also of the journey into the mythic dark which true writing requires.

Paradoxically, again, it is humility that links us to humanity and makes our writing more likely to be publishable. I know several people who have thought that writing a formulaic Romantic novel, of the Mills and Boon, or Silhouette kind must be easy, but, on trying, they found out the romantic truth that their heart was not in it and they gave up the attempt. Humble sincerity may not be a guarantee of quality, but it is a guarantee of the writing succeeding on its own merits, on its own gift credit, or credibility. The last of

Pullman's 'list of responsibilities' is that 'we have to pay attention to what our imagination feels comfortable doing', which is another way of being true to the depth of our art and to what the art itself demands, which may not be so comfortable perhaps. Here, Pullman calls on his title-word 'service' and the service the writer gives to his material is another aspect of Hyde's 'gift economy', under which art flourishes. 'And finally, as a faithful servant, I have to know when to let the story out of my hands' towards 'editors' and towards the public, he says.

My own model for a tribal level of useful art and what I call a 'culture of creativity' is not limited to the publication, or public space, which the classroom provides, although that space is included. The classroom can give much communal feeling to the value of writing and sometimes student writers find it difficult to continue outside that close community. This is explained often by feelings that stimulation is gained from the setting and even from the teacher. I think that the making public of art has another, deeper relevance. When we are sharing our insights with a community, they feel as if they have a life beyond us, which is essential to the writer, especially to one who understands the healing role of bringing back the easily forgotten mythic truth.

Writing for and about our community, our tribe, friends, family and locality provide us with a tough but demanding audience. Building success from a local level, like the Beatles in Liverpool's Cavern Club, is a well-established path. The fact that the Beatles did Campbell's separation – initiation – return trip to Hamburg, where they played all-night gigs, before returning to Liverpool transformed, reinforces the parallel. The singers of traditional folksong which so inspired composers like Vaughan Williams were only heroes in their own pubs and homes, where their songs were valued. Yet these songs contained the essence of English music for which Vaughan Williams had been searching. As the Arabic proverb has it, 'Often in tiny streams may be/ Something you can't find in the sea.'

The state of difficulty for the writer is a mythic necessity. The return is as full of mythic uncertainties as the journey itself and this is part of the process, part of the difficult truths we might offer. The writer can transcend this by making the gift weave its own mythic spell, by it having the journey written within it, so that the song is self-renewing for itself. This, in turn, will bring its value to the attention of those who seek, whether they know it or not, the same truths.

The story of art not being given its proper value is an old one, and one expressed by modern writers too. Kenneth Rexroth's 'The Advantages of Learning' (*Penguin Modern Poets 9*, 1967) gives, in its title, an ironic view of a gift which is not obvious in the poem itself. He paints a picture in the poem of a defeated, pointless and damned being, a useless, friendless poet. But he has defiance and he drinks and writes happily away in the night. In writing the poem, so confessional, so apparently cynical, but resilient in its seriousness about its gift, it does what it demonstrates and justifies its mocking title. It gives a picture of a local journey which has a universal truth about real value, even in apparent failure. A good poem about failure is an act of contrary strength, an adventurous, mythic success.

Even further back, an Irish poem by Mahon O'Heffernan, shows a similar heartfelt defiance to the unpropitious time the writer is confronted with, and with which we end this chapter. This contemporary translation emphasises the crudity of the defiance, as well as the exorcising of the negative power of the times, as it calls on the 'ancient wisdom' of myth.

The unpropitious time is ours and the time is always now.

Who Will Buy a Poem?
From the 17th century Irish poem of Mahon O'Heffernan (by A.M.)

Who will buy a poem?
It's got the grand old wisdom
That makes you live forever
And I'm only passing through
Who will buy a poem?
Fucking no-one, that's who

Who will buy a poem?
Made solid from the hidden lore?
I have hawked it from door to door
And in the market places too
Who will buy a poem?
Fucking no-one, that's who

Who will buy a poem?
No-one says why they don't want it
The rich and poor refuse
I'd sell it for a pound, a penny would do
Who will buy a poem?
Fucking no-one, that's who

Who will buy a poem?
Is this a dignified trade?
Should this art die out?
Should I sell the Big Issue?
Who will buy a poem?
Fucking no-one, that's who

Who will buy a poem?
Who appreciates what comes for free?
Where's the reward for what's true?
Where are the generous few?
Who will buy a poem?
Fucking no-one, that's who

Who will buy a poem?
Once the well-off knew the value
Of gratuity, not the price
With them gone, I can't continue
Who will buy a poem?
Fucking no-one, that's who

Who will buy a poem?
I'm like a brandy bottle, spirit gone
An object of empty mockery
Is it vanity even asking you?
Who will buy a poem?
Fucking no-one, that's who

Writing

Find a local story, or a story particular to a group of people you know and retell it in a way that reveals its relevance.

Write a celebration of how writing shares deeper truths.

Write about an artist who finds an audience in an unexpected way or place. This can be fiction or researched biography turned into a creative piece.

Describe a separation from a social group which brings about a return with an insight.

Write of a famous writer's attempts to regain anonymity.

Write a protest piece about what people do not want to hear.

Reading

'Preface' to *Nigger of the Narcissus*, by Joseph Conrad (old); 'Who Will Buy a Poem?' (old/new); Lewis Hyde's *The Gift* (new/critical).

POSTSCRIPT

Theories and Fairies,
Myth and Magic

◆

THE PROFESSOR OF FABLES (by A.M.)

The Professor of Fables was sad because everybody else kept getting the meanings wrong. Like a far-off bell the thought rang that this way of thinking might be the symptoms of a madness of right-man-ness, but he knew so much about the fabulous that their very opulence and every suggestion was known and doubly known.

He had once heard a student call him the Fabulous Professor. He remembered it, as he was feeling especially weary and heavy with driven knowledge at the time and it had lifted his spirits. He did not know that the student, a girl with no sense of respect, had used the expression as a joke, thinking the opposite.

Beside this unknown, a thought that could have been thought but wasn't, the memory was not one that made him happy this time. Instead, it just increased his sense that he had it right and everyone else got it wrong.

He lived in a house by the sea and was retired from teaching now, alone with his theories of fairies and their tales. His wife had died and now his daughter had died, while giving birth to a girl, whose father had long ago abandoned her mother. He sent money to the granddaughter, but had never wished to see her.

In his work he was unassailable, as no one knew as much as he did. In private he looked out from his high window over the sea and wept for his daughter. Something fabulous had gone from him and he was inconsolable.

He wept huge tears, seascapes of tears. His hair grew longer and whiter. The tears flowed over the window-ledge to a brook which joined the sea. He wrote about motifs of coastal erosion in fairytales, while his hair and beard grew longer, till they twined round his chair and into the floor and into the wooden frame of the very building and he was held fast. Meanwhile the tears were a sad, undrinkable wellspring.

His granddaughter, her mother having been called Mab, and her name being Fiona, had been called Fab. It was a nickname that stuck. She had been brought up in a town just a few miles away from the sea, where the Professor had taught at the university. But it was an area of town where he had never been, being a poor area, allegedly full of crime, an area devoid of the fabulous. Fab was also an ironic name, as Fab never dressed well, or fashionably, or even in trendy sixties style, as the name might have suggested. She wore the kind of clothes you might get out of a skip. She never paid money for clothes.

She had been brought up by an old woman friend of her mother, who had worked with her as an agency office cleaner. Although they lived on the Verdant Estate, Else had kept chickens in her garden for many years and sold a few eggs to posh, organic shops locally, in the better parts of town, near the university. Else was too old to clean and Fab now looked after her, and the chickens.

Her one other friend was an immigrant gipsy boy from Poland, who could play the fiddle brilliantly and used to play his soulful tunes, strange but happy, to the hens. The hens liked it and laid more eggs. When she wasn't out looking for old, abandoned clothes, in bins and skips and behind charity shops, Fab would dance to his tunes. He taught her gipsy dances and she danced to the chickens and they laid even more eggs, like a kind of applause.

There was a big celebration at the university and the Chancellor sent the Professor an invitation. The university was fifty years old and the Professor of Fables had been there since the very first day of the first term. He was the only one left alive who had. He was to be guest of honour. He had the builders in to cut him free of his hair and the doctor call to attempt to dry his tears by chemical means and then he set off to the campus.

There was also an organic food festival in the ground of the university, as part of the celebrations, and Fab and the boy fiddler had decided to go. They had trained their chickens to move as one when the fiddle played and they travelled across the footpaths, fields and roundabouts to the campus, all in one jolly and strange band. People laughed and gawped at them, with their procession of music and orderly, hypnotised hens. They were like a fable come to life, like some old fairytale.

There was a celebrity coming to the celebration day. He was an ex-student of the university and had actually known the girl who called the Professor 'Fabulous' as a joke. Jack Smyth had failed his degree but gone on to write a book about the history of nature which had been a popular success. His series on TV was massive. He was giving it all up to go into the church, but he had kept that a secret. Another secret was that he had split up from his 'business-woman of the year' wife. He was doing this gig for the money and would talk about the books he read while at university, so as not to talk about why he had left without a degree.

On the day, Smyth's car was held up at the roundabout traffic lights, even though they were green. He saw Fab and the boy fiddler and the hens crossing. A man in a four-by-four was shouting abuse at them. Smyth watched them cross, neatly and musically, but slowly, and the four-by-four speed off. He saw the girl and the boy and the hens take the road up to the university and he overtook them slowly, giving them plenty of room. He waved to them. Fab waved back and broke into a dance.

Instead of going into the main hall, Smyth went into the grounds where the organic fair was taking place. He saw the girl, Fab, at the entrance. She was being told she could not go on, as she was not a registered stall-holder. Him in his smooth, expensive clothes went up to her in her strange, carefully patched rags to intervene, using his celebrity. He approached and they exchanged smiles as if the smiles were in a world outside the one they were both confronting.

There was no need for his celebrity. A wise woman security officer, who happened to have bought eggs from Fab and Else, approached and said that it was OK to let her in. The officer looked sardonically at Smyth, as if she had expected to see him, as if she had seen it all and said: 'Health and Safety eh, Jack?' She turned and walked away, bristling with the walkie-talkies and torches of her profession.

Smyth, like a child at all this, said to Fab, without knowing why, 'Will you all come in to the hall later, to hear me speak?' The fiddle began playing and the jolly procession went in, as he went away. No one had answered except the fiddle, but he felt they would come all the same.

When Fab, the boy fiddler and the chickens entered the hall, for some reason no one stopped them. Smyth was just about to speak. The Professor, already seated on the platform, looked at them and knew somehow that it was the granddaughter he had never seen, and he turned away and the tears welled up, stemmed a little by the doctor's chemicals.

When Jack Smyth saw Fab, he stood up, astonished at what he was seeing in front of him.

There was a bright light shining from Fab's clothes, like gold, too dazzling to keep your eyes on, but too brightly compelling to keep them away from.

He looked to see if everyone else saw them and he saw that they did. Some looked hypnotised, others smiled, wide-eyed, but all gazed on her. Only the Professor's eyes were averted, swollen, blindly looking at the floor. The Professor of Fables could not look at her.

Smyth walked towards her. Taking her two hands in his, he said, without knowing why, but to all assembled, 'You are welcome here'. The golden light began to fade, but he still felt it like a kind of energy source.

She stood at the back of the hall while he spoke. The golden light seemed to light up his words, though now only he could see it and had it within him.

As the applause rose up, he walked slowly towards the golden light, forgetting the time for questions from the audience. Fab and Jack Smyth left hand in hand.

At last, the Professor went home. His big weeping soon began again, as the sea encroached. Else got well and was able to tend the chickens and attend the marriage of Fab and Smyth.

If you go to the sea, you can see the Professor of Fables in his high window, as his is the last house on the crumbling land, always looking as if it will fall to the beach at any minute. He is still working on motifs of coastal erosion. The tears still flow down to the eroding earth and on into the sea. 'Nothing can be saved', he writes. The Professor of Fables is always sad, and sad because everybody else keeps getting the meanings wrong.

***

This story, a version of 'Tattercoats', as collected in Joseph Jacobs' *More English Fairy Tales* (1894), is a warning about those who deal with the mysteries of myth becoming complacent about them and becoming disconnected from the magic of the ordinary world. For although we have a strange relationship with the strange, we still can find life full of wonder and magic. We cannot quite believe that we still believe in such things. The golden being, especially the golden child, represents the glory and wonder at the centre of things and the gift there for those who can see it. Just as we began with the wonder of creation, so now we return to the marvellous with proper trepidation, but also with promise. We are like Silas Marner, in the George Eliot novel of the same name (1861) who sees the arrival of a golden haired child as a miracle, which it, in a sense, proves to be. It is worth noting that the novel *Silas Marner* also appeared unbidden to its author, who was at the time engaged on a longer, more deliberate work of fiction. Given the right attitude, the magic and the myth will come as a blessing.

It is worth pointing out that *Silas Marner* is a realist novel and reminding ourselves that myth need not show, in any overt way, its magic connections. 'The Professor of Fables' could easily be presented without the tears, hair or golden light elements seeming magic, for example. However, in this postscript we will allow a little look at the magic element, which is there, however hidden.

When we talk about the kind of mysteries of myth we have been talking about here, it is necessary to remind ourselves that *we do not know what we are talking about.* Discussing the role of the unconscious, we make guesses and advance theories, but what is out of sight retains its mystery, especially to us here, in the West. We console ourselves with the idea that we do not have to believe in anything. But, confronted by real faith, we feel incomplete and weak, and thus we become prey to any evangelism and even to extremism. Every theory has its shadow, even a theory of the shadow. We know somehow that, in our relation to the magic of life, we are lost. It is worth asking Mercia Eliade, from the opening pages of *Myths, Dreams and Mysteries* (1960), to remind us that, in the societies that created them, traditional myth

> is thought to express the *absolute truth*, because it narrates a *sacred history*; that is, a transhuman revelation that took place at the Great Time, in the holy time of the beginnings . . . Being *real* and *sacred*, the myth becomes exemplary, and consequently *repeatable*, for it serves as a model, and by the same token as a justification, for all human actions. In other words, a myth is a *true history* . . . In *imitating* the exemplary acts of a god or of a mythic hero, or simply by recounting their adventures, the man of an archaic society detaches himself from profane time and magically re-enters the Great Time, the sacred time.

In the face of this, our attitude must be one of being aware of our limitations of faith and being unconsciously bound to the comforting myth of rationalism, while we acknowledge that the creative element common to all humanity is the best we can offer. We must give our creative efforts as much of our own energy as we have. This does not mean being falsely reverent to myths. But we pay them our own kind of best, creative respect, even if it might at times look to outsiders like disrespect. If we have taken this stuff seriously, we know otherwise.

Most English or Literature departments in universities, it seems to me, are either away with the theories or away with the fairies. I am obviously of the latter party, on the team of myth and the creative. 'The Professor of Fables', above, is similarly a warning against theorising our fairytales too much. The magic is in the writing process and in the living of it, the unknown remains unknown and whatever you say about myth is true, but only as far as it goes and no one meaning is ever absolute.

On the other hand, we cannot leave the mysterious, or magic alone. As G.K. Chesterton suggested, the time of no religion means mad religion, as there is no such thing as no religion. We have to have a view, of some kind, about what is beyond us. On the whole, we like the unknown, the uncanny, the coincidence, the love-at-first-sight lighting up of the world: we are mythic and often off with the fairies. Our superstition, our sense of magic, is impossible to get rid of totally.

Does magic exist? What is magic? Is it what we used to believe in? Magic, like myth, is about underlying meaning and about seeing the world differently, like writing. The *OED* says it means either 'influencing events by compelling the agency of spiritual beings' or 'bringing into operation some occult [= hidden] controlling principal of nature'. So it is either 'pretended' or a 'hidden principle', either a conjuring trick or a real power. As with myth, the danger is inbuilt, the ambiguity and paradox of the truth is unfixed, like a Trickster who does magic tricks. And is it a 'principle of nature' or to do with 'spiritual beings'? They could be the same thing.

Magic is often acknowledged by writers and other artists whose material seems to find them. Writing creatively is not about what we know, but is a process of discovery, a practice, as opposed to a theory, to enable us to approach the mystery of life, in order to reveal its 'hidden principles'. Spooky coincidences abound in writers' stories of their composition. Tom Wolfe tells in his introduction to *The Bonfire of the Vanities* (1987), a novel about a character's mythic descent, of having his protagonist carry his expensive shoes in a bag on the subway, so he was not robbed of them. He then observed this happening in real life *after* he had written the idea, but before the book was in print. This is just one example of many instances of the natural magic that happens when writing.

Again, if magic seems to happen, it is no guarantee of quality. We must still allow proper help to come, by the proper attitude of diligence and craftsmanship. Ambition and desire for power over magic is 'black magic'. Richard Cavendish, in *The Black Arts* (1967) defines Black Magic as 'the hunger for power', which appears mythically, as the serpent in Genesis saying 'Ye shall be as gods', or in the story of Prometheus, who stole fire from the gods by a trick. Cavendish also insists that magic is 'poetic rather than rational thought', dealing with 'the regions of which science has nothing to say'. This is no 'thing of the past', but 'deeply embedded in the human mind'. His definition of magic, from the opening of the book, is worth quoting: The 'pagan but not ignoble conviction that everything has its place and function in the order of the universe and that all types of experience are potentially rewarding'.

To believe in magic is to see that the universe has meaning, which may be an unfashionable idea these days, but those of us who aspire to be mythsmith writers must often believe the same thing. This is not the contemporary world's cynicism, as defined by Oscar Wilde, that knows 'the price of everything and the value of nothing'. We seek, rather, true value and the connection between all things, the divine spark. All systems of myth, religion, divining and fortune-telling describe various forces at work in the universe and attempt to 'channel between . . . inner impulses and the forces outside', as Cavendish says, which is 'imagination'.

This could also be described as 'sympathetic magic', which is Sir James Frazer's phrase. Frazer wrote *The Golden Bough* (1922), the great classic of magic, myth and religion. 'Sympathetic magic' means like affecting like, even at a distance. The ritual mimicking is then a cause and effect and this is extendable then to imagination and writing. Writing is imagination, but imagination is powerful action.

Oracular divining is a way of finding patterns when the intention is focused to see them. These patterns likewise reveal hidden 'sympathetic' connections and give us what Prometheus had, which is foreknowing. If time contains meaning, then the concentrated moment contains seeds of meaning and foreknowing. Our minds seek patterns, which can become theories, but the magic is in revealing the hidden connections, showing life in process, as living embodiments of the imagination, which is what fairies are, when they are real.

A world-renowned expert on fairytales was once asked by a student, I was told, if she actually believed in fairies. She said 'No'. Fair enough. But I think I would have said 'Yes'. The proper attitude for a writer, to me, is that magic serves the purpose of making writing an enhancement of the wonder, and awe, of life. I certainly do not *disbelieve* in magic, or in fairies.

Even the stage magic of the trick is not far from real magic and not far from writing. We are capable of being tricked and of magical leaps of imagination and wonder. To write is to suspend disbelief, just as readers desire to, in 'poetic faith' as Coleridge suggested. Writing is both the trick and the magic. Writing is not real. I wonder if you have noticed this recently? It is the magic trick of mere marks on paper and we are magicians. We do the old mythic trick, but the trick also has the seeds of all magic in it. The magic is the reanimating power of myth and of the self-renewing song.

Writing

Use the major arcana of the Tarot or the *I Ching* to find an image or subject. Write about a writer who seeks, disbelieving, to summon up the power of the image found. The writer is interrupted by the appearance of the image in unlikely human form (friend, stranger, cleaner, boss, enemy etc.) and then finds, through the encounter, that something in them is changed by the experience.

Use a sequence of cards from the major arcana of the Tarot as the shape for a story.

> When you stop—you keep going,
> confident in the moving bond with flat nature.
> Slippery exuberance, needless joy from the coldest time. (by A.M.)

Guess what this refers to: one suggestion was 'death', others include 'writing' and 'running'. It is a riddle, the meaning of which is actually 'skating'. Write a riddle which seeks to be ambiguous or surprising in its meaning(s). For inspiration/ research, read the *Exeter Book* (see translation by Kevin Crossley-Holland in bibliography) (circa 975) riddles (trans. Crossley-Holland, 1978), which are still, rightly, puzzling people.

Reading

The story of the Muses, in Hesiod, *The Exeter Book* riddles (old); John Fowles' *The Magus* (1966, revised 1967) (new); Richard Cavendish's *The Black Arts* (1967), Colin Wilson's *The Occult* (1971), 'Spookiness for Writers' by A.M. in *Writing in Education* (no. 23, summer 2001) (critical).

Fifty-seven mythic subjects from a writer's point of view.

INTRODUCTION

This part of the book is a dictionary of subjects and topics, looked at from the point of view of a writer seeking to make mythic and symbolic connections. The point is to give a practical guide which shows that to write from a mythic perspective is a way of approaching *all* writing and, which is the point of the whole book, that all writing is mythic. Under each topic can be found references to, and examples of, relevant mythic and literary material and approaches which might be of practical help to a writer. Each of the fifty-seven topics here offers a short, indicative demonstration of some mythical approaches, designed to help writers develop their own researches and approaches to any subject they may be writing about.

AGE

See 'About Time' in Chapter 10, The Daily Myther and YOUTH. Ages can be seen in a linear way, as a symbolic straight line of pessimistic material inevitability, but the truly symbolic and mythic way is to see life as a cycle, corresponding to the times of day and seasons of the year, for example, as well as to cycles of fertility. Much writing is about exploring the promise of youth and the move from innocence to experience, but figures like the archetypal Mentor are usually depicted as an older person who has wisdom as well as experience and who sees the cyclical and is able to pass on what is good and useful. In the very passing on of the good, the Mentor also demonstrates the cyclic, traditional, on-going nature of mythic understanding. The term Mentor is taken from the character of Mentes in *The Odyssey*, who advises Telemachus, Odysseus' son. The old man Mentes is inhabited by the goddess Athena, immune to age of course, who works through him.

AIR

Aeolus is the Greek god who controls the winds, but the most significant aspect of air is its place as one of the elements: the others being fire, water and earth. We still speak of someone being 'all hot air', or, positively, 'a breath of fresh air' and air thus represents the non-material, the intellectual and the spirit of human beings. Air is inspiration, which means 'breathing in' and also the space between heaven and earth. Air is the breath of life, without which life cannot exist. In this sense, it is pure and invisible, but a changeable, and mythically 'female' element, like water. A hurricane is the manifestation of its power, just as much as a breath of life.

The word, and speech are carried in the air, as is the invisible aspect of the intellect, so the word is sometimes associated with intellectualism, when someone has their 'head in the clouds'. Air is the medium for light, smell, colour and for all sounds and vibrations, just as it stands for flight, sails and quickness, 'like the wind'. Freedom, as in Bob Dylan's song 'Blowin' in the Wind', and spaceflight, or 'flights of fancy' illustrate these symbols of lightness and speed. Ghosts and dreams of flight, 'flights of fancy' and being 'airy fairy' show the imaginative and abstract sides of the element. Sci-fi is the genre most obviously associated with air, in terms of its flights of imagination and travel through space.

Storms at sea have always provided a metaphor for human troubles, as well as the literal place of confronting the elements. Poseidon must call up the winds to create storms in *The Odyssey*. Pegasus is the winged horse of Apollo and also the Muses' horse. Pegasus brings thunder and lightening and creates springs with a stamp of a hoof.

The most famous myth of flight is that of Icarus. Daedalus and his son Icarus seek to escape imprisonment by flying away on wax wings, but Icarus flies too close to the sun and falls. This is the subject, the fall from air, the fall from flight being a metaphor for man's high ambitions, or for 'the fall', as in Adam and Eve being cast out of Eden, in Genesis. In literary terms, W.H. Auden's 'Musée des Beaux Arts' (1938) discusses Brueghel's painting *Icarus* in terms of how 'suffering' happens in the ordinary world, while life goes on all around. The airy myth we make much of is earthed by its ordinariness. In some sense this could be seen as a poem which attacks myth for its airy pretension, but also one that acknowledges myth's ability to tackle human failings.

W.B. Yeats' poem 'An Irish Airman Foresees His Death' (1919) describes a man becoming spirit-like in the sky, where his flight to death is 'A lonely impulse of delight', where everything is seen clearly and 'balanced'. This seems both a metaphor for death and perhaps for the flights of art, of poetry. Daedalus was, after all, a great inventor and he escaped on his wings, even if his son did not.

Poet of the Second World War John Pudney wrote his poem 'For Johnny' in 1941 and it was very popular and much quoted at the time, notably being recited by Michael Redgrave in the wartime film *The Way to the Stars* (Dir. Asquith, 1945). The poem asks the reader not to mourn the warrior pilot, because he dies flying. From these two poems one gets the feel of war almost as a kind of intellectual, airy suicide.

J.G. Ballard's early novels deal with elemental forces which threaten the world and *The Wind from Nowhere* (1962) is a good example of sci-fi, using its primal element.

Witches are supposed to be able to fly after anointing themselves with 'flying ointment'. The supernatural flies towards us in the world of dreams and stories, where flight is the norm. In Shakespeare's *The Tempest*, Ariel is 'an airy spirit'. The dangers and benefits brought in the air are ever present. The best air is that of inspiration, while the worst is a fall or a too-high and dry air of abstraction. Aeolus' sons and daughters married each other and this must be a symbol for the aridity of the air, unmediated by the other elements, like that of intellectualism. On the other hand, Ariels and sprites, the demons of the air, can bring us flights of fancy and flying carpets, lightness and the spirit of life, or even the Holy Spirit.

ANIMALS

The mythic significance of animals cannot be overestimated and myths about animals are many and varied and probably best studied by researching the individual animal. Animals offer us both the animal nature of ourselves and our lives and an insight into what might seem a more primal aspect of the self and its archetypes. The archetypal nature of animals can be seen in common phrases like 'cunning as a fox' and 'strong as a lion'. Animals then represent both our selves and the other sides of the self.

Part of our relationship with animals can be traced to hunting, where the identification with the hunted is a kind of respect for the life of it. This is perhaps connected to animism, where the life force in the animate is worshipped in a form of nature religion. Animal spirits are often the source of healing in shamanic ritual and the source of other spiritual powers beyond the human world. Animals are our others and their being more deeply attuned with the natural world represents something we have lost and must be reminded of. They are the instinct and honesty we tend to veil in ourselves.

Animals, as food, pets or familiars are our companions and victims and guides. They are in our stories and in our dreams and contemporary writers like J.M. Coetzee have written novels about animal rights (*Elizabeth Costello*, 2003). Paul Auster, among others, including Virginia Woolf, has written in the first person as an animal (*Timbuktu*, 1999).

Fairytales are full of animals and the Greek myths are full of mythical beasts, who are often supernatural in aspect, like the centaur, having a man's upper body and a horse's lower body. Jorge Luis Borges' *The Book of Imaginary Beings* (1967) is devoted to these supernatural animals who embody powers and archetypes and especially, here, the imagination. Sirens are winged women, Cerberus is a dog with three heads who guards the underworld, Satyrs are hairy-legged lust-bags of the forest, the Sphinx is a winged woman with the body of a lion who devours those who cannot answer a riddle (see *Oedipus Rex* by Sophocles). The myth world is full of fabulous beasts. For the writer these offer both precedent and scope for invention, as a political writer like George Orwell found when writing *Animal Farm* (1945).

The word 'anthropomorphism' means the attribution of human form or behaviour to an animal, or a god. In a sense, mythical animal thought works in the opposite direction, where animal or godlike attributes are borrowed by man, for various mythic purposes. The imagination works in a two-way street here, as it does with most mythic work. What differentiates true mythic writing is the use of animals to remind ourselves of essences, instincts and otherness. To see animals as more in tune with the natural world is not mere sentimentalism and to use the mythic exchange and possibility of change between ourselves and our close relations is actually as well as mythically useful and relevant, as well as freeing to the imagination.

For the writer, such things as playing a game of giving animal aspects to characters to help define them has always been a part of both planning and writing itself, while the observation of animals is both attention to detail and to character beyond our word-worn descriptions. It might be anthropomorphic to see an endangered species and identify with it, but if the animal is part of the world soul, then things are more complicated and interesting. Pets grow like their owners and owners grow like their pets and metamorphoses happen. We still need to learn from animals, including our own human, animal selves.

APOCALYPSE

See Chapter 11, Dooms and Dead Ends. The word in some way resembles the modern journalistic world of secrets revealed or the 'scoop', as it means an uncovering or a disclosure, but has come to mean the 'offing' of humanity rather than the 'offing' of a cover. This might be partly due to the smacking relish of the word in English, as the 'pock' leaves your 'lypse'. The strict meaning of the word is rooted in the Book of Revelation as discussed in Chapter 11.

APPLES

Symbolically and mythically apples stand for available fruitfulness. Their instantly edible shininess and sun-like roundness have the quality of offered completion. While an apple is *not* specified in the Bible as the fruit of temptation, its place as the symbolic fruit is assured in mythic stories, often, however in a reversed way. So it appears as poison, as temptation and as discord, as if its availability reversed becomes too available to be good, or, too good to be true.

The Greek story of Paris' Judgement is a story of 'the apple of discord'. Pelius and Thetis are at their wedding feast with the gods, and Eris, who is discord, throws an apple of gold to be given to the most beautiful woman. These are Athena, Hera (Roman name Minerva) and Aphrodite (Roman name Venus). Paris has to choose and picks the latter. His impossible choice is disastrous, as it leads to the Trojan War. All three promise him gifts if he will choose them, but Aphrodite offers him the love of Helen, the most beautiful woman in the world. This event leads to the war, the subject of *The Iliad*.

This apple of strife has something in common with the story of Snow White (Grimms' fairytale no. 53). Snow White's stepmother is also obsessed with beauty and the gratuity of beauty is again symbolised by the reversed-meaning apple. The enticing apple is the last attempt of the stepmother to kill her too-beautiful stepdaughter and she succeeds. But Snow White is brought back to life by a Prince dislodging the poison apple and the stepmother dies a cruel death. The apple illustrates the abuse of the gratuitous, which is both beauty and innocence. So, even in these two classic apple tales, the apple has its power for available good as well as for temptation.

In Arthurian myth, the dying King Arthur goes to Avalon, which is the Island of Apples. Likewise, the golden apple which causes such trouble for Greek myth is one of the Golden Apples of the Hesperides, who guard this fruit of immortality. Here we have the positive, sweet and fruitful extreme of the mythic nature of apples. As a fertility symbol, it stands often for marriage and love.

If you cut an apple transversely, it reveals, in the pip chamber, the five-pointed star, which is the pentagram, symbolising mystical power and knowledge.

Writer on computing Phil Manchester tells me that the sign of Apple Computers, with the bite missing, may be a reference to Alan Turing, computer pioneer, who was said to have died by eating a poisoned apple. Gratuity and its abuses obviously are troubled areas in computing, just as they were for Paris and Snow White. Thus apples are life and fruitfulness and powerful in their offer of completion and fullness, or its reverse.

The immortality apples offer is echoed in our 'apple a day keeps the doctor away' saying and in their ability to last, if stored well. The positive Celtic myth of apples in shown in W.B. Yeats' poem 'The Song of Wandering Aengus' (1899), which speaks, in its final two lines of 'The silver apples of the moon,/ The golden apples of the sun.'

BIRDS

Birds are archetypal symbols of flight, flights of imagination, the mind, freedom, and connection with the higher universe, or the gods. Prophets read flights of birds for signs from above, of the future. Birds 'of ill omen' can be dark, while bright, especially golden birds ('bird of paradise') can signify positive sides. The white dove is a symbol of peace and Noah first sends a 'raven' to see if the flood has abated, before sending the 'dove', which eventually returns with 'an olive leaf' (Genesis 8:7–12).

The classic myth of a man who seeks to be a bird is that of Icarus, who, in escaping imprisonment with his father Daedalus, flew too close to the sun, which melted his wax wings (see AIR and Ovid, *Metamorphosis*, Book VIII). W.H. Auden's poem 'Musée des Beaux Arts' (1938) discusses Brueghel's painting *Icarus*, where the ordinary world seems more pervasive, in its down to earthiness, than the failed attempt at flight.

Mythical birds abound, with their various qualities of transformation, from the phoenix, which arises from the ashes of its nest, to the basilisk, or cockatrice, with its look that can kill. Jorge Luis Borges' *Book of Imaginary Beings* (1969) is a good source on these and other mythical beasts, as is a dictionary of symbols for specific birds.

The eagle is the bird that signifies Zeus, the major divinity of the Greeks, and Athena takes the form of different birds in Homer and elsewhere. In

Virgil's *Aeneid*, the Harpies, which means 'the snatchers', monstrous storm-bringers, are pictured as hag-faced vultures; they also appear in the story of Jason and the Argonauts. In the *Mabinogion*, Rhiannon's three magic birds' singing could wake the dead and cause the living to fall sleep, as could the Sirens' song in the *Odyssey*.

Individual birds, in their 'messengers of the gods' role, are often associated with qualities: the owl with wisdom, etc. The mythology of the crow is explored in all its resonances in Ted Hughes' *Crow* (1972). A Greek tale says that the crow was originally white, but was changed by Apollo as a punishment for bringing bad news. Thor Heyerdahl's, *Aku-Aku* (1957) is about the bird cult on Easter Island.

Birds are often seen as souls of the dead and charming the birds from the sky, or talking to them, is a sign of magical blessing, in fairytales and elsewhere. See Grimms' tales 'The Crows', 'Fitcher's Bird', 'The Golden Bird', 'The Mouse, the Bird, and the Sausage', 'The Raven', 'The Three Little Birds', 'The Wren', etc.

The wisdom of birds, these higher creatures, is reflected in the ancient Sufi poem *The Parliament of the Birds*, by Farid al-Din Attar, which was very influential in English Literature, via Chaucer and Edward Fitzgerald, for example. The association of birds with the souls of the dead is shown in the existential nursery rhyme 'Who Killed Cock Robin', which is said to be a version of the death (gods are not supposed to die) of the Norse god Balder.

BODIES

The body, not being directly conscious, operates on a more primal level and provides symbols which offer enduring images of ourselves. Our bodies are alike and show us elements we have in common, so that we can see the frailty and wholeness of the world in ourselves. As a link between mind and matter, the body gives us messages, often in symbolic form.

Animals (see ANIMALS) in literature often represent the body making its demands and presence felt, where it might have been repressed sexually or in its basic material life. The senses also link us to the body, as well as to the mind, which is why they are often emphasised as vital to describe in writing, to make it live.

Parts of the body express parts of ourselves, as when we talk of 'putting your foot in it' or of 'healing hands'. 'Losing your head' is the symbolic cliché of allowing the primal to act without reason, while the bones offer an image of structure, the blood of inner life, breath of inspiration and the eye an image of the ego. The spine is often used to depict the will and the heart as strength.

The five points of the body stretched out like a wheel – the head, the arms, the legs – is the mythical image of the wheel of life and symbolises the body in harmonious movement. This is sometimes shown as a five pointed star.

The ages of the body are the ages of life too, where, for example, we might see the old like children and so, again, the body provides the archetypal place to observe our seasons of life. The body is the place of birth and of death. Disease shows us the dis-ease of the body and the fact that the head and body are one, as do psychosomatic illnesses. The body image of women has been an area of richness for writers, as have such issues as bulimia and anorexia. Here the body expresses the mind's difficulties, or, maybe it is more mythically correct to say, the difficulties of the whole being and its interrelatedness.

One major example of the mythic struggle with the physical sphere is in Odysseus' encounter with the Cyclops, who is said to have a single eye. It is hard not to feel sympathy for the Cyclops in book nine of *The Odyssey*, as he is a creature of nature, peacefully tending sheep until enraged by the devious hero of the epic. The Cyclops, whose name is Polythemus, is shown as a horrible giant, but his hospitality is abused and he is provoked to violence. Giants are defeated by cunning, but there is always ambivalence in their treatment. These stories often then represent the battle of the mind and body, the battle of 'civilisation' and nature. The myths are then often secretly on the side of the body against mere cleverness, as in the arguably despicable cheap trick Odysseus plays on Polythemus and the mockery he offers him.

Ovid's *Metamorphosis* is an anthology of people changing bodily into their obsessions and offers many examples of the body telling us its mythic, symbolic and useful archetypal messages.

CHANGE

Yet another definition of myth might be that myths tell us about how we manage change. The narrative nature of myth would suggest that something is happening and that we need to address it. The Chinese divinatory book of wisdom in nature symbols and archetypal patterns is called the *I Ching*, or *The Book of Changes*, while Ovid's *Metamorphosis* sees this connective pattern of myth at its basic level.

Transitions from stasis to fluency, birth to life, the darkly creative to the brightly public are all given voice in mythic processes and stories. Mythic writings, like myths themselves, are narratives of change. To handle change well, with mythic help, is to renew the self, as well as the myth.

The great shape-shifter of Greek stories is Proteus, the god of the sea, who can change shape at will, the sea being an image of constant change. He does this often to avoid telling the truth about the future, which, as a god of change, he, of course, knows. He is one of the key figures of myth in that he embodies the mythic mystery, which only reveals itself through ritual, through story, through its process of the revelation of change. Proteus appears in Homer's *The Odyssey*, in Virgil's *Georgics* and in Euripides' *Helen*. Menelaus tackles the monster of change in *The Odyssey*, but he gets an answer by his persistence with the myth.

We know that everything is in motion but the human rational mind likes stasis, which seems real but, in fact, is not. We see the changes when they happen fast, but change, like the gods, will come, whether we are ready or not.

Writing is often about rites of passage, related to changes and to time and myth. We cross the adventurous threshold to another state and have to deal with our own ability to change. Change reveals itself via a journey from the unconscious to the conscious, where the awareness of change is revealed. Meanwhile the seasons and the days, the rivers and the plants all remind us of the change we must live with. The great effort of change from winter to the return of fertility is the one mythic festival we in the West have yet to banish – the one we call Christmas celebrates the symbolic change which is always most necessary. Winter is the stasis and the spring growth is the renewal.

CHAOS

Chaos is an old Greek word, related to 'chasm', or empty space, meaning undivided, unformed, undifferentiated matter, out of which comes creation. It is 'without form' and 'void', as genesis, and the book of Genesis begins. The modern word 'gas' is related to it by sound and by the nature of unformed potential, of spirit awaiting form. A chasm can also be an open break in the earth, from whence form might be born, linking it to the underworld, or unconscious.

In the mythic sense, though, there is a way in which chaos is not just disorder, far from the way we tend to use it now. Chaos can be seen as the one-ness before creative dividing (see Chapter 1, Starting Creation). The wildness of nature, of the wilder world beyond our control, has a unity of 'otherness', which might be the unity of a monotheistic god.

Writers on myth have often divided the world into 'chaos and cosmos', where 'chaos' is the world beyond the control of humans and 'cosmos' means what mankind controls. The wilder world of mysterious nature, creation in birth and destruction in death, the weather and the universe itself, is the unknowable 'no-thing', which we can only describe by its absence.

In the way that chaos is seen to move towards creation, it can be related to the unconscious, but perhaps even that does not do justice to its primal potential. The gods of constant change hold the keys to creation and the paradox of change and of becoming is the creative exchange of living between what seems ours and what we must adjust to, in the mythic way.

Battles with monsters, especially those of the deep, are our battles for creation. Tennyson's Kraken awakening ('The Kraken Wakes', 1830) could be compared to the threat of primal chaos which is still posed for us now by atomic war. Our perceived enemies often represent chaos to us, as in George Orwell's *1984* (1948), where a fictional war is reported on daily, to answer this need for some representative of chaos to hate. The 'war on terror' might be today's chaos icon of hate for us, just as the communists were in the Cold War era. Chaos is then reversed creativity here, in its association with evil and death, but mythically the unknown is always a help to defeat the monsters of nihilism and pointlessness. Chaos reflects us and defies us, but it also gives us birth, one way or the other.

CHILDHOOD

See Chapter 9, Modernising Myths. In fairytale, children are, as always in myth, symbols of innocence and spontaneity. They provide a balance with the devious world of the adult or monstrous. Our own culture's obsession with childhood safety and those that violate it is a trope of lost innocence and fear of spontaneity. To be childlike, rather than childish, is a universal mythic virtue, from the ancient Chinese to the sayings of Jesus. The honesty and vulnerability of children are powerful tools for the writer who would go to the archetypal depth of a story.

Hermes is the messenger of the gods, often depicted as a child, as he symbolically brings new life to the world. He was a rebellious child who made the first lyre from a tortoise shell. Both of these aspects show restless creativity embodied in youth. His whole story is one of young creative energy winning over all.

Whereas *Peter Pan*, by J.M. Barrie (1904), shows both sides of childhood, creation and the failure of growth, the golden child in *Silas Marner* (1861) by George Eliot gives the fairytale aspect of the child being god-like in purity and potential for good. The crowned child is the alchemist's symbol of the Philosopher's Stone, which stands for gold and youth and health. William

Blake's 'child' is the song of innocence renewed (*Songs of Innocence and of Experience*, 1794).

CITIES

The city is human potential in its symbolic form and is the capacity for great good and great evil. The city is paved with gold or is depraved with sin. Cities can then represent a kind of heaven or hell on earth, ultimate civilisation or its opposite, utopia or dystopia. In *The Epic of Gilgamesh*, Uruk embodies both aspects. It represents strength, achievement and invincibility in its powerful walls and yet corruption has entered. The strong place has become a prison and decadence has taken over. The opening of the epic sees the ruler, bored, over-civilised, corrupting youth and running riot. The very modern dilemmas are there from the first in the tale. Likewise, in the Bible, Sodom and Gomorrah are places of evil and the old myths seem to give a view of the city as a place of human vanity, where humans shut out the mythic balances. In *Gilgamesh*, the gods must create a man of nature, Enkidu, as an opposite force to the corrupted hero. The modern city, such as LA in 'Hotel California' by the Eagles, is still seen as a place of corruption.

On the other hand, as a utopia of human achievement, the bright city offers the opposite to the dark wood. The political ideals of the city as a place of virtue were there from the Greeks onwards. Rome is still seen as a glorious achievement, while Constantinople was a new model of all that was impressive in the human world, by its riches of art and culture and architecture. Cities are also great places of religion, just as, in the evil aspect, they are great places of sin. Security and the settlement of ordered peoples in an ordered place are both a strong pull in the human mind.

Adventure and the natural world in a sense offer another opposite to the city. The retreat to the country, or the escape in the journey, are as old as cities. This is the retreat to where the world is less certain of its human strength and where humility is found to counteract the potentially corrupting stasis of the walled place of human vanity.

In literary terms, the richness of the city in material and variety is appealing, which can be seen in Joyce's *Ulysses*, for example. Cities have their sources in nature of course, such as being by rivers, having harbours or being holy meeting places, so their positive side may have an older mythic source of virtue. The city has the archetypal aspect here of the mother figure, nourishing the children in the home. The epic hero must found a city, while the mythic hero must save it, perhaps from itself.

As a mythic subject the city is an overwhelming one and many books are devoted to it. Human ambition is the theme of every city, with all the potential for greatness or its opposite implied.

CLOTHING

If bodies represent the unconscious, then clothes represent the conscious or self-conscious mind. Clothes also act as signs of the inner self in the sense of conformity or individuality. The human body is natural and has its own mythical power, while clothes can symbolise anything we choose to associate them with, like flags of communication. In Genesis 3, Adam and Eve are punished for *not* being naked, where human division from the natural, or naked, has made them cover their genitals. The sin was wearing clothes, while for civilisation nakedness is often the crime.

Humans must clothe themselves, which is both their ingenuity and their inability to be naturally warm, or of signalling their identity authentically. Status and endless signals to be read, of such status and of power, invitation and defence, are embodied in clothes. Symbolically we might say that the tie and the shoe represent male and female genitals, but that is just a hint of the kind of fetishisation or acting out of obsessional aspects of the body or mind that clothing affords. Just as a cloak can be a symbol of magic, of containment of power and protection, so we give dress every kind of image of ourselves. Clothes obviously have their ritual aspect, preparing the outer person for a task or duty.

Colours of clothes offer signs of purity and light, in white, while the cliché cowboy baddy wears a black hat. Examples of colour symbolism are every-where in literary clothing. New clothes can symbolise newness of changes of state and the gift of clothes can be seen as both hospitality and new identity. The whole subject of disguise and appearance versus reality can be brought in, for a writer.

Potipher's wife, in Genesis 39, tries to seduce Joseph, but he escapes by slipping out of his clothes, as she tries to hold him. His nakedness, like that of Adam and Eve, thus becomes a virtue, but obviously no one believes his story, as she lies about him. Hans Andersen's fairytale 'The Emperor's New Clothes', where the emperor is naked and only a small boy will admit as much, show likewise how empty vanity versus honesty, revelation versus concealment can be played with through clothes and the naked. The emperor walks on proudly where all can see his emptiness. Clothes, or the lack of them, show how we have to create our identity, as well as our own protection and attest to the human need for the useful, renewing arts.

CONSPIRACY

At first glance, it might seem that this subject is a feature of the modern world only, with no mythic connection, but popular superstition is a feature of all human society and indicates a break or problem with the mythic. If it is a disease, it is a mythic problem, like the curse of the Sphinx, as addressed by Oedipus. The need for myth is turned in on itself and creates strange monsters. Whether the response to the industrial, to anonymous societies and authorities is appropriate in terms of the break between ourselves and what might over-power us, as shown in the work of Kafka and in Orwell's *1984* (1948), for example, is another matter. The function, though, is mythic in essence.

Jung pointed out that in a world of dislocation, we seek symbols of unity or completeness, which is one way of looking at UFOs, especially in relation to another world and the disc shape of 'flying saucers' (*Flying Saucers*, 1976). If we are talking about superstition, what is overwhelming is the desire to believe, the desire for some startling revelation, because we have given up the old gods and there is a vacuum in us for the healing myths.

In this way, conspiracy theories are kinds of creation myths, or even creativity myths, gone wrong. They create worlds of connection where we fear that no connection can be made. In this sense, like urban myth, conspiracy theories are a great potential source for a writer, inasmuch as the themes of the need for myth and the suppression of myth have caused this indicator of projected and paranoid desire to exist. An old story might appear to mend the new.

That secrecy, lies and our ambiguous relationship with 'truth' are mythic should be no surprise to us (see Chapter 3, The Truth Lies). Thus science fiction becomes *New Maps of Hell* (1960), as Kingsley Amis' book has it. What belief in conspiracies does show is that we need to seek truth which is not apparent from living on the material surface of the world. The problem is that we seek to salve this need by creating news, itself a kind of commodity, which feeds on itself and the desire for sensation, rather than offering any real satisfaction to the unconscious seeker after myth. Proper use of myth aids a deep understanding, while improper or unconscious projections of the mythic may only add to the confusion.

DEATH

See Chapter 5, Dark Matter and Chapter 11, Dooms and Dead Ends. Death is the great myth and the enduring destroyer which confounds all human vanity. Every end has its beginning and every beginning has its end. The figure of Death, a skeleton with a scythe, is a symbol of the death of all vanity, of the ego. If the ego lets go, then renewal can take place. So the mythological function of death is decidedly not one-dimensional, or in any way final. In Last Judgement paintings, a huge Hell's mouth consumes the sinners, but always in myth, the disintegration is a move towards transformation. For the viewer of the painting, the experience of seeing this nightmare coming to life, this reminder of death, is intended to give a new relish for life and for goodness. The old cliché that a condemned man will eat a hearty breakfast is another example of a *memento mori*, a reminder of death, like the skull displayed on the shelf.

Encounters with underworlds (see UNDERWORLDS) or with vampires often symbolise parts of the story, or of a life, not normally available. Their point is that they are to be survived.

Eurynomus is the Greek consumer of all flesh in the underworld, while all gods obviously have power over life and death. Thanatos is death in person and the brother of Sleep. Sleep and orgasm are sometimes known as 'little deaths', while the phrase 'in the midst of life, we are in death' is another mythic balancing that thoughts of death seem to demand, coming from 'The Burial of the Dead' in *The Book of Common Prayer*. The opening line of Dante's *Commedia* (*The Divine Comedy*), is possibly the source of this, where death is the 'dark wood', where the hero is lost.

Death is symbolically the release from the material world into the mythic realm, so its multifaceted quality echoes the fact that, to reverse the service, in the midst of death, we are in life. Death provides the context in which we strive for meaning. We take our hats off at funerals to acknowledge the significance of death to the living. As a symbol of great sacrifice, death belongs to the element of earth, where myth and life become agricultural, with their god Dionysus, and death-myths are therefore about new life coming from the earth.

DEVIL

A relatively recent arrival, at least myth-wise, the great personification of evil has risen like a monster with our own sense of disbelief in good. The devil is definitely of the world and is to do with materialism, human vanity, weakness and desire for selfish power. Homer's underworld, in *The Odyssey*, is without the devil. The devil is only the snake in Genesis in retrospect. By the time we get to Dante's *Inferno* and thence to Milton's *Paradise Lost*, the devil is becoming ever more present, to the extent that William Blake claims the devil to be the hero of the latter. The alternative word Satan means adversary, so the devil as a classic Shadow archetype (see Chapter 5, Dark Matter), as the great villain has become central in literature.

In black magic, the devil is God reversed and a parody of God. But in magic generally he can represent worldly energy, the opposite of the holy spirit, or an abstract God. The Rolling Stones' song 'Sympathy for the Devil' is an example of the need for the darker forces of change. Often, Christians labelled old gods as devils. Likewise the snake, an old symbol of god in changeability and fertility, is seen as the devil, in Revelations, for example.

In the Gospels, the devil offers Christ the world and, like all evil in myth, offers the chance to be like gods. The mistake is one of human vanity, just as, at the start of *The Odyssey*, a conference; and discusses how foolish humans are to blame all their evil on gods. Evil is thus, as always, rooted in the human, not in the divine. In this way the devil is our wishful thinking: someone to blame and someone to embody our petty ambitions. It could be argued that the devil was the result of monotheism, where one all-powerful God seems too exclusive for human life.

For those who see life as evil, like the Gnostics, or the Cathars, who saw different views on evil, the devil is a more ambiguous figure. The devil here seems to be our need for dualistic ambiguity, where Lucifer, another synonym, might be depicted as a half-shining being, in the upper body, and beast from the waist down. Dionysus and Pan, as gods who deal with human darkness, might offer useful parallels in our need to exercise or exorcise our evil, or darkly energetic, sides.

Goethe's *Faust* (1832) offers the great pact with the devil motif, where the soul is sold, while the devil is often present in folklore and fairytale, often as a force which needs to be tricked out of its dull greed. The devil here often appears in animal form, as a black cock for instance, and if we 'talk of the devil, then he will appear'. The Devil's Dyke in Sussex, UK, where legend says the devil tried to flood the land, is an example of large, unexplained items of matter being given devilish aspects. Adding a noun to the devil, makes a good starting point for writing: the devil's computer, the devil's ukulele, etc.

The devil can be both energy and fixity, an aspect of character which performs a liberating function or a regression into vanity and stasis. He can be fun and he can be cold evil. His oxymoron is coldness and the fires of hell (see Dante's *Inferno* (part of *The Divine Comedy*)). The devil himself has his ambiguity and, for writers, will respond well to this being explored.

DREAMS

Myths are where dreams make sense and perhaps dreams are then pure, undiluted, unrefined myth and so, as such, sometimes indigestible. For the individual, unconscious mind, dreams offer representations of insights into our needs, fears, desires and potentials. For the mythic writer they have always been invaluable. Many writers, such as Jack Kerouac, have kept dream journals and many works have been dreamed before being written. Coleridge's 'Kubla Khan' (1797) and Stevenson's *Dr Jeckyll and Mr Hyde* were famously dreamed inspirations. The Old Testament is full of the significance of dreams and the Native Australian 'dreamtime' is a time both then and now, of ancestry and connection.

Dreams are, in one sense, unreal, but to our own creative minds they are a kind of raw reality and direct insight. They can be creative, responsive and reflective and of vital use to the mythic writer. Obviously writers must beware of 'it was all a dream' clichés, but the visiting by the dead or the prophetic in dreams are both well-worked motifs in writing. Traditional songs like 'The Unquiet Grave' describe the dead night-visiting to give messages to the living and so represent in dreams a kind of underworld of transition, of testing and changing. Dreams of course must be allowed their obscurity too, just as myths will demand something beyond analysis from us, but they offer a place where one's own symbolic associations can be traced in a direct route to the mythic. Dreams, like myths, are often narrative, visual and symbolic.

Nakedness in dreams, to give an example, can represent the need for honesty and for delving under the surface of life and a myth will often work in the same way. The experiment of control of dreams through ritual, religious discipline or drugs can be a strong effect for writers who want to reflect the mythic search in their work. Day-dreaming to some purpose is the mythic way, while wish-fulfilment day-dreams might result in mere fantasy work. Writers will often ask the old question: are we dreaming the dream or is the dream dreaming us?

Dreams can do the future, creative journeys, the secrets which underlie the world and the individual's needs and desires. They can be warnings or present archetypes. Like creativity itself, we need dreams to keep us sane. The creative dream is the mythic way of keeping sane. Myth itself can be a guide to creative day-dreaming, while some might say the internet is the dream-place of the fantasy of technological omniscience.

Psychology and psychoanalysis, especially in Freud and Jung, offer a central importance to dreams, while writing has always been a world which has drawn on dreams' significance. Sleeping on a creative problem, or any problem, will often offer an answer to the mythsmith: the unconscious will respond to proper attention. The constancy of our dreaming selves, visible or not, is testament to our need for creative balances.

DRUGS

Drugs offer an instant method of transformation, which can obviously go either way. A classic old drug-escape myth appears in *The Odyssey* (Book 9, lines 82–104). Book 9 contains various alternative societies, from the world of Alcinous' hospitality to the world of war and violence, thence to a world of total peace via the Lotus Eaters, and finally to the Cyclops' land. Civilisation, extremes of war, then of peace, then of primitive life are placed side by side, with only the first finding merit with the brutal warriors. Below is a version of the short, but beguiling Lotus-stoned world of 'The Eaters of Flowers'.

The Eaters of Flowers (by A.M.)

Passive, sexy, expansive –
we were blown well off course, us blokes
from feasts, from killing and from cursing hurricanes
when we put a washed-up foot on their island,
those stoned, stress-free hippies –
the eaters of the flowers

Like three naïve cops in a posh crack-house
or some tranced-out dope-blowers
my guys went in, and didn't come back.
Lovely temptation is such a relief
wallowing, untrying, hypnotised, endlessly smiling
letting go, gone, lost and flowing free
loving everyone, easy, blessed-out forever –

We dragged them out and tied them up
weeping like babies for the sweet taste
but as I cursed the soppy fuckers
and wondered who I could kick the shit out of next
I couldn't help thinking of the hidden sex goddess
and how she's had me –

Make no mistake, there's stuff here
to change the narrow mind, the narrow pain
and I plug the real danger for effect –
having a point to us, I get us out

don't mention my doubt
just a soldier turning off my sense of peace –
She'd had me years of endless, ripe, blooming love
but fuck that – we're going – someone's going to get it and
we've got to get back

This poem is intended to bring out the ambivalence we feel about 'peace and love', that our resistance is a kind of vanity. The 'sacred blue' Egyptian lotus is actually a euphoric drug, akin to ecstasy, by the way.

Drugs, of course, can themselves offer vanity. In *Grimm's* fairytale no. 118, 'The Three Army Surgeons', for example, these arrogant men think they have the universal balm that can heal anything. It all goes wrong for them, like the power offered perhaps by drugs like cocaine, where the world is cock-eyed, or turned to stone by arrogance, as in Cockayne. This is the land where the ego Cock will turn what he sees to stone. To be stoned then can be to escape the physical world or to be entombed in it. Extreme myth may not be so useful, but rituals involving drugs are part of many cultures' contact with the supernatural. Our own cultural heritage in the United Kingdom sanctions the dangerous drug of alcohol to get us out of our minds and talking to God.

Drugs, like alcohol, of course belong to the world of Dionysus and wild celebration, fertility and the proper acknowledgement of the irrational. See Chapter 8, Myth Madness.

See also works like Carroll's *Alice in Wonderland* (1865) and de Quincey's *Confessions of an English Opium Eater* (1821), plus the writing of William Burroughs, Aldous Huxley, etc.

EARTH

The most solid of the four elements, the down-to-earth, earth goddess, earth mother, mother earth, Gaia is our ground and our base and the place from whence we spring and return. This still-powerful symbol represents the stable, fertile, receptive, material side of the symbolic, where promise and support are vital riches to us. Nourishment and openness, permission, sensation and intuition operate through the earthly powers. Negatively, the earth is the place of the dead, the underworld, the weakly passive, the stubborn, the bound, the static, the decaying. Dionysus is there, as the agricultural god, giving the earth its fertility via life above, via decay and rebirth. The ecologist might use Hesiod's name for earth, Gaia, to symbolise how the world is one being and must be treated with respect. The creatures of the earth, gnomes and elves, appear as small but powerful elemental forces in the world, while Adam is *adamah* in Hebrew, 'of earth'.

Earth is a potential Eden, or earth, in some views, is actually hell, as the opposite of heaven. Humility is tied up in the down-to-earth, via the humus, the soil. The earth mound is a place of burial, but the roundness of earth is also a sexiness of earthiness, where the plough and the planting is the agricultural symbol of sexual fertility, of mud and fundamentals. Man, in many creation myths, is moulded of clay, of earth.

Earth Calling The Mythsmith! We, like the late Pope, kiss the scared ground in our mud bath of potential growth. Writings about gardening, gardens, farming, ploughing, tending plants and crops, earthquakes, owning ground and the sense of place are often celebrations of earth, as are elegies of burial and black humour of worms and death.

In writing, often a character close to the earth, an old gardener say, acts as a mentor figure, or a reminder of basic truths and a slower reality. A good example of this is Adam in Shakespeare's *As You Like It*. The play begins with Orlando seeking the long view from Adam the old servant, before returning to earth via exile in the greenwood. A New Age Traveller version of this play might work well, where the 'civilised' find a way back to earth.

See John Michell's *The Earth Spirit* (1975) and Jonathan Bate's *The Song of the Earth* (2000) about nature, weather and English literature, and the poems of John Clare.

EVIL

See Postscript on Myth and Magic, plus Chapter 5, Dark Matter, on the Shadow, plus Chapter 11, Dooms and Dead Ends; also entry above on the DEVIL.

We are all attracted to evil in a kind of uncanny fascination, which is why darker characters are interesting and why we are drawn to any manifestation of decay, death or destruction. The mysteries of annihilation and of sex mixed with death are strongly present in contemporary culture. The danger for writers is that of caricature. Georges Bataille's *Literature and Evil* (translated 1985) gives the picture of our fascination, and how in writing, these things become compelling. Dionysus' prophet Tieresias points out, in Euripides *The Bacchae*, that the evil is indeed in humankind, rather than in the god who might release it. Is evil our greatest invention? No, because that could be seen as just a reversed kind of sentimentality. On the other hand, it is a sign of our defiance of static order.

The poet Baudelaire's *Flowers of Evil* (1857) is a seminal text for those who want to see evil explored well, and a source for other writers associated with decadence. The naughty honesty of decadence is very attractive, but, again, the only problem with decay is its infertility, ultimately. The great condemnations of mankind in the Bible, such as 'Every imagination of the thoughts of his heart were only evil continually' (Genesis 6:5), from the Flood in Genesis, have a power too, in the hell-fire preacher way. The obsessed-with-evil character is a strong feature of writings around the paranoia about witchcraft and a good source of the instability of morality.

The power and energy of evil are what makes them tempting for a writer, where real power or energy seem too good to be true. As a force of change, of death bringing about rebirth, evil performs its useful function in the reversals used by myth. Evil alone is not just a lack of empathy, of course, but may be a lack of creative imagination.

EYES

The Elizabethans believed that the eyes were not just 'windows to the soul', but that looks wielded power. Shakespeare is full of visual metaphor and English still uses 'seeing' as meaning 'understanding', or, to use another shade of eye-related meaning, taking a view on something. Is this how you see it? The power of where you are looking, who you are looking at, the downcast, staring or evil eye still say much to us about relationships. The look in the eyes of a loved-one is still a look of love, in the dilation, or something else in the closing of the pupil, like an opening up of mind and being to another, or the closing off. The colours of eyes too hold their place in us, their colour giving colour to the world, themselves like twin worlds.

The force of the gaze is mythically depicted in the Gorgon, or the Medusa, who will turn you to stone, or in the mythical beast the Cockatrice, who will kill with a look. The directed beam of the eye is then still the primal sense, where the eye of God might be the invisible omnipotence. The electric, or lazer beam, the radio wave, the influence, the evil eye are all there in the gun, the ray-gun in space, the lighting up, the lightning, lightening, the investigation. Eyes are powerful magic. The eye is the ego, the light of the mind, which echoes the light of the sun and moon. The one-eyed, like the Cyclops, is a primal, primitive vision, unified or limited, while two eyes give focus and form, or duplicity, to the world. H.G. Wells' story 'The Country of the Blind' (1927) echoes the Cyclops' story and the proverb, 'In the country of the blind, the one-eyed man is King'. Light and darkness, such a feature of Greek tragedy in terms of imagery, are one of the most powerful representations of human understanding and insight, or of the lack of it.

The eye of the writer is, of course, like the eye of a film director, who uses the camera as an eye, seeing the tale revealed. Where the eye sees from and how the eye sees are all important in writing: the viewpoint, both physically, character-wise and opinion-wise. It is all in the eyes, just as 'all looks yellow to the jaundiced eye' and beauty is said to be 'in the eye of the beholder'.

FAME

See Chapter 12, Myths of Fame. Fame is an airy quality and just as easily dissipated as generated, in fading warmth of feeling. The worldly quality we associate with fame is as ephemeral as it seems. The journey of the heroic writer through myth is an inner journey, which may result in a difficulty in bringing the discovery back to an unreceptive world. This is the harder route of true heroism, deserving of fame, which may be denied or may come as a by-product of achieving something of real creative worth. The abstract, airy quality of fame is a negative, masculine trait, which is a type of vanity, rather than something to admire. In a world where a 'celebrity' is someone you have never heard of, with no visible talent, fame is a good topic for heroism perverted in a hero-free world. The craving for fame reveals only a hunger for a truer example of the heroic.

FEMININE

Mythically, to talk of the female principal may not be so unbalanced or gender prejudiced, as the feminine forces are often seen as more powerful magic than the 'man's world' abstract, controlling power of the male side might be. A good place to start might be *The Woman's Encyclopedia of Myths and Secrets*, by Barbara Walker (1983). While ancient myths might offer worlds, or societies, where women are not equal, the language of mythic symbol has proved powerful for female writers in the twentieth century, such as Margaret Atwood and Angela Carter, Anne Sexton, Stevie Smith and Marina Warner. The struggle of male and female is the struggle of mythic opposites, where each must be well balanced to achieve unity. Nature, feeling and receptivity are not the same as unintellectual or passive attributes and can obviously be quite the opposite.

Creativity is essentially a feminine quality, requiring knowledge and confidence beyond the self-consciously questing mock heroics of many male moves towards the creative. Dante's Beatrice in *The Commedia* is a higher figure than Dante, just as Faust's saving grace (as in The Three Graces, perhaps) is

The Eternal Feminine. The Virgin Mary is another symbol of female power. Understanding the creative process means that, if the feminine is associated with the unconscious, then the source of mythic power in writing is the power of the anima, the feminine energy-force counterbalancing the less-inspired male side.

The word 'charity' comes from the same source as grace, as in the Three Graces, who, like the Muses, embody the power of the feminine. All goodness, all creativity seems to flow from these ancient images of the great Goddess of the world. The inconstant image of the 'femme fatale' is merely the reflection of the negative power of the feminine, where there is such need for a positive power in the world.

When writing about mythic characters, or characters from fairytale, subverting the stereotype is a good way of exploring the feminine power which might be hidden in older versions of the tale. This has been a great source for all types of women writers. Cinderella from the ugly sisters' points of view, for example, could be a very strong take on the tale, as could a version from the point of view of the stepmother. The only danger for the writer in doing this is the trap of shrillness, but many writers have demonstrated that wit and energy can rebalance old stories and make them new, revealing hidden energies, rather then overlaying an agenda. Myth is a ripe area for the writer who would challenge the narrower aspects of the masculine world in a creative way.

Marina Warner's work on the feminine in literature and fairytale are another good place to start to explore this topic of huge potential and importance. Classic works of feminist critique also explore the symbolism of the feminine to strong effect, and in old myth, when Circe turns men into pigs, we get the picture. Orpheus is torn apart by women but it is his hidden passion, his repressed creative side, that is doing the tearing apart. Each negative symbol like the Sirens who lure men to death can be countered by, or in writing, combined with, an opposite. The Sirens' opposite are the Muses, who inspire all songs and try to help you sing.

FIRE

One of the four elements (with water, earth and air), but the most powerful, fire is full of potential energy and its converse, consuming destruction. The sun is its source and symbol and we live by its light and heat, its essential goodness. The burning and withering destructive power of fire reaches its ultimate form in the nuclear bomb. The Greek myth of Prometheus, who stole fire from the gods, shows both the power and the danger. Fire can melt solids and represents the spark of life in us and, if we have it, we shall be as gods. Knowledge of fire, in industry and technology, seems godlike but is open to hubris and pollution. Prometheus' chains and torture punishment is a reminder, renewed every night, of his human and physical limits, which counteracts his act of materialistic grasping of the power of fire. Ted Hughes' *Prometheus on his Crag* (1973, in *Collected Poems*) explores this and Blumenberg in *Work on Myth* (1985) has a wide discussion of the myth. This is the human dilemma in strong terms: our knowledge of good and evil that sets us apart in both this myth and in the creation story in Genesis.

Jorge Luis Borges, in his *Book of Imaginary Beings* (1969), among many mythical animals, gives an overview of the Phoenix, the tale of this bird who burns then rises from the ashes. He traces the phoenix to Egyptian myths of eternal life, which took root in Greek and Roman mythology. D.H. Lawrence famously took the phoenix as his symbol and wove a tapestry of it. The bird rising from the flames is a common symbol, used by insurance companies among others, to symbolise renewal, or the survival of being consumed. It is known that fire can regenerate, and is necessary to, some forest areas of the world. There is an Anglo-Saxon version of a Roman phoenix poem and Dante, Milton and Shakespeare all refer to the phoenix, as well as many classical writers. The salamander, less known, but also written about frequently, is a fire-dragon, said to be able to live in, and possibly on, in terms of food, fire. In these stories, fire is our struggle with the concept of immortality, while T.S. Eliot says, in 'Little Gidding' IV, from *Four Quartets* (1944, in *Complete Poems and Plays*), 'Love is the unfamiliar Name/ Behind the hands that wove/ The intolerable shirt of flame.'

FISH

The secret nourishment in the depths is the world of the symbolic fish and represents the emotional, non-intellectual world under the surface. Negatively, it is the place of the growing monster, like the Kraken. The Fisher King is one who can bring up the treasure from the depth (see Terry Gilliam's 1991 film of that title). In legends of Arthur, he is the one who guards the Holy Grail and lies wounded, neither dead nor alive, and a knight must come to revive him and, of course, thus revive the whole land. Herman Melville's *Moby-Dick* is both monster and treasure, obsession and destruction, in the great American novel. The English fairytale 'The Fish and the Ring' (see Joseph Jacob's collection) tells of love, symbolised by the ring, lost and then found in a fish's belly, caught by the lover. The fish is also used in Christian symbolism, partly in reference to the fishermen in the Gospels and the 'fishers of men' (Mark 1:17) symbolism, where the depth of the soul is saved. Jonah (the Book of Jonah, in the Old Testament) and the whale is another biblical story of survival in the depth, or a trial in the unconscious realm, and a testing by water.

FLOOD

See Chapter 11, Dooms and Dead Ends, especially 'Always the Flood'. The human world is never without tales of floods. Even those who have never been near a church will know the story of Noah's ark. The destruction of the world and the saving of the few is a universal myth, still with us in religious faith and cults, science fiction and post-apocalyptic writings of all kinds. It is a myth about death and rebirth, but reinforced by the real danger of its literal meaning. We fear death by drowning, we fear inundation. With fire, flood is probably the biggest metaphor we have for destruction and the power of water has immense symbolic power.

The word itself derives 'in the primary sense' as the *OED* says, from the word flow, and means 'the action of flowing'. The tides, thus ebb (go out) and flow or flood (come in). Shakespeare uses flood in this sense, in *Julius Caesar*, IV, iii: 'There is a Tide in the affairs of men,/ Which taken at the Flood, leads on to Fortune.' Here flood, in the sense of flow, means when things are coming your way. So flood in a positive sense is something we need. When we talk, when we write, when we are in tune with the 'tide in the affairs of men' and we are absorbed in things and things go right, we say that we 'go with the flow'.

In Genesis 6, we get the destructive, capital 'F' story of the Flood. Verse 5 says: 'And God saw that the wickedness of man was great in the earth, and that every imagination of the thoughts of his heart was only evil continually.' This killer sentence is the power of the King James' translators at their best. More, from verse 7: 'And the Lord said, I will destroy man whom I have created from the face of the earth; both man, and beast, and the creeping thing, and the fowls of the air; for it repenteth me that I have made them.' Verse 17: 'And, behold, I, even I, do bring a flood of waters upon the earth, to destroy all flesh, wherein is the breath of life, from under heaven; and every thing that is in the earth shall die.' Putting aside how we see these stories, there is a beguiling quality about this destructive language, where we can feel the palpable wrath of God and even share in a kind of thirst for the inundation to come. This thirst for destruction is a powerful negative force in us, at once appeasing our sense of attraction to evil and quenching it and letting it fall away.

The world is awash with flood stories. In *The Epic of Gilgamesh*, we find the usual parallels, but also some clue as to the function of such stories. We should note, in passing, that flood was a particularly real danger for the people of the city of Uruk, as this Mesopotamian city was built between two rivers. In chapter five of N.K. Sandars' version (1960), we have the gods being angry in the same way at all the row made by the expanding human world. Humans were noisy neighbours. Sandars uses the word 'babel' with a small 'b' in this passage, aware of the Biblical echo. Gilgamesh seeks out the man who lived through the flood and thus is immortal. This is Utnapishtim, which means 'he who saw life'. Gilgamesh is told of the flood and here we can see the Flood as a kind of initiation, a baptism, a renewal by ordeal and a passage from one state to another. In Genesis 10:29, we are told that 'the days of Noah were nine hundred and fifty years', so there is something almost immortal there (a logical impossibility). But Noah, like Gilgamesh, does face death eventually. There is a human acceptance, an epic acceptance you could say, of the falling from life, as if the baptism, the survival or rebirth prepares them both for the finality of being overwhelmed.

Karen Armstrong's article 'Believers in the lost ark' (*Guardian*, 9.8.2003) insists that we must not treat myth as literal truth. Those seeking to find the ark are getting it wrong. The story of the Flood is about what it means to be human, confronted with death. Floods also talk of the break with God, the Fall and disconnection from innocence and direct access to the divine. Water is mystery. It is the living embodiment of what we cannot grasp and the Flood is its ultimate expression.

See Ted Hughes' version of Ovid's flood, in *Tales from Ovid* (1997), 'Water' by Philip Larkin, the opening section of 'The Dry Salvages' (1954, in *Collected Poems*), from T.S. Eliot's *Four Quartets* (1944), and *The Drowned World* (1962) by J.G. Ballard, among masses of writings about water. Also, see WATER.

FOOD

For the mythsmith, food might be an easily overlooked symbol of significance to human relationship and sustenance of life. The 'Last Supper' of the disciples is re-enacted in communion, where the blood and flesh are drink and meat. We sustain and/ or are consumed by one another in many symbolic ways. Food is a powerful motif in fairytale and all myth, in its offering, sharing, symbolic 'gift of life' way. The taking of meals is a ritual of community and an acknowledgement of shared need and has a narrative in-built.

Ambrosia means 'not mortal' and is the food of the gods. Likewise 'manna' is supplied to the Israelites in Exodus 16, and means 'what is it?' Both are wonder foods, then, and symbolise life, which is given free. This food is only available to the virtuous, of course and, if stolen, or misused, like the Lotus Eaters (see DRUGS), there is a price to pay. Nectar is the drink of immortality, combining in its roots the source of the word 'noxious', which is the drink of death. The ambiguous meaning suggests some good fiction of death and immortality being easily mistaken.

The stolen aspect of Prometheus' fire is used for cooking and is then a symbol for civilisation, for giving food extra life, while differentiating it from its raw or dangerous stage. The 'primitive' god Dionysus is the god of plenty and of agriculture, also of wine and excess. The growing and getting of food, with its link to the seasons, makes food the hidden mythic technology which means life or death to humankind. We still need to be in tune with this mythic growth and sustainability.

GIANTS

Giants are huge in myth and symbol and they are everywhere, representing the feared, the repressed, the primitive, physical urges and the monstrous. Fairytale and processional giants with their 'Fe, Fi , Fo, Fum!' are popular in our children's and folkloric cultures, but the origins of giants can be seen mythically in Genesis and in the Hesiod's *Theogony*, as well as appearing in texts like *The Epic of Gilgamesh*, for example. The Titans, in Greek myth, seem to represent the greedy, selfish, brutish side of life, whose strength and threat needed both gods and men to get together to defeat. Here they are unconsciousness, or innocence, in a corrupted form. They could be the gods' first experiment in human life, gone wrong.

In Genesis 6:4, the giants seem a source of the evil which the Flood will destroy: 'There were giants in the earth in those days; and also after that, when the sons of God came unto the daughters of men, and they bare children to them, the same became mighty men which were of old, men of renown.' It appears that the giants became good here, if 'after that' means after the flood, by Godly intervention perhaps, yet this is in the tale just before God decides to destroy the world. In Samuel 1:17, David kills the giant Goliath with a sling and this is a classic of the small and clever overcoming the great force. Humbaba, the giant in *Gilgamesh*, guards the trees, which are sought by the hero and is an example of the mythic tyrant who wants to own everything. For a writer, this could be a most useful example of mythic potential, as the world teems with these greedy giants, some might say. Heroes are needed to overcome such men who destroy the world with their greed.

The good, or gentle, giant is hard to rouse, but is there in some old stories. Usually a magician can get a good giant to help, here representing the forces of the unconscious coming to our positive aid.

GOD(S)

God and the gods are the great life-force, unifying and all-encompassing. What belongs to the gods or to God is what is beyond our control: nature, the cosmos, the unknown, the unconscious, death and the spark of life. As mythic and symbolic power, they hold the strength we seek to summon, whatever our particular belief or lack of belief. Karen Armstrong's *A History of God* (1993) describes the functions God fulfilled for people through the ages and is useful for a mythic use of the deity. Greek gods have their own individual, more human, stories, which is part of why they still appeal so widely, while still being gods anyway.

God tends to be seen as an authority figure, as paternal and judgemental, while a contemporary view might challenge this stereotype. The goddess figure is a powerful force and God as neither gender, or as female, calls back to an older, matriarchal myth. The creative creator is a parallel with the writer who 'plays God' with his creation. To write is to imitate a power we may not deserve to have and the gods or God may be jealous of this creative force. It comes at a cost.

The pure, or perfect, essence of being, the 'I am that I am' in Exodus 3:14, is also a powerful image with a ritual repetition and contradiction, paradox and circle built-in. All are useful for writers. The question of whether God is an interventionist force or not is also worth exploring, when many give reasons for disbelief involving the lack of good in the world. The conflict between God and older, local, multiple gods has been a source for writers on myth, embodying the conflict between the Puritanism of monotheism and the pantheistic openness of the old gods. Losing both is obviously nowadays a good subject for the anti-materialist mythsmith.

Heroes, in myth, epic and elsewhere, must be part god and the glimpse of the unknown power in the self can be a manifestation of this subject. Like the last subject, this one is too big to encompass fully here, but the one-ness and the otherness of God/gods will always be the ultimate symbol of myth and mythic writing. Like myth, the gods and God are immortal, so we partake of something godlike, even if we remain sceptical.

HAIR

The extraordinary amount of attention given to human hair shows its symbolic significance. The hair is associated with ego and the growth of sexual identity and so the cutting off of hair symbolises the loss of ego, but also the possibility of a new self, more in tune with the inner, or true self. That is why it is probably a good idea for balding men to have the short hair of the serious monk, seeking a new and stronger self, than to try to cling on to a vanishing youthful ego. The cutting off of hair symbolises a humiliation of the ego, such as in the case of women in the Second World War who had slept with German soldiers, or the emergence of a new self, such as in monks and soldiers, who sacrifice their ego for the greater good.

The biblical story of Sampson, whose strength was in his hair, is the classic myth of the subject. His association with the outward self can be seen in his name, which means 'sun man'. In the Book of Judges, Sampson is a larger-than-life character, a man of ego, the epitome of strength, on an epic scale. Samson, amid his woman and war trouble, locates the source of his strength in his hair, which has never been cut in all his life. His natural ego is untouched by the world's restraint. Delilah has him shaven while he sleeps and his strength is gone. But hair grows again and he pulls down the pillars of the house of his captors and dies with them. His overextended ego, when cut off, turns negative. The story is a tragedy of strength, which Milton's *Samson Agonistes* (1671) explores.

Songwriter Richard Thompson has a powerful song ('She Cut Off Her Long Silken Hair', from *You? Me? Us?*, 1996) about a woman cutting off her own hair and how he regrets the loss of her old, natural beauty, where she might feel caught, by her own conformity to feminine image. Brian Wilson's Beach Boys song 'Caroline, No', from *Pet Sounds* (1966) uses a similar trope, where youthful beauty and innocence seems cast off by the loss of hair. Baudelaire's prose poem 'Un hémisphère dans une chevelure' (A Hemisphere in a Woman's Hair, 1862) likewise explores the sensual delight in the natural, unaltered sexuality of hair. The fairytale of Rapunzel (*Grimm's* fairytale no.12) also has natural sexual allure as its motif. Rapunzel's name itself means a kind of green lettuce and her natural abundance of youthful vibrancy is what the Prince climbs up. This mythic tale has received and deserves much attention, but it also gives rise to the mythic jest: Let down your hair, you never know what might come up.

HEAD

The head is the whole, round, central image of strength, as well as the place of the mind and the spirit. The separation from the head, losing one's head, is to lose one's soul and spirit and strength. When the head appears, disembodied, the self is disconnected from the world. Our heads are our burden of self-consciousness personified, which, like Orpheus, continue to sing after our deaths. They are our disintegration as well as our unnatural ability. The uncanniness of the head is why severed heads seem so powerful, either as trophies or as messengers from the world of death. Medusa's head had power, including the power to turn those it looked at to stone. The burial of heads often symbolises a power to protect the living, which must not be disturbed.

The multiple head symbolises the power of the monstrous to change and come at you in a new life-form. Mythical monsters, such as Hydra, have many heads, hence many life-forces. Multiple heads are all-seeing. Wisdom and stupidity are in the head. The two-headed shows the contradictory natures needing balance (see references to Janus in Chapter 2, Birth Myths). Heads are also there in flowers and in the growth of grain and thus the dismembering of Dionysus is a sign of death and rebirth, through agricultural ritual. The English folksong 'John Barleycorn' shows the sacrificial ritual in the personification of grain, where the head is cut off, with his capacity to rise again in the life-giving quality of beer.

The gods' messenger Hermes is often seen looking in two directions, to show his connection to travel and to being able to see before and in front. He is a good god for the writer, seeking to balance the inner and outer worlds and making his current connections from the mythic past work towards the future. The head can be control and rule, but is also the spirit and self and needs its connection to life. It can wear a crown, or the dunce's or fool's cap. The presence of the disconnected head throughout myth, fairytale and folklore all speak of the old power we have tended to neglect and to which the living need to reconnect.

HERO

See Chapter 6, Late Heroes. For the purposes of writing, the writer who understands this book *is* the hero. The writer might not be heroic outside the creative process, but the practice of mythic writing will tend to suggest a better, i.e. more heroic, way of life.

INCEST

The story of Oedipus, as told by Sophocles, is the classic myth of mother/son incest, as in the 'Oedipus Complex' while the lesser known, not much used

'Electra Complex' is said to be that of the daughter and the father. Electra hated her mother, who had murdered her father, so her case for incest does not really add up, however.

The story of Myrrha might be a better one for a daughter's incest with a father, as it is told in Ovid's *Metamorphoses*, Book X. Myrrha is overwhelmed with suitors. She tries to resist her own love of her father Cinyras with argument, but she knows that animals make no distinction and seems to know that the gods seem to be able to make new gods from incest. Furthermore she has heard of primitive people who use incest as a communal bond. Ovid warns us that we will not like the story, like a pornographer, threatening and tantalising with the hardcore nature of his goods.

She tells herself to flee, excessively conscious of all the problems her forbidden love might bring. Ovid is brilliant here at painting her as no innocent and at depicting the pressure around her. Cinyras asks her to choose a suitor and she says she wants one like him, whereupon he kisses her for her devotion, not realising her passion. At night, tortured by doubt and pressure, she decides to kill herself. Her old nurse rescues her from hanging and gets her to talk. The nurse gets the truth from her eventually, and decides in fear that it is best to have what you want, however bad, rather than die by your own hand. The nurse colludes in tricking the father into allowing the daughter into his bed, during the Dionysian harvest ceremonies of wild licence, saying to Cinyras that she has the same name as his daughter. They repeat the incest, but eventually Cinyras brings a lamp to see her and realises their crime. He draws his sword, but she escapes, to pray for deliverance.

The gods turn her into a myrrh tree, which oozes her tears. But she is pregnant and eventually gives birth to her son Adonis, the beautiful, beloved of the goddess Venus.

It is amazing and characteristic of myth in general and of Ovid in particular that such a dangerous topic can be tackled so lightly and persuasively. This may be because the underlying psychological force of the madness is understood more deeply in these tales, more perhaps than we can do with our talk and systems of abuse and addiction. The idea of incest as a mental stage that a child may go through to reach a more mature attachment is implicit in the Myrrah story, while the Oedipus/ Electra 'complexes' have a sense of a kind of hidden desire that can undo us. This has been especially appealing to the suppression of sexual desire seen everywhere in early psychoanalysis.

The gods can be incestuous because they are not human and therefore not subject to human vanity through self-love. Their self-love is not available to us. Our desire for stasis leads to physical and moral degeneration, to the breaking of the healthy cycles of birth and death, where new life must come from otherness, to give a proper sense of change. The unchanging gods are our opposite.

To write about incest, myth offers some warnings and pointers, beyond the taboo horror of the deed. It gives what is behind the prison of fatally abusive vanity, which is perhaps what incest now means to us.

JESUS

There is a sense in which Jesus is a descendent of Dionysus, inasmuch as he is a sacrificial figure of new life. For the modern mythsmith, though, using Jesus mythologically could get you into trouble, in offending both the literalist religious and the rationalist who might be sick of crass forms of evangelistic propaganda. This might be a good thing, if that is what you want to do, but the myth might get lost in the clamour of worldly opinion. Myth needs a bit of strangeness to make it do its demanding job of the contradiction of our self-aggrandisement. Some myths are best approached sideways, or at least in a fashion which is aware of the prejudice surrounding the topic, either way.

That said, the story of Jesus holds many of the tropes of myth discussed here and the Gospels are full of useful source material and verbal wonder, so I would not advise avoiding them altogether. It might be said that we need to know them well, if only to understand where so much of our cultural identity, and hence our sense of myth or the lack of it, arises. Many writers have used Christian myth to useful purpose, such as C.S. Lewis.

KING

Myth, liking old symbolic power, means it is in favour of such things as Kings, you might say. The King represents earthly power and the positive use of power, unhampered by lowlier desires. A good male boss might be like a King, who has both strength and fairness. The aspect of the heroic (see Chapter 6, Late Heroes) will be present in the figure. Via Shakespeare and via the modern world, we mistrust such figures, but are presented with the bureaucrats and businessmen pursuing their own interests through power. We wonder if we made a mythic mistake. The old figure of the benign King seems far from our sordid world. The King is the force of the conscious and communal worlds, ritually renewed to create order and peace. Have we neglected this renewal? There is nothing worse than a bad King and nothing better than a good King. The Sun and the Lion are his symbols of strength.

Often, the bad King will be rigid and inflexible, lacking the renewing force of the feminine side and a writer might use such a figure to represent the country in one personifying figure, which is also the role of the King, symbolically. Jazz musicians have traditionally used aristocratic terms for stage-names and we probably all know someone we might think of as having these qualities, in a half-joking way. On the other hand, what would it be like to believe in the old virtues, mythically earned? There are many Kingly and Queenly opportunities for writing.

LIGHT

Light is the positive force of consciousness and the bringer of life and new days. The actual and symbolic power of light cannot be overestimated. The dark and the light, the day and the night – these are the positive and negative of our symbolic life at the most primal level. There is also the quality of lightness, as opposed to heaviness and as opposed to seriousness. To be light-hearted is not necessarily to be unserious, however. To balance the weight of solemnity, we need that which is quick, at the speed of light, to animate ourselves in balance. Seeing the light has long been a symbolic indication for understanding and Jesus is often called 'the light', representing all that is good. On the other hand, light pollution and the unnatural, killing bright light of nuclear weapons shows that even this basic quality can be made into a negative thing. Apollo is the great god of light and order, according to Nietzsche, in *The Birth of Tragedy* (1872), as opposed to Dionysus, who represents a darker power, of earthy fertility.

Italo Calvino's essay on 'Lightness' in *Six Memos for the Next Millennium* (1988) is instructive on the quickness of the best thought, among other things, while W.H. Auden's introduction to his Oxford anthology of light verse (1938) argues well for the seriousness of the light.

Sun worship is worship of the light and the visible force of all life and perhaps the source of all worship. The power that animates us, that blesses the children, is the one we can see. The tarot card of the Sun always shows two children beneath, with the blessing falling on them. Droughts and danger from too much sun are familiar to us too, but the return of the sun in winter is the only ritual many still adhere to, believers or not, and the most necessary boon. The destruction and especially the creation of the sun are often used by writers of science fiction and other mythic creators. Light is the immediate source of real and symbolic seeing.

LOVE

See Chapters 7, Happiness Writes and 8, Myth Madness. Love is the most present aspect of mythic behaviour and thinking left in Western culture. We permit the irrational nature of Romantic love, where perhaps we permit little else which addresses transformation or metaphors of new life. We all have our favourites from the great love stories, which allow us doom and glory.

Poet Hilary Llewellyn-Williams tells me, in a personal message, that 'love and erotic passion have always been central to human existence and it was only in extreme patriarchal societies, such as Ancient Greece and Rome, and from thence to early Christianity that romance was banished or trivialised'. She also says that there is 'a rich and varied tradition of love stories and poetry from the far East, India, Persia and Islamic Spain: a tradition that evolved via the Crusades to southern France and Italy from the eleventh century onwards and fired the European imagination'.

Creative Writing students are often advised to avoid love as a topic, but, because of the above and the possibility there of seeing it in a wider context, I would say that one only need avoid the clichéd expression of love. Love then can be the pathway to the mythic for us, as it might open the door to a deeper mythic journey, literally and in terms of writing.

Eros is the god of love, or the snake or rope which holds the world as one and offers the place of transformation. The binding together of love is the hold the world has on the person and the person has on the world. The love of the opposite principal is the journey from self to world and from world to self. Eros is always present in human life, whether it is in prime desire or a retreat from it. Eros is, in a sense, the male muse, inspiring the active side of love. The mythic aim is the union of opposites to create a fully realised power, where 'the other half' is sought to achieve wholeness.

D.H. Lawrence's *Lady Chatterley's Lover* (1928) is a love story which shows the union of opposites, just for one example of many. The failure of the class system and of the divisions between men and women are challenged by the lovers moving outside the societies they seem bound by. They become, by the end of the novel, a symbol of hope for a more tender understanding between genders and classes: one working title for the novel was 'Tenderness'. The erotic nature of the book was also an attempt to claim an honest language of sex, a point notoriously missed by the scandalous success of the 1960s uncensored publication.

MADNESS

See Chapter 8, Myth Madness. Myths seem often mad because they deal with what we find mad in us or in the world. But myths are there not to drive us mad but to help us understand the power and limits of the irrational and our attitudes to it. The mythic realm is in the area of the unconscious, where the madness, like the ever-changing Proteus, needs to be wrestled with to find the sense in it. Madness and nonsense are the prime examples of mythic hiding, which myths tend to do, if not attended to properly. The madness of myth is a potential sanity of creativity. There is real madness there, but confronting the monster is part of the adventure and the testing of the adventurer. These things are not to be taken lightly and real madness is no joke in its danger or capacity to destroy. However, the opposite strength of the mythic seeker of true and earned sanity is arguably more powerful still.

The view of myth is that we are responsible for our madness and not the gods. They only allow access to the realms of possibility. This is spelt out by Tiresias in Euripides' *The Bacchae*. Dionysus is not mad, he is the cure for the inclination to madness, but will also reveal those who have madness in them by vain attitudes. The gods are supposed to drive people mad, before destroying them, but this seems to say that we must be responsible for our madness and our own mythic sanity. Madness is tragedy, but true mythic sanity is comedy (see Chapter 7, Happiness Writes), although the Greek proverb 'Whom the gods wish to destroy, they first make mad' is quoted in Euripides' *Fragments*.

MEN

The irony of men in myth terms is that the heroism they aspire towards has become non-mythic. That is, the materialist, rationalist society they have created amounts to an uptight, unbalanced view of the world, lacking in intuition and feeling. For the heroic discussed at length, see Chapter 6, Late Heroes. The character of Pentheus in *The Bacchae* by Euripides would be the classic view of men's capacity to lose touch with the mythic. Robert Bly's *Iron John* (1990) uses a fairytale of initiation, Grimms' 'Iron Hans' (fairytale no. 136) to discuss men's problems. This book began the men's movement, which seeks to redress this imbalance. Powerful men still rule the world with their money and they seek immortality, while failing to see that they must die in their material selves, in order to live at all. Mythically, men are not grown up, as Bly asserts in his neglected follow-up book, *The Sibling Society* (1996), so all of society lacks mythic initiation. Myth and fairytale, as all literature, is full of tales of vain and foolish men (tragedy) and the fools who see through them (comedy) and there is much scope for the writer to explore both society as it is and as it might be, perhaps better, or indeed, worse. Elvis Costello's album *All This Useless Beauty* (1996) has many songs about the crisis of masculinity and, probably the classic text for the post First World War crisis in men is Hemingway's *Men Without Women* (1927). *Money* (1984) by Martin Amis shows the greedy male 'John Self' in all his tragic-comic glory.

NAMES

There is a mythic, magical idea that all things have a secret name that reveals their nature and power. Names are given, therefore a gift, therefore mythic in their value beyond the material. We rarely name ourselves and, if we do, we risk becoming materialistic by nature. Seeing ourselves as an object with a name, rather than having the gift from the world which names us is potentially a dangerous thing. The names in classic myth have a meaning, such as Odysseus meaning 'Trouble'. If you are writing about a classic mythic character, look up the meaning of the name. It will deepen your insight into the character and suggest a modern alternative (see Chapter 9, Modernising Myths).

Books of names, used by new parents, are useful, as they often include meanings. I use *The Magical Name* (1991) by Ted Andrews, not for its new-age agenda, but for the meanings of names, useful for characters in fiction. We all know how significant names of organisations can be and people pay consultants much to find a good one. Your favourite band's name will have significance for you, above its apparent meaning. Names are loaded by the human imagination with mythic power. Nicknames are also powerful, as another given thing, especially if they work against the self-image of the character.

Titles also have a ritual, ceremonial power, even in their absurdity, as do descriptions of mythic roles, such as Sage, or Witch. If I wrote about a character called 'Hilary Sage', she might, by meaning, be a cheerful wise woman and this helps me make my imagination work: it has just told me she wears a bright yellow raincoat. Naming of literary works is important too, like a short art-form. The right title is essential, to resonate mythically far beyond itself.

OPPOSITES

Opposites working together are an essential element of creativity. In creation myth (see Chapter 1, Starting Creation) the unity of chaos is divided to create life. New life is then (re)created by uniting opposites, which partakes of the original creative unity. For the mythic writer, this might be the unconscious working through myth into the conscious, in the form of the created work. Thus creativity becomes an attempt at a kind of unity between the inner and outer worlds, between the personal and the universal (again via the mediation of myth) and between nature, or the gods and mankind. Both danger and evil and great potential for good come from the joining of opposites and the writer might choose any dynamic pairing to represent this. The obvious one is male and female, represented by love. In this sense, love is our metaphor for the creative. But you might also take summer/ winter, sun/ moon, animal/ human, or indeed good and evil. Creativity is a kind of balancing, or rebalancing of something suppressed or seemingly at odds with our conscious idea.

Koestler's *The Act of Creation* (1964) talks, in the opening chapters, of the comic analogy, which is the simple simile in language terms, as being at the root of all creativity. We compare, we draw the unexpected together, and something fresh happens. How often have writers put two seemingly separate ideas together to create something new? If you write a list of ideas for writing, quickly, then try linking two (or more) in your mind, often you will find the sparks begin to fly. Here is my own experiment: Seaside, moving house, institutions, compost heaps, feeding many cats: that is my instant list, unthinkingly written. The mind already makes analogies and begins to make a narrative. Myths work on analogy and on narrative. The seemingly disparate are close to opposites. Someone buys a house by the sea and finds many cats to feed. Maybe he is a comic Oedipus, who will be good to his new-found people (or cats) and free them from a curse and, against the myth, not be cursed himself, or free himself too via kindness to cats. The quality of the idea does not matter. The point is the suggestions which arise from seemingly anomalous ideas. Notice how the tribe of cats suggested an opposite from another story to build a dynamic to animate (!) the tale. Another, obvious way to make creative opposition is just to introduce an opposite. Dogs, perhaps?

Creativity reveals the hidden connection between things and the hidden unity of life. When the opposites work together the creative magic can happen, which is the fruitful, multiple world of that which flourishes and multiplies. As Blake says 'he who made the Lamb' also made 'The Tyger', combining the opposites of fierce and meek in his dynamic poem.

PERSONAL

See Introduction, plus Chapter 12, Myths of Fame. Writing, and especially writing using or influenced by myth, however personal, *becomes* public when it is published. So writing is, in a sense, always both personal and public and tends to move from one towards the other. This traditional or mythical role is inherent and it is useful to keep this in mind. As John Donne says, in *Devotions* (1624) (Meditation XVII), 'I am involved in mankind'. If someone asks you if your writing is autobiography, the proper answer is that, since it has become public, it has moved beyond the personal realm entirely. As myths are written to be of some use to the society they were created for, mythic writing tends towards helping the individual be communally and therefore perhaps morally involved via their work.

POLLUTION

E.R. Dodds, in *The Greeks and the Irrational* (1951) says, in chapter two, that there was an underlying hatred of pollution and yearning for purification in the Greek psyche. The Greek for the Latinate word we use is 'miasma', which for us means a poisonous gas, a kind of poisoning of the air. All this seems to point to the way the Greek duality is hard-wired into our consciousness. The cathartic act of purification is a creative act, the theme of tragedy and the purpose of art, if the idea is taken to its logical extreme. Bringing the good from darkness is the classic creative/ mythic act which is our own mythic work.

Dudley Young, in 'Pollution and Chaos', part of chapter six of *Origins of the Sacred* (1991), says that 'pollution in every culture means the bad breath of divinity' and that it is like a virus, full of life-force but too powerful or untameable to do any good. The analogy for a writer might be that we could purify the dangerous unconscious of our selves or our society by the catharsis of creation, which is a ritual of dealing with these powerful poisons, perhaps turned to better use. What is important again is the maintaining of a balance between the human and what is beyond our control. The essence of many classic myths is in the workings out of the polluted and the pure, which is the balance of health, both personal and societal.

Good and evil are seen in terms of what is good for all, or pure, and what is bad for all, which is unclean. This is religious, mythic thinking which demands proper ritual for the potentially dangerous. Taboo does not, though, forbid what is risky, but rather seeks to make its potential useful. This is where, perhaps, the fundamentalist goes wrong, enforcing a total ban rather than an understanding of the process needed to make things good. The mythic writer, however, will tackle, like a religious shaman who seeks to purify health, the polluted aspect and devise a creative ritual which allows the strength to emerge in a useful way.

The connections with modern science are obvious then and the dangers of, for example, nuclear energy, are not gone from the world, as there is some doubt still about their miasmic power. The anxiety about this is our traditional anxiety about unmediated power, as we invoke the creative god without mythic knowledge, at our peril.

QUEST

This is the slightly fantasy-edged term for the hero-myth, although the search for something to bring fertility back to the world does put the emphasis on the boon, which is the reseeding of the barren land. The problem with the word, perhaps, is its easily mocked associations. You can add any absurd object or quality to 'The Quest For . . .' and get a cheap laugh. There is scope and purpose though behind mocking the mock-mythic. So a writer's quest might be a comic one, in terms of humour and of happy endings.

The quest is a specific journey, mythically, to find something which symbolises a greater loss. If the loss is in the inner world as well as the outer, then the quest is for a missing part of the self, which needs restoration. A writer might say that we are questing for a myth that will bind us back to the world we have become separated from.

In Arthurian myth, the great quest is for the grail, which is the wine cup Christ used at the Last Supper, where he told his disciples that the wine was his blood. The grail is a vessel which preserves life and represents the female principle of the creative. Here death is overcome by new life, so the vessel is the symbol of the human and natural ability to preserve and renew life. The creative individual who heals the world, potentially, is the symbolic holder of the grail, which, in turn, symbolises the creative quest.

RINGS

As a circle the ring means completeness or unity. Thus it can mean time as well as a symbol of marriage. It can represent the link of a chain too, where the one symbolises a complete connection. The circle is also a boundary, a strength of unification and is a symbol of democracy and equality among people, as in the 'round table' of King Arthur. Prometheus has to wear a ring after escaping his fate of being tied to a rock, to symbolise his submission to the chain of punishment. His ring is iron and has rock as a stone. A ring of fire is life and death in their powerful forms. It is a powerful symbol of unity and strength and appears in many mythic works, such as the English fairytale

'The Fish and the Ring', where a couple's lost ring, dropped into the sea, is found in a fish they are served for a meal (see FISH).

SCIENCE

We live in a scientific age, but science is in all kinds of mythical trouble, from nuclear bombs to pollution. The mythic writer might be tempted then to fall for the cliché of the mad scientist, driven to the edge of madness by excessive rationality. But perhaps better, and at heart more mythic, would be to create a sane scientist, who understood this. That would also create a more two-dimensional character. Science now tells of the need for myth.

Chapter 1, Starting Creation explores the ideas of science having trouble with beginnings and ends, as Dudley Young suggests in chapter one of *Origins of the Sacred* (1991). Scientists are the new myth-makers, as we can see in science fiction, which deals with the big societal and worldly concerns where the mythic enters the world.

In the subject of alchemy, the scientist and the myth-magician were one. Alchemists sought to understand the elements of the universe and control them to find the secret of life. As an image for a myth-maker, they are profoundly involved in connecting the analytical with the moral and process-based activity of the creative life, which seeks the same through different but parallel means. Alchemists could be the creative others of our divisive views of the world. The outer world of science and the inner world of the mind are linked by alchemical understandings, in the same way we seek links via myth. Jung wrote about alchemy, and its symbols still hold the doors open between perceptions and instincts. Mercury, the quick, or quicksilver, messenger of the gods is still the fast, adaptable life of understanding. The elements and the planets still have their alchemical values.

For the writer, the use of science can bring the questions and questioning of myth and of human limits into sharp focus. The temptations of science are those of illusions of order, while the temptations of myth are of illusions of ritual disorder, disaster and power, and we are all prone to both. Many creative works have these dualities at their centre.

SEA

The sea is the great symbol of the unconscious, of the other side of the world, beyond the human realm and of 'otherness' in general. As a symbol and as a source of stories, myths and monsters, it is inexhaustible. Seek out the lyrics to 'Sea Song' by Robert Wyatt for a brilliant personification of the sea (from the album *Rock Bottom*, 1974).

The sea symbolises limitlessness, bottomlessness, travel to unknown places, changeability, the surface we float upon, 'female' power; ignoring the depths, depth itself, other worlds of creatures, monsters and vegetation, a place of wreaks and death. The tides and storms, calms and winds, have rich imagery for writers too. From classical myth, where Poseidon, god of the sea, rules the travellers' success, to today where the sea is the last great element which can overcome us in its watery power, the call of the sea has been present. We seek solace and confrontation with ourselves through it and beside it. Poseidon was the younger brother of Zeus, who ruled, but was always rebellious and untamed, like his kingdom. He was also the god of watery nourishment, when springs gave natural water to men.

Mermaids and mermen represent all the above features and their interaction with humans gives a place for our conflicts between the instinctive and transitional versus our ideas of what is dry and ordered. Islands, too, give small worlds more immediately in contact with the big watery aspects of life, where new/ old lives can be experienced in mythic works.

Hephaistos, the fire god, was deformed and thrown out of Olympus by his mother, the great goddess Hera, but was saved by sea goddesses. He has the balance of life restored by a journey into the sea, just as Jonah, in the Bible, is given new life by the whale who swallows him.

In science, as in myth, the sea is the place of the birth of life and its power is always there for writers. See also FLOOD and FISH.

SEASONS

The movement of the seasons is a prime subject for writers, as it is a structure, supported by nature. For our purposes it also echoes in the inner world of man, tied by mood, by agriculture and by the need to control the environment. The obvious symbolic and mythic resonance of the seasons has meant that some might consider it hard to write something new about them. But writing is more like the Spring than critics would know, who only have one, frosty season. Write about the seasons, then, but use their returning and renewal to make the way you say it fresh. The seasons, then, are a symbol of freshness and of what is on-going. Seasons deliver us into warmth and out of stasis. It is no wonder that we still celebrate mid-winter with a festive attempt to bring the sun back by generosity. It is no wonder that the Standon Morris, in Hertfordshire, UK, dance the sun up on May Day. The 'pathetic fallacy' is overloading emotions onto nature, but the gloomy day is partly our gloom, as is the sunny morning. We are part of nature and one another. Writers return to the seasons and return with them. See also AGE and TIME.

The seasons, structurally, can work as childhood, youth, maturity and old age. The four elements can also be aligned: the feeling towards intuition of the waters of Spring, the passionate fire of Summer, the high intellectual insights in the winds of Autumn and the seed waiting in the cold earth of Winter.

The seasons are a primal cyclic, mythic pattern and we live by them and through them. This is myth as part of us and a palpable presence beyond our closed world.

SEX

Sex, as a taboo, having special significance and symbolism, is a proper subject for myth (see INCEST and LOVE). The pleasures of sex and its romantic significance are more the sphere of modern writers, while myths deal with its ritual significance. A writer can explore these two views of sex usefully. Sex is, obviously, the significant union of a balance of opposites in a myth which calls on images of fertility, or, if forced, is a breaking of a natural order by human lust–greed. Again, we have the mythic challenge to one simple view, where all social pressures can operate for or against and discriminate, rightly or wrongly, between what is natural and what is right.

Yeats' poem 'Leda and the Swan' (1928) is about a mythical sexual encounter between Leda, a princess and Zeus, the greatest god, in disguise. It is impossible to resist a god but the poem wonders if the encounter gave her his 'knowledge' and 'power' for a moment. This is a poem perhaps not so much about sex as about sex's potential to give an experience of something beyond the human, in however terrible or violent a form. Sex with a god is not human sex, however, and such an excuse would not be valid for us. Sex has a power beyond itself and therefore is a focus of mythic energy. The challenging nature of what is good and right and what is potentially damaging is the area that myth addresses. The unmediated power of nature is only helped through the proper rituals of union. Myth might then have a conservative view of sex, just as well as an 'it was the god not me' kind of licentiousness (see POLLUTION).

SHADOW

See Chapter 5, Dark Matter. The Shadow is a symbol used to denote the unknown side, or opposite side of a person. Shadows and shades can also be places of refuge and we talk about 'shadow boxing' and of someone being a 'shadowy figure' and about being out of the light, hidden or repressed in someone's shadow. Shadow puppets might be comic or revealing of shadow sides, or a trick of light. Shadows are potent contrasts for writers, who want to see behind the apparent.

TIME

See Chapter 10, The Daily Myther; AGE and SEASONS. Time as a line and time as a circle represent two ways of seeing it and the split in our minds between progress and inevitability on one hand and seasonal returning and renewal on the other. The attitude of myth is that things go round and that the straight line is the ego of mankind seeking to impose itself on an older order. Time, in terms of writing, is a primary structure which is very flexible in creative work and also where these seasonal and progressive tensions can be depicted.

TRICKSTERS

See Chapter 8, Myth Madness. A Trickster is a figure who occupies the borders between the real and the unreal, or the conscious and the unconscious. The Trickster is a personification of the imagination and a writer is therefore a Trickster, for our purposes. There are many Trickster tales in all cultures under different names: some Shakespearean fools are Tricksters, who can play with the truth and speak the unspoken. Chapter 3, The Truth Lies in essence deals with the nature of paradoxical truth of the kind the Trickster reveals. Writers can search their local culture for Trickster figures or return to the fund of Native American Indian stories. The trick can be magic, just as it can be a con. If we manipulate our material well, rather than a base humiliation of a victim or an act of robbery, it will be both entertaining and magic.

UNDERWORLDS

The journey into the dark, to be tested and emerge with new insights, is one of the oldest literary tropes, from Homer's *The Odyssey* to Carroll's *Alice in Wonderland* (1865) or a modern thriller. For the writer, the aim is to make the journey as meaningful and significant as possible, where the symbolic reaching into the dark shows us something worth seeing. See Chapter 5, Dark Matter. In one sense, the underworld is the place of the past and of death. All that is unresolved or unknown of ourselves lies there forgotten, awaiting rediscovery or reinterpretation. In the mythical underworld, the river of Oblivion is called the Lethe, where the dead may drink to forget life. In some stories there are also springs of memory, where what is lost may be regained in the mind.

The hero in the underworld is the exception, as heroes stay alive in the place of the dead. This is their test of vision and strength and they emerge with knowledge of time, both past and future. Odysseus, Aeneas and Dante are the heroes of epic literature who have underworld journeys. Ultimately the underworld is a symbolic death in order to gain new life. As a primal aspect of mythic writing, the underworld, which might be anything from a small encounter with difficulty, to a full-blown life-threatening theme, is the big one. It is night before day, storm before calm, the monster before it transforms into the god.

The mythic process, or descent to find the truth, for the writer, is a journey to the underworld. The hero has to find the way in, which might be to follow the sun to its end. Where the sun goes down is the intersection of day and night, or conscious and unconscious. There are guards, Threshold Guardians, to be tackled, who might hold a symbolic key or stick, to help or hinder us. As Dante had the poet Virgil, we might need a mentor figure of a past writer, as our guide into the world of the dead. We hope to return transformed.

We are tested to the full there and have to fight monsters, which are the suppressed darkness and desires of the world.

The underworld cannot be conquered, but must always be approached with the best attitude. The secrets of the past and the future reside there for us, but, as in *The Odyssey*, we go there to face the dark for its necessary balance and to bring ourselves and our message of transforming hope back. In a sense, just as Dante is rescued by Beatrice, we are rescued as writers by our writing from the land of the dead and made new.

WAR

The main topic of epic, war is a hard mythic subject for the world of gentle mythic writing, but nevertheless, and perhaps because of its difficulty, most significant. As a symbol, albeit overused, of struggle between forces of life, war appeals in its absolute declaration of conflict. It is the struggle for a single aim and direction. Its symbolic power is that of disunity towards unity. War is also the testing place of the human spirit, where all things are extreme. This is one reason why war is so used by writers as a life-struggle. Meaning and meaninglessness work side by side. War is still the subject we sing about, as the opening line of *Aeneid* says.

The warrior, as a symbol of someone prepared for any trouble, can be a more positive image, where the peace comes from the sense of defence of the individual truth being protected. Then the warrior becomes the hero. If war is the battle between the unconscious and the conscious worlds forced into the open, then the warrior may be the person in whom these forces are balanced. The warrior is thus able to protect the world, inside and outside, by being ready for any monstrosity. The writer, with pen as sword and paper as shield, may be the warrior of peace, or of protecting life. Given the tide of bad stories in the world, the mythic writer needs to be a warrior, restoring the balance within and resisting the bullshit without. I think this was what D.H. Lawrence meant in his poem 'It's Either You Fight or You Die' (from *Pansies*, 1929, in *Complete Poems*).

War is a troublesome subject for us, because of its pointless death and awful destructive power, made more meaningless and unfair by modern weapons. But war is the darker, even unavoidable side of humanity, shown in all its mythic disorder and display of power and should not be avoided by the mythic writer. As a focus for the symbolic opposite of peace, it is a symbol of how the world often presents itself in its incoherence and impossibility. Our weapons may be just pens or lutes, but we have our own arms to sing of and our own fights, internal and external, to win. War is the myth we must do battle with sooner or later.

WATER

Arguably water is the most essential of the four elements, with air, earth and fire. Water is the great giver and transmitter of life, but it is also changeable, in shape and character, capable of bringing death (see FLOOD). We are, famously, largely made of water ourselves and water is also our means of cleaning both literally and symbolically. Water is needed for re-growth and renewing the seed. The hero brings back water to the dry world, so that the element is the transforming one between the inert and the living.

Baptism is the ritual of water, the giving of life through immersion in the life-element, so that fluency may be attained. The tides that flow in symbolise things coming your way, while life ebbs away in its season. Crossing the water is the passage to new life, the potential dangerous, potentially renewing task towards change. Meetings by the water have the power of change built in, with the element of constant change at hand.

For writers, water is their power of mutable creativity. The rain changes the mood, just as the sun does and eyes can light and weep in the same way. Water imagery runs throughout literature, as do flood stories. For a positive view of water, try Philip Larkin's short poem 'Water', from *The Whitsun Weddings* (1964), where water is seen religiously. Springs were holy places, where the life-source came up spontaneously and people still visit holy wells to ask questions of Saints and leave coins in the wells for luck. The emotional resonance of turbulence or calm, of depth and high cloud, of tears and of ritual washing are called on again and again by writers. The only problem is to be able to make the watery image fresh, by attention to detail rather than easy calling on the over-used.

Water is also symbolic of all liquid fecundity, as the sea (see SEA; FISH) is of the unconscious. As a means and symbol of transport, its movement haunts us. The transparent quality of water again adds the symbolic and literal power, arguably the one most powerful force in the world and the imagination.

WORDS

'Word' is an old English word and old words are especially mythic, as they have shifting narratives of origin and interaction with the human world all through them. It is a truism to say that words are our basic material, but a truism that is true. We speak myth in loaded sound, we call on the past and the changes inside a word. Words are not indifferent or flat. My word can be my promise of trust and words make us from their mythic and traditional past. This is the word. Mythic and magic texts understand how significant words are and how the right word can open the door. The magic words are easy to forget and it is easy to forget that they are magic.

The alphabet is also a system of thought, of order. It is a structure with symbolic meaning that can be used by writers. The alpha and omega are the Greek beginning and end letters and signify life and death. Eric Partridge, whose etymological dictionary *Origins* (1958; 1966) is a must for writers, who will want to share his inspired insight into words. His *Comic Alphabets* (1961) shows many possibilities for using letters creatively. Ambrose Bierce's *The Devil's Dictionary* (1911) gives a cynic's take on words and a view of creative definition. 'Mythology' is a culture's 'body of primitive . . . beliefs . . . as distinguished from the true accounts which it invents later.' This is a properly creative and ambiguous view of the truth as being outside our own realm, which is the mythic (as well as the cynic) truth. The hum of the middle letter of our own alphabet, 'M', is the hum of life. Words hold massive mythic power in every aspect of their ordinary, often overlooked, currency. They are a kind of wealth.

No-nonsense English blues songwriter, Wilco Johnson, ex of Dr Feelgood, has the full multi-volume *OED* on his shelves, in a room dominated by black electric guitars and amps. Writers never underestimate the words they use. Words are myths and symbols, as are the letters of the alphabet, and words have tales to tell.

WORK

The mythsmith's work might be seen to be invisible, or, in writing, immobile and therefore look like leisure. The idea of work being related to material production has arguably made creative work feel under siege at times. But work is not the opposite of myth. The mythsmith has a magic forge, where mysterious new truths are made in the fire of creative work. As most of us know, work can be fulfilling, if its purpose is for the good of all, otherwise it rots the soul. Is myth silent on work? Sisyphus, who has to keep rolling the rock back up the hill, is the pointlessness of work. Work, as a nature myth, can be like putting new growth forth, like a blossoming and a life-enhancing game in the convivial, humane market of the world. If you bring a cheer and something true from yourself, you are contributing to the mythic, gift economy, far more valuable than wage-slave goods and money (see Chapter 12, Myths of Fame).

Fictionally, writers may reveal their characters through the work they do and through their attitude to it. The mythsmith can test the Sisyphus against the communal craftsman, who works in a mythically useful way.

XENOPHOBIA

Xenophobia is one for mythic writers to stand on its head. If we use a myth, we are, some might say, excluding others from our work, if they do not understand it. But the more you understand myths and can present them usefully, the richer your understanding of all human nature.

If I take myth to include 'Old Uncle Tom Cobley and All', you might not know what I meant. But if I set the reference up to include the story of the traditional English song 'Widdecombe Fair', where eight riders get on one horse, to go to the fair, including 'Old Uncle Tom Cobley and All', you would understand that I simply meant 'everyone'. With myth, strangers become friends and strangeness is made the familiar of change and truth.

YOUTH

See also TIME and AGE. Many myths, or even all myths, are about rites of passage to some extent, and the movement from youth to adulthood echoes the creative process, from unconscious to conscious. The negative side of youth is demonstrated in Oedipus' killing of his father and Cronus (which means 'crow', see BIRDS) devouring his children (Hesiod's *Theogony*). Youth and age, and their relationship, is often the theme, or metaphor, of conflict and of failure to grow, or of the need to grow. Peter Pan is the modern eternal youth, but Adonis (see Ovid, *Metamorphosis*, Book X), Ganymede (shiny genitals), the play-thing boy of the gods (depicted well by Marlowe in *Dido, Queen of Carthage*) and Narcissus (see Ovid's *Metamorphoses*) are his predecessors. Youth is associated with sacrificing itself to achieve adulthood, or a refusal to do so, to become death in life by stasis. Sir James Frazer's *The Golden Bough* (1922) links Adonis with cycles of agricultural growth, thereby the link with Dionysus is reached.

Dionysus, in Euripides' *The Bacchae*, is the spirit of youthful changeability, sexual ambiguity and rebellion, energy, drunkenness and fertility. He drives the women crazy and demands that all worship him. The uptight father figure Pentheus resists and is destroyed. Donna Tartt's *The Secret History* (1992) is about students of Greek literature who enact the killing in youthful arrogance. In *The Bacchae*, the old men go to the dancing rituals willingly, if comically, thus combining youth and age positively.

Fairytales, such as 'Jack and the Beanstalk' offer images of growing and of responsibility, of the transformation of a child to the adult realm, as does Cinderella. Children's stories generally are often, naturally, concerned with this motif.

The classic youth in literature is Telemachus, in Homer's *The Odyssey*. Books one to four are often referred to as 'The Telemachy', as they are his epic of growth, helped by his Mentor (the source of the term), a man called Mentes, who is the goddess Athene in disguise. Thus the female element combines with a substitute father to encourage the unpromising youth to transform.

Youth and growing are a strong element of much myth, and of writing and literature in general, but *Hamlet* is perhaps the classic of brooding youth. Hebe, the Greek goddess of youth was conceived by eating lettuce and stayed fair. She became cup-bearer to the gods, but fell into an indecent posture once, when pouring out nectar. She was replaced by Ganymede (see above). She married Hercules and had the power of restoring youthful vigour to gods and men. She is also known as Dia and, in Roman mythology, Juventas and is depicted as a young virgin, crowned with flowers.

ZOMBIES

Zombies are a symbol of the non-creative life, where we are mechanical and controlled. This is behind all zombie tales, beliefs and writings. They are the fear of self-annihilation in an indifferent world. Paradoxically the word itself is a corruption of an African good luck word 'zumbi', which has come to mean its opposite, revealing our ambiguous view of magic. The word is also used to describe the part of software viruses which spread the virus to others indiscriminately. Here, again, is the myth of our own fears of our non-mythic, conspired against and mechanised selves, made mythic so that we can get our heads round them and regain some true mythic power.

BIBLIOGRAPHY

◆

Publications, films, LPs

Abbey, Edward. *The Brave Cowboy*. 1956; Avon: New York, 1992.

Adams, Richard. *Watership Down*. 1972; Penguin: London, 1974.

Aesop. *Aesop's Fables*. Trans. E.S. Vernon Jones. Wordsworth: Ware, 1994.

Aeschylus, *The Oresteian Trilogy*. Trans. Philip Vellacott. Penguin: Harmondsworth, 1959.

Amis, Kingsley. *New Maps of Hell*. Gollancz: London, 1960.

Amis, Martin. *Money*. Cape: London, 1984.

Andersen, Hans Christian. *Fairy Tales*. Trans. W.A. and J.K. Craigie. OUP: London, 1914.

Andrews, Ted. *The Magical Name*. 1991; Dragonhawk: Jackson TN, 1998.

Angwin, Roselle. *Riding the Dragon*. Element: Shaftesbury, 1994.

Arabian Nights. *Tales from the Thousand and One Nights*. Trans. N.J. Dawood. Penguin: London, 1973.

Armitage, Simon. *Sir Gawain and the Green Knight*. Faber: London, 2007.

Armstrong, Karen. *A History of God*. 1993; Vintage: London, 1999.

Armstrong, Karen. *In the Beginning*. 1996; Harper Collins: London, 1998.

Armstrong, Karen. 'Believers in the lost ark', *Guardian*, 9.8.2003.

Armstrong, Karen. 'Look on the dark side of life', *Guardian*, 21.2.2004.

Armstrong, Karen. *A Short History of Myth*. Canongate: Edinburgh, 2005.

Arnold, Matthew. *Selected Poems and Prose*. Dent: London, 1978.

Asquith, Anthony. Dir. *The Way to the Stars*. 1945.

Attwater, Donald. *The Penguin Dictionary of Saints*. Penguin: Harmondsworth, 1981.

Auden, W.H. *Forewords and Afterwords*. Faber: London, 1974.

Auden, W.H. *Collected Poems*. Faber: London, 1991.

Auster, Paul. *Timbuktu*. Faber: London, 1999.

Ayto, John and Crofton, Ian, Eds. *Brewer's Britain and Ireland*. Weidenfeld and Nicholson: London, 2005.

Ballard, J.G. *The Drowned World*. Gollancz: London, 1962.

Ballard, J.G. *The Wind from Nowhere*. 1962; Penguin: Harmondsworth, 1967.

Ballard, J.G. *The Overloaded Man*. Panther: London, 1967.

Baring-Gould, Sabine. *Curious Myths of the Middle Ages*. 1866; New Orchard: Poole, 1987.

Bataille, Georges. *Literature and Evil*. 1957; Trans. A. Hamilton. Marion Boyars: London, 1985.

Bate, Jonathan. *The Song of the Earth*. Picador: London, 2000.

Baudelaire. *Selected Verse*. Trans. Francis Scarfe. Penguin: Harmondsworth, 1968.

Baudelaire. *The Poems in Prose*. Trans. Francis Scarfe. Anvil: London, 1989.

Bede. *Ecclesiastical History of the English People*. Trans. Leo Sherley-Price. Penguin: London, 1990.

Benedict, Ruth. *Patterns of Culture*. Penguin: Harmondsworth, 1946.

Bergman, Ingmar. Dir. *The Seventh Seal*. 1957.

Bettelheim, Bruno. *The Uses of Enchantment*. Knopf: New York, 1976.

Bible, King James Authorised Version.

Biederman, Hans. *Dictionary of Symbolism*. Trans. James Hulbert. Facts on File: New York, 1992.

Bierce, Ambrose. *The Enlarged Devil's Dictionary*. 1911; Penguin: Harmondsworth, 1967.

Black, Matthew, Ed. *Peake's Commentary on the Bible*. Nelson: London, 1962.

Blake, William. *Songs of Innocence and of Experience*. 1794; Folio Society: London, 1992.

Blake, William. *The Marriage of Heaven and Hell*. Dover: New York, 1994.

Blakeney, E.H., Ed. *Smith's Smaller Classical Dictionary*. J.M. Dent and Sons: London, 1934.

Blumenberg, Hans. *Work on Myth*. Trans. Robert. M. Wallace. MIT Press: Massachusetts, 1985.

Bly, Robert. *Iron John*. Addison-Wesley: Reading MA, 1990.

Bly, Robert. *The Sibling Society*. Hamish Hamilton: London, 1996.

Book of Common Prayer. 1662; HM Printers: London, 1968.

Booker, Christopher. *The Seven Basic Plots*. Continuum: London, 2004.

Borges, Jorge Luis. *The Book of Imaginary Beings*. 1967; Penguin: Harmondsworth, 1974.

Bouquet, A.C. *Sacred Books of the World*. Penguin: Harmondsworth, 1967.

Brande, Dorothea. *Becoming a Writer*. 1934; Macmillan: London, 1996.

Brown, Mary Ellen and Rosenburg, Bruce A., Eds. *Encyclopedia of Folklore and Literature*. ABC-CLIO: Santa Barbara, 1998.

Brunvand, Jan Harold. *The Vanishing Hitchhiker*. Pan: London, 1981.

Burroughs, William. *Nova Express*. 1964; Penguin: London, 2010.

Calvino, Italo. *Six Memos for the Next Millennium*. 1988; Vintage: London, 1996.

Campbell, Joseph. *The Hero with a Thousand Faces*. 1949; Fontana: London, 1993.

Campbell, Joseph. *Oriental Mythology*. Penguin: London, 1962.

Campbell, Joseph. *Oxidental Mythology*. Penguin: London, 1964.

Campbell, Joseph. *Creative Mythology*. 1968; Arkana: Harmondsworth, 1991.

Campbell, Joseph. *Primative Mythology*. 1969; Penguin: London, 1976.

Campbell, Joseph. *Myths to Live By*. Souvenir: London, 1991.

Campbell, Joseph, Ed. *The Portable Jung*. Penguin: Harmondsworth, 1976.

Carey, John, Ed. *The Faber Book of Utopias*. Faber: London, 1999.

Carlyle, Thomas. *On Heroes and Hero Worship*. 1840; Ward, Lock: London, 1900.

Carter, Angela. *The Bloody Chamber*. 1979; Vintage: London, 1998.

Cave, Nick. *Murder Ballads*. Mute 1996.

Cave, Nick. *Murder Ballads*. Mute, 2003.

Cavendish, Richard. *The Black Arts*. 1967; Pan: London, 1969.

Cavendish, Richard. *The Tarot*. Chancellor: London, 1986.

Chambers, R., Ed. *The Book of Days*. 1864; Chambers: London, 1869.

Chaundler, Christine. *Everyman's Book of Ancient Customs*. Mowbrays: London, 1968.

Chetwynd, Tom. *Dictionary for Dreamers*. Paladin: St Albans, 1974.

Chetwynd, Tom. *A Dictionary of Symbols*. Granada: London, 1982.

Chetwynd, Tom. *A Dictionary of Sacred Myth*. Unwin: London, 1986.

Chetwynd, Tom. *The Age of Myth*. Unwin: London, 1991.

Chevalier, Jean and Gheerbrant, Alain. *The Penguin Dictionary of Symbols*. Trans. John Buchanan-Brown. Penguin: London, 1996.

Child, F.J. *English and Scottish Popular Ballads*. 1882–98; Cooper Square: New York, 1962.

Cirlot, J.E. *A Dictionary of Symbols*. 1971; Dover: New York, 2002.

Clare, John. *Selected Poems and Prose*. Eds Eric Robinson and Geoffrey Summerfield. OUP: Oxford, 1966.

Clarke, Lindsay. *Essential Celtic Mythology*. Harper Collins: London, 1997.

Coetzee, J.M. *Elizabeth Costello*. Secker and Warburg: London, 2003.

Cohen, Leonard. *Various Positions*. Columbia, 1984.

Cohen, Leonard. *Ten New Songs*. Columbia, 2001.

Coleman, J.A. *The Dictionary of Mythology*. Arcturus: London, 2007.

Conrad, Joseph. *The Nigger of the 'Narcissus'*. 1897; Pan: London, 1976.

Cook, Peter, etc. *Beyond the Fringe*. EMI, 1961.

Cooper, J.C. *An Illustrated Encyclopedia of Traditional Symbols*. Thames and Hudson: London, 2008.

Cope, Wendy, Ed. *101 Happy Poems*. Faber: London, 2001.

Costello, Elvis. *All This Useless Beauty*. Warner, 1996.

Costello, Elvis. *Momofuku*. Lost Highway, 2008.

Coupe, Laurence. *Myth*. Routledge: London, 1997.

Crossley-Holland, Kevin, Trans. *The Exeter Riddle Book*. Folio Society: London, 1978.

Crossley-Holland, Kevin. *Folk Tales of the British Isles*. Faber: London, 1985.

Crossley-Holland, Kevin. *British Folk Tales*. Orchard: London, 1987.

Crowley, John. *Little, Big*. 1981; Millennium: London, 2000.

Dante. *The Divine Comedy*. Trans. John D. Sinclair. OUP: Oxford, 1961.

Dodds, E.R. *The Greeks and the Irrational*. University of California Press: Los Angeles, 1951.

Donne, John. *Devotions Upon Emergent Occasions*. Vintage: London, 1999.

Dostoyevsky, Fyodor. *Notes from Underground, The Double*. Trans. Jessie Coulson. 1864; Penguin: Harmondsworth, 1972.

Drury, Nevill. *The Watkins Dictionary of Magic*. Watkins: London, 2005.

Dylan, Bob. *Bringing It All Back Home*. Columbia, 1965.

Dylan, Bob. *John Wesley Harding*. Columbia, 1968.

Dylan, Bob. *Blood on the Tracks*. Columbia, 1973.

Dylan, Bob. *Chronicles, Volume I*. Simon and Schuster: New York, 2004.

Eldon, Jim. *Golden Arrows*. Stick Records: Hull, 1991.

Eliade, Mircea. *Myths, Dreams and Mysteries*. Harvill: London, 1960.

Eliot, Alexander. *The Universal Myths*. Meridian: New York, 1990.

Eliot, George. *Silas Marner*. 1861; Penguin: London, 1967.

Eliot, T.S. '*Ulysses*, Order and Myth', in *The Dial*: London, November 1923.

Eliot, T.S. *Selected Essays*. Faber: London, 1951.

Eliot, T.S. *The Complete Plays and Poems of T.S. Eliot*. Faber: London, 1979.

Eliot, T.S. 'Tradition and the Individual Talent', in *Selected Essays*. Faber: London, 1951.

Euripides. *The Plays of Euripides, Volume I*. Trans. Shelley, Dean, Milman, Potter and Woodall. Dent: London, 1942.

Euripides. *Alcestis and Other Plays*. Trans. Philip Vellacott. Penguin: Harmondsworth, 1953.

Euripides. *The Bacchae and Other Plays*. Trans. Philip Vellacott. Penguin: Harmondsworth, 1972.

Euripides. *Alcestus / Hippolytus / Iphigenia in Tauris*. Trans. Philip Vellacott. Penguin: Harmondsworth, 1974.

Euripides. *Orestes and Other Plays*. Trans. Philip Vellacott. Penguin: Harmondsworth, 1980.

Folklore, Myths and Legends of Britain. Reader's Digest: London, 1977.

Ford, Richard. *Independence Day*. 1995; Harvill: London, 1996.

Fortune, Dion. *Applied Magic*. Aquarian Press: Wellingborough, 1987.

Fowler, Roger, Ed. *A Dictionary of Modern Critical Terms*. Routledge and Kegan Paul: London, 1987.

Fowles, John. *The Magus*. 1966, rev. edn 1967; Pan: London, 1977.

Frazer, James George. *The Golden Bough*. 1922; Macmillan: London, 1959.

Gardner, Richard. *The Tarot Speaks*. 1971; Universal Tandem: London, 1974.

Goethe. *Faust*. Trans. Theodore Martin. Dent: London, 1954.

Ghiselin, Brewster, Ed. *The Creative Process*. Mentor: New York, 1952.

Ginsberg, Allen. *Howl and Other Poems*. City Lights: San Francisco, 1956.

Ginsberg, Allen. *Kaddish and Other Poems*. City Lights: San Francisco, 1961.

Goleman, Daniel. *Emotional Intelligence*. 1995; Bloomsbury: London, 1996.

Gordon, Stuart. *The Encyclopedia of Myths and Legends*. Headline: London, 1994.

Grant, Michael. *Myths of the Greeks and Romans*. 1960; Phoenix: London, 2001.

Graves, Robert. *Poems Selected by Himself*. 1957; Penguin: Harmondsworth, 1961.

Graves, Robert. *The Greek Myths*. Penguin: Harmondsworth, 1960.

Graves, Robert. *The White Goddess*. Faber: London, 1961.

Graves, Robert, Ed. *New Larousse Encyclopedia of Mythology*. Hamlyn: New York, 1970.

Gray, John. *Black Mass*. 2007; Penguin: London, 2008.

Grimal, Pierre. *Dictionary of Classical Mythology*. Penguin: London, 1991.

Grimm, Brothers. *The Complete Fairy Tales of the Brothers Grimm*. Trans. Jack Zipes. Bantam: New York, 1987.

Habeshaw, Sue and Evans, Colin. *53 Interesting Creative Writing Exercises*. Technical and Educational Services: Bristol, 2006.

Hamilton, Edith. *Mythology*. Mentor: New York, 1955.

Hammond, N.G.L. and Scullard, H.H., Eds. *The Oxford Classical Dictionary*. OUP: Oxford, 1984.

Hardy, Thomas. 'God's Funeral', *The Works of Thomas Hardy*. Wordsworth: Ware, 1994.

Harrison, Jane. *Themis*. Merlin: London, 1977.

Harrison, Tony. *The Mysteries*. Faber: London, 1985.

Hedsel, Mark. *The Zealtor*. Century: London, 1998.

Hemingway, Ernest. *Men Without Women*. 1927; Penguin: Harmondsworth, 1955.

Herbert, George. *A Choice of George Herbert's Verse*. Ed. R.S. Thomas. Faber: London, 1967.

Hesiod and Theognis. *Hesiod and Theognis*. Trans. Dorothea Wender. Penguin: London, 1973.

Heyerdahl, Thor. *Aku-Aku: The Secret of Easter Island*. Rand McNally: New York, 1958.

Heylin, Clinton. *Bob Dylan Behind the Shades*. Viking: New York, 1991.

Hillman, James. *The Dream and the Underworld*. Harper and Row: New York, 1975.

Hillman, James. *Healing Fiction*. Station Hill: New York, 1983.

Hillman, James and Ventura, Michael. *We've had a Hundred Years of Psychotherapy and the World's Getting Worse*. Harper Collins: New York, 1993.

Homer. *Iliad*. Trans. Lord Derby. Dent: London, 1910.

Homer. *Odyssey*. Trans. Richard Lattimore. 1965; Harper Collins: New York, 1991.

Homer. *Odyssey*. Trans. A.T. Murray. Harvard University Press: Cambridge, Massachusetts, 2002.

Homer. *Odyssey*. Trans. Alexander Pope (1726).

Howatson, M.C. and Chilvers, Ian, Eds. *The Concise Oxford Companion to Classical Literature*. OUP: Oxford, 1993.

Hughes, Kathryn. 'Doris Lessing did what no politician would dare to do', *Guardian*, 27.10.2007.

Hughes, Ted. 'Myth and Education', in *Writers, Critics and Children*. Eds Geoff Fox *et al*. Heinemann: London, 1976.

Hughes, Ted. *Winter Pollen*. 1987; Faber: London, 1994.

Hughes, Ted. *Tales from Ovid*. Faber: London, 1997.

Hughes, Ted. *Collected Poems*. Faber: London, 2003.

Huxley, Aldous. *Island*. 1962; Penguin: Harmondsworth, 1964.

Hyde, Lewis. *The Gift*. Vintage Books: New York, 1983.

Hyde, Lewis. *Trickster Makes This World*. 1998; Canongate: Edinburgh, 2008.

Jacobs, Joseph. *English Fairy Tales*. 1894; Everyman: London, 1993.

Jacobson, Howard. *Seriously Funny*. Viking: London, 1997.

James, Henry. 'The Private Life', 1892, in *The Aspern Papers and Other Stories*. Oxford: OUP, 1983.

Jamison, Kay Redfield. *Touched with Fire*. Simon and Schuster: New York, 1993.

Jung, C.G. *Memories, Dreams, Reflections*. Fontana: London, 1963.

Jung, C.G. *Aion*. Trans. R.F.C. Hull. 1959; Routledge and Kegan Paul: London, 1968.

Jung, C.G. *Four Archetypes*. Trans. R.F.C. Hull. Princeton University Press: Princeton, 1970.

Jung, C.G. *Flying Saucers*. Trans. R.F.C. Hull. Princeton University Press: Princeton, 1976.

Jung, C.G. *Psychological Reflections*. Ed. Jolande Jacobi. Ark: London, 1986.

Jung, C.G. *Aspects of the Masculine*. Trans. R.F.C. Hull. Ark: London, 1989.

Jung, C.G. *Modern Man in Search of a Soul*. Ark: London, 1992.

Jung. C.G. *Jung on Active Imagination*. Ed. Joan Chodorow. Routledge: London, 1997.

Kaplan, Stuart R. *The Classical Tarot.* Aquarian: Wellingborough, 1984.

Koestler, Arthur. *The Act of Creation.* 1964; Arkana: London, 1989.

Larkin, Philip. *Collected Poems.* Marvell; Faber: London, 1988.

Lawrence, D.H. *Phoenix.* Heinemann: London, 1936.

Lawrence, D.H. *Collected Poems.* Heinemann: London, 1972.

Lawrence, D.H. *Lady Chatterley's Lover.* 1928; Penguin: Harmondsworth, 1994.

Leach, Edmund. *Genesis as Myth.* Cape: London, 1969.

Lempriere, J. *Classical Dictionary.* Milner and Sowerby: Halifax, 1864.

Llewellyn-Williams, Hilary. 'Actaeon', in *Scintilla*, 6. Llantrisant, 2002.

Lodge, David. *The Art of Fiction.* Penguin: Harmondsworth, 1992.

Logue, Christopher. *War Music.* 1981; Penguin: Harmondsworth, 1984.

Lorre Goodrich, Norma. *Ancient Myths.* Mentor: New York, 1963.

Mabinogion. Trans. Gwyn Jones and Thomas Jones. Dent: London, 1974.

May, Adrian. 'Spookiness for Writers', *Writing in Education*, 23 (2001), 33–35.

May, Adrian. 'Mything You Already', *Writing in Education*, 24 (2001), 25–28.

May, Adrian. *An Essex Attitude.* Wivenbooks: Wivenhoe, 2009.

May, John. *How to Make Effective Business Presentations.* McGraw-Hill: Maidenhead, 1983.

May, Rollo. *The Art of Counselling.* Souvenir: New York, 1989.

Metzner, Ralph. *Opening to Inner Light.* 1986; Century: London, 1987.

Michell, John. *The Earth Spirit.* Thames and Hudson: London, 1975.

Miller, David. Dir. *Lonely Are the Brave.* 1962.

Milton, John. Ed. Alastair Fowler. *Paradise Lost.* Longman: London, 1973.

Mitchell, Adrian. *Out Loud, annotated edition.* Publishing Cooperative: London, 1976.

Nichols, Sallie. *Jung and the Tarot.* Weiser: Boston, 1984.

Nietzsche. *The Birth of Tragedy.* Trans. Shaun Whiteside. 1872; Penguin: London, 1993.

O'Flaherty, Wendy, Trans. *Hindu Myths.* Penguin: Harmondsworth, 1975.

Osborne, John. *Damn You England.* Faber: London, 1994.

Ovid. *Metamorphoses.* Trans. Arthur Golding. 1567; Penguin: London, 1973.

Ovid. *Metamorphoses.* Trans. A.D. Melville. Oxford University Press: Oxford, 1986.

Partridge, Eric. *Comic Alphabets.* Routledge and Kegan Paul: London, 1961.

Partridge, Eric. *Origins.* Routledge and Kegan Paul: London, 1966.

Pearson, Carol. *The Hero Within.* Harper and Row: San Francisco, 1986.

Perrault, Charles. *The Complete Fairy Tales.* OUP: Oxford, 2009.

Pinkola Estes, Clarissa. *Women Who Run with the Wolves: Myths and Stories of the Wild Woman Archetype.* Ballantine: New York, 1996.

Polti, Georges. *The Thirty-Six Dramatic Situations.* 1921; The Writer Inc.: Boston, 1977.

Preminger, Alex and Brogan, Terry V.F., Eds. *The New Princeton Encyclopedia of Poetry and Poetics.* Princeton University Press: Princeton, 1993.

Priestley, J.B. *Literature and Western Man.* Penguin: Harmondsworth, 1960.

Price, Simon and Kearns, Emily. *The Oxford Dictionary of Classical Myth and Religion.* OUP: Oxford, 2003.

Public Enemy. *Public Enemy.* Def Jam, 1987.

Pullman, Philip. 'Voluntary Service', *Guardian* 'Review', 28.12.02.

Radice, Betty. *Who's Who in the Ancient World.* Penguin: Harmondsworth, 1975.

Rexroth, Kenneth. 'The Advantages of Learning', in *Penguin Modern Poets 9*. Penguin: Harmondsworth, 1967.

Rilke, Rainer Maria. *Letters to a Young Poet.* Trans. M.D. Herter Norton. Norton: New York, 1993.

Rimbaud, Arthur. 'A Season in Hell', in *Rimbaud, Collected Poems.* Trans. Oliver Barnard. Penguin: Harmondsworth, 1962.

Ritsema, Rudolf and Karcher, Stephen. *I Ching.* Element: Shaftesbury, 1994.

Ritsema, Rudolf and Sabbadini, Shantena Augusto, Trans. *The Original I Ching Oracle*. Watkins: London, 2005.

Roob, Alexander. *Alchemy and Mysticism*. Taschen: Cologne, 2006.

Roth, Philip. *Operation Shylock*. Cape: London, 1993.

Roud, Steve. *The English Year*. Penguin: London, 2008.

Sampson, John. *Gipsy Folk Tales*. 1933; Robinson: London, 1984.

Sandars, N.K., Trans. *The Epic of Gilgamesh*. Penguin: Harmondsworth, 1960; 1964.

Schmidt, Michael. *The Story of Poetry*. Weidenfield and Nicholson: London, 2001.

Shelley, Percy Bysse. *The Poetical Works*. Frederick Warne: London, 1942.

Simpson, Jacqueline and Roud, Steve. *Oxford Dictionary of English Folklore*. OUP: Oxford, 2003.

Smith, Stevie, *The Frog Prince, and Other Poems*. Longmans: London, 1966.

Smith, Stevie. *The Collected Poems of Stevie Smith*. Penguin: London, 1985.

Snyder, Gary. *The Practice of the Wild*. North Point Press: New York, 1990.

Sophocles. *The Theban Plays*. Trans. E.F. Watling. Penguin: Harmondsworth, 1947.

Stevens, Wallace. 'Towards a Supreme Fiction', in *Selected Poems*. Faber: London, 1965.

Storr, Anthony, Ed. *Jung: Selected Writings*. Fontana: London, 1986.

Sumner, William Graham. *Folk Ways*. Mentor: New York, 1940.

Suttie, Ian D. *Origins of Love and Hate*. 1935; Peregrine: Harmondsworth, 1963.

Swift, Jonathan. *Gulliver's Travels*. 1726; Penguin: Harmondsworth, 1967.

Tales from the Thousand and One Nights. Trans. N.J. Dawood. Penguin: London, 1973.

Tartt, Donna. *The Secret History*. 1992; Penguin: London, 1993.

Tennyson, Alfred. *Poetical Works and Plays*. OUP: Oxford, 1953.

Terry, Philip, Ed. *Ovid Metamorphosed*. Vintage: London, 2001.

Terry, Philip. 'Dante: Inferno I', in *Oulipoems 2*. Ahadada: Toronto, 2009.

'The Cruel Mother', in *Oxford Book of Ballads*. Ed. James Kinsley. OUP: Oxford, 1969.

Thomas, Edward. *Collected Poems*. Faber: London, 2004.

Thomas, Keith. *Religion and the Decline of Magic*. Penguin: London, 1978.

Thompson, Richard. *Rumour and Sigh*. Capitol, 1991.

Thompson, Richard. *You? Me? Us?* Capitol, 1996.

Tressider, Jack, Ed. *The Complete Dictionary of Symbols*. Duncan Baird: London, 2004.

Virgil. *Eclogues and Georgics*. Trans. T.F. Royds. Dent: London, 1946.

Virgil. *The Aeneid*. Trans. C. Day Lewis. OUP: Oxford, 1986.

Vogler, Christopher. *The Writer's Journey*. 1992; Pan: London, 1996.

Walker, Barbara G. *The Woman's Encyclopedia of Myths and Secrets*. Harper Collins: New York, 1983.

Warner, Marina. *Managing Monsters*. Vintage: London, 1994.

Warner, Marina. *From the Beast to the Blonde*. Vintage: London, 1995.

Wender, Dorothea, Trans. *Hesiod and Theognis*. Penguin: London, 1973.

Weston, Jessie L. *From Ritual to Romance*. Doubleday: New York, 1957.

Weston, Mike. *Philosophy, Literature and the Human Good*. Routledge: London, 2001.

Wilhelm, Richard, Trans. *The I Ching Book of Changes*. Routledge and Kegan Paul: London, 1968.

Wilson, Colin. *The Occult*. 1971; Mayflower: St Albans, 1973.

Wolfe, Tom. *Bonfire of the Vanities*. 1987; Vintage: London, 2010.

Wordsworth, William. *Poetical Works*. OUP: Oxford, 1904.

Wright, David, Ed. *Anthology from X*. OUP: Oxford, 1988.

Wyatt, Robert. *Rock Bottom*. EMI, 1974.

Yeats, W.B. *Collected Poems*. Macmillan: London, 1983.

Young, Dudley. *Out of Ireland*. Carcanet: Cheadle, 1975.

Young, Dudley. *Origins of the Sacred*. St. Martin's Press: New York, 1991.

Zipes, Jack, Ed. *The Oxford Companion to Fairy Tales*. OUP: Oxford, 2000.

INDEX

───── ◆ ─────

Abbey, Edward, 75
Abraham and Isaac (Bible), 101, 104–105
absurdity, 89
Act of Creation, The (Koestler), 90, 194
Actaeon story, 51–57, 59, 60, 61; poem,
    54–55
Adam and Eve, 123, 160, 170
Adonis, 205
'Advantages of Learning, The' (Rexroth),
    145–146
Aeneid, The, 68
Aeolus (Greek god), 160
Aeschylus, 40
Agamemnon (Aeschylus), 40
AGE, 159–160
ages of man, 116
AIR, 160–161
alcohol, 176
al-Din Attar, Farid, 165
All This Useless Beauty (Costello), 193
alpha and omega, 203
alphabet, 203
'Always the Flood', 134
ambrosia, 184
Amis, Kingsley, 171
Amis, Martin, 193
Andersen, Hans, 170
Andrews, Ted, 193
Animal Farm (Orwell), 162
ANIMALS, 161–163
animals, mythic significance, 165; snakes,
    symbolism of, 42–43, 172; *see also* birds, as
    mythic subject
animism, 51
Anna Karenina (Tolstoy), 80
anthropomorphism, 162
anti-hero, 77
antinomy, 141
apocalypse, 125
APOCALYPSE, 162
Apollo, 40, 41, 42, 89, 165; as god of light and
    order, 190
APPLES, 163–164
Applied Magic (Fortune), 64–65
archetypes, 25, 60, 62, 64, 65; and animals, 162;
    hero *see* heroes
Arctic Monkeys, 141

Aristotle, 81
Armitage, Simon, 3
Armstrong, Karen, 16–17, 65, 183
Arnold, Matthew, 74–75
Ars Poetica (Horace), 20
art and artwork, 143, 144, 145
Art of Counselling (May), 94–95
Art of Fiction, The (Lodge), 20
Artemis *see* Diana (hunter figure)
Arthurian myth, 163–164, 181, 196
'As I Walked Out One Evening' (Auden),
    120
As You Like It, 118, 177
Atwood, Margaret, 179
Auden, W.H., 120, 160, 164
Auster, Paul, 162
awe, 16

Bacchae, The (Euripides), 92–93, 113, 177, 192,
    205
bad news, 84
ballads, 119–120
Ballard, J.G., 126, 134, 161, 183
banishment, 113
baptism, 202
Baring-Gould, Sabine, 9
Barnard, Oliver, 125
Barrie, J.M., 168
Bataille, Georges, 64, 124, 177
Bate, Jonathan, 51, 177
Baudelaire, Charles, 177–178, 186
Beatles, 141, 144, 145
beauty, 41
Beckett, Samuel, 84
Becoming a Writer (Brande), 9, 25–28, 37–38
beginnings: creative, 19–23; ways of beginning,
    101–106
Bible, 14, 21, 35, 39, 101, 163; condemnation of
    mankind in, 178; Sodom and Gomorrah, 169;
    see also Genesis; New Testament; Old
    Testament; Revelation
Bierce, Ambrose, 203
bipolar disorder, 28
BIRDS, 164–165
birth myths, 24–34; Taliesin, story of,
    29–34
Birth of Tragedy, The (Nietzsche), 81, 190

bisociation, 90, 94
Black Arts, The (Cavendish), 153
Black Magic, 153, 173
Black Mass (Gray), 133
Blake, William, 24, 25, 56, 86, 168–169, 173
Blood on the Tracks (Dylan), 27
Bloody Chamber, The (Carter), 108
Blumenberg, Hans, 100, 181
Bly, Robert, 7, 76, 177
Bob Dylan Behind the Shades (Heylin), 27
BODIES, 165–166
Bonfire of the Vanities (Wolfe), 153
Book of Common Prayer, The, 172
Book of Days, 91, 92, 106
Book of Imaginary Beings (Borges), 162, 164, 181
Book of Judges, 186
Book of Revelation, 125
Booker, Christopher, 50
Borges, Jorge Louis, 162, 164, 181
Bradbury, Malcolm, 25
Braine, John, 25
Brande, Dorothea, 9, 25–28, 33, 37–38, 39, 102
Brave Cowboy, The (Abbey), 75–76
Brave New World (Huxley), 84
Buddha, story of, 68–69
Burch, Nigel, 43
Burroughs, William, 42
Burton, Tim, 81
Butler, Tom (Rev), 97
Byatt, A.S., 3

Cadmus, 93
Calvino, Italo, 190
Campbell, Joseph, 4, 62, 69, 83, 128–129;
    Hero with a Thousand Faces, 7, 9, 28, 50,
    68, 79, 81, 105; *Primitive Mythology*, 140;
    'separation-initiation-return', 60, 68
Carlyle, Thomas, 78
Carter, Angela, 108, 179
Cassandra story, 40–42, 44, 45, 59, 60, 61
Cathars, 173
cauldron image, 29, 32
Cave, Nick, 120
Cavendish, Richard, 153
celebration, 85, 87
Cerberus, 162
Chandler, Raymond, 87
change, 15
CHANGE, 166–167
CHAOS, 167–168
character, 108
charity, 180
Chaundler, Christine, 92
Chesterton, G.K., 153
Chetwynd, Tom, 17, 62, 115–116, 127, 128
childhood, 101, 102, 106–107
CHILDHOOD, 168–169

Christ, 35, 44, 49, 173, 189, 190
Christ, see JESUS
Christian mysticism, 50, 181–182, 189; *see also*
    Christ; New Testament
Christmas, 91–92
Chronicles Volume I (Dylan), 114
CITIES, 169–170
Clapton, Eric, 20
Clare, John, 177
Clarke, Lindsay, 21
clichés, 85–86, 139
CLOTHING, 170
Coetzee, J.M., 162
Cohen, Leonard, 14, 15, 52, 53
Coleridge, Samuel Taylor, 174
collective unconscious, 113
comedy, 80–88; dark humour, 81; 'light', 82;
    meanings, 80, 90; of sex, 95
Comic Alphabets (Partridge), 203
Commedia, The (Dante), 71, 172, 179
concept of myth, 1–2
conflict, 83
Conrad, Joseph, 44, 142, 142–143
CONSPIRACY, 171
Cook, Peter, 122
cosmos, 167
Costello, Elvis, 90, 193
Coupe, Laurence, 3
courage, 24, 37
creation: beginnings, 19–22; defined, 18; myths
    see creation myths
creation game, 22
creation lists, 18–19
creation myths, 13–19; elements, 19; purpose,
    18–19; types, 18
Creative Mythology (Campbell), 129
Creative Writing courses, 24, 80, 83, 191
creativity maps, 47
creativity story, 59, 65
creativity/creative expression, 48, 89, 90, 96, 179
Crow (Hughes), 165
Crowley, John, 80
crying and laughter, 90
cryogenics, 115
Curious Myths of the Middle Ages (Baring-Gould), 9
customs, 117
Cutler, Ivor, 88
Cyclops, 166, 175, 178
cynicism, 81, 82, 154

Daedalus, 160, 161, 164
Daily Myther (imaginary newspaper), 112, 114
Damn You England (Osborne), 44
Dante Alighieri, 52, 53, 73, 172, 179
'Dante: Inferno I' (Terry), 135–137
darkness/dark matter, 58–66, 125; and comedy,
    80, 81, 82

Dark-to-Light, 59, 65
dawn, 13
day-dreaming, 174
'Days' (Larkin), 116
death, 2, 33, 84, 123–124
DEATH, 171–172
death: and body, 166; souls of dead, bird
    association, 165
'death of God', 123, 128–133
defamiliarisation, 14
developing, 107–109
Devil, 124, 129
DEVIL, 172–173
Devil's Dictionary, The (Bierce), 203
Devil's Dyke, Sussex, 173
Devotions (Donne), 195
Diana (hunter figure), 51, 52, 53, 56, 59
Dickens, Charles, 85
Dictionary (Lempriere), 9, 40
Dictionary of Modern Critical Terms, A (Fowler), 70
Dictionary of Sacred Myth, A (Chetwynd), 127
Dictionary of Symbols, A (Chetwynd), 17, 62,
    115–116, 128
Dionysus, 173, 176, 184, 187; and Apollo, 190;
    and madness, 89, 92, 93, 94
discovery, 117
divisions, 15, 16
Dodds, E.R., 195
dogs, 94
Donne, John, 195
doom, 122–138; dooms of God, 128–133
Dostoevsky, Fyodor, 76–77, 84
doubt, 68, 69
Douglas, Kirk, 75
'Dover Beach' (Arnold), 74–75
Dr Jeckyll and Mr Hyde (Stevenson), 174
DREAMS, 174–175
dreams and dreaming, 37, 105
Drowned World, The (Ballard), 134, 183
DRUGS, 175–176
duality, mythic, 25, 36
dust, man made of, 15, 16
Dylan, Bob, 27, 39, 40, 41, 42, 140, 160;
    autobiography, 114

EARTH, 176–177
Earth Spirit (Michell), 177
Ecclesiastes, 4
eco-criticism, 51
eco-hero, 78
ecology, 51
Eden, 84
education, as initiation, 60
egoism, 4
Egyptian myths of eternal life, 181
Eldon, Jim, 77, 78
elegy, 114

Eli (Biblical priest), 39
Eliade, Mercia, 152
Eliot, George, 151–152, 168
Eliot, T.S., 5, 125, 181, 183
Elizabeth Costello (Coetzee), 162
Emotional Intelligence (Goleman), 26
'Emperor's New Clothes, The' (Andersen), 170
'End of the World, The' (Cook), 122
enjoyment, 85
Enlightenment, 124, 128
epic hero, 70
Epic of Gilgamesh, The, 3, 123, 169, 183, 184
epic poems, viii, 71
epithalamium (wedding song), 114
Eros, 191
escapism, 2, 6–7, 36, 81
Estes, Clarissa Pinkola, 76
eternal life, Egyptian myths of, 181
Euripides, 92–93, 113, 177, 192, 205
Eurynomus, 172
Everyman's Book of Ancient Customs (Chaundler), 92
evil, 16, 123–124, 173, 195
EVIL, 177–178
existential angst, 24
Exodus, 185
extremity, 103
exuberance, creative, 86
EYES, 178–179

facts, 35, 36, 43
fairytales, 9, 61, 115, 152, 154, 176; giants,
    184–185; men, portrayal of, 192–193;
    modernising myths, 104, 108; and youth, 205
faith, 128, 152
FAME, 179
fame, myths of, 139–147
fantasy, 91
Farewell, My Lovely (Chandler), 87
Faust (Goethe), 173
feasts, 117
FEMININE, 179–180
festivals, 117
FIRE, 180–181
FISH, 181–182
Flaubert, Gustave, 103
flight, 160–161
FLOOD, 182–183
flow, 26, 27
Flowers of Evil (Baudelaire), 177–178
fluency, 27, 37
folklore, 9, 61
FOOD, 183–184
fool, wise, 36
'For Johnny' (Pudney), 161
Ford, Richard, 21
Fortune, Dion, 64–65
Four Archetypes (Jung), 93–94, 96

Four Quartets (Eliot), 181, 183
Fowler, Roger, 70
Fragments (Euripides), 192
Frazer, Sir James, 154, 205
free-writing, 27–28, 102
Freud, Sigmund, 25, 83, 174
'Frog Prince, The' (Smith), 100
fruit, symbolic, 163–164

Gaia, 51, 176
Garden of Eden, 84
Gardner, John, 25
Gardner, Richard, 105
Genesis, 123, 133, 153, 167; Adam and Eve, 123,
    160, 170; creation myths, 14–15, 16; fire, 181;
    flood, myth of, 183; giants, 184; modernising
    myths, 104–105; *see also* Bible; Old Testament
Genesis as Myth (Leach), 1
genius, 38
genre, 109
Gestalt psychology, 56
Ghost of Frankenstein (film), 64
giants, 16
GIANTS, 184–185
Gift, The (Hyde), 143
gift economy, 143
Ginsberg, Allen, 4, 43, 44, 57
Gnostics, 50, 173
God, 124, 125, 128–133
GOD(S), 185
gods and goddesses, 16, 59, 70, 92, 160, 173;
    see also specific gods, such as Apollo
'God's Funeral' (Hardy), 129–132
Goethe, Johann Wolfgang, 173
Golden Apples of the Hesperides, 164
Golden Bough, The (Frazer), 154, 205
Goleman, Daniel, 26, 27
Gospels, 173, 182, 189
Grant, Michael, 8
Graves, Robert, 8, 60, 88, 107, 141
Gray, John, 133
Greek drama, 95
Greek myths, 50, 104, 167; Actaeon story *see*
    Actaeon story; Cassandra story *see* Cassandra
    story; Titans, 184; *see also specific Greek characters
    such as* Prometheus
Greek Myths, The (Graves), 8, 107
Greek names, 107
Greek tragedy, 113
Greeks and the Irrational, The (Dodds), 195
Grenfell, Joyce, 90
growing, 106–107
Gypsy Folk Tales (Sampson), 61

HAIR, 186
Hamlet, 83, 205
Hanged Man, The, 96

happiness, 80–88; happy endings, 81
Hardy, Thomas, 129–132
Harpies, 165
Harrison, Tony, 5, 114, 117
harvests, 118
Hawk in the Rain, The (Hughes), 75
HEAD, 186–187
Healing Fiction (Hillman), 35, 43, 61
Heaney, Seamus, 3, 82
Hedsel, Mark, 56
Hemingway, Ernest, 193
Hephaistos, 198
Hermes, 168, 187
Hero with a Thousand Faces, The (Campbell), 7, 9,
    28, 50, 68, 79, 81, 105
heroes, 67–79, 93; dark, 64; eco-hero, 78; and
    gods, 185; heroic decline, 70; hero-worship,
    78; post-heroic texts, 75, 77, 78
HERO, 187
Hesiod, 15, 16
Heylin, Clinton, 27
Hillman, James, 35, 43, 61
hip-hop, 33
history, 117, 121
'Hollow Men, The' (Eliot), 125
home, 113
Homer, 164, 166; *Iliad*, 107; *Odyssey see Odyssey,
    The* (Homer)
'Hometown Mystery Cycle' (Maxwell), 117
Howl and Other Poems (Ginsberg), 43, 57
Hughes, Kathryn, 36
Hughes, Ted, 5, 53, 54, 94; *Crow*, 165; *Hawk in
    the Rain*, 75; 'Myth and Education', 48–50;
    Prometheus on his Crag, 181; *Tales from Ovid*, 52,
    107, 183
humility, 144, 177
humour, 91, 94; dark, 81; *see also* comedy;
    laughter
hunting, 161–162
Huxley, Aldous, 84
Hyde, Lewis, 94, 96–97, 143–144
hypnosis, light, 39

I Ching, 105, 106, 154, 166
iambic line, 119
Icarus, story of, 113, 160, 164
Iliad (Homer), 107, 163
image, 15, 16
imagination, 36, 62–63
imitation, 37
improvisation, 102
In the Beginning (Armstrong), 16–17
INCEST, 187–189
incubation, 39
Independence Day (Ford), 21
individuality, 4, 37–38, 77
'Infant Sorrow' (Blake), 24

Inferno (Dante), 52, 53, 73, 172
initiation/initiation rites, 60, 66
inner world, 47, 49, 51, 87
innocence, creation of, 21
innovation, 4, 5
insight, process of, 49
inspiration, 24–25, 87
Iphigenia story, 101, 102, 104, 107, 109
'Iron Hans' tale, 76
Iron John (Bly), 7, 76, 177
irrationality, 89
Island (Huxley), 84

Jackson, Ian, 113
Jacobs, Joseph, 151
Jacobson, Howard, 91, 95
James, Henry, 28
Jamison, Kay Redfield, 28
Janus (Roman god), 28–29
Jason and the Argonauts, 165
Jesus *see* Christ
JESUS, 189
John (Biblical figure), 127, 128
John Wesley Harding (Dylan), 39
Johnson, Wilco, 204
Jonah, 182
Jove, 43
Joyce, James, 5, 101, 169
Judgement Day, 125
Julius Caesar (Shakespeare), 182
Jung, C., 62, 93–94, 96, 171, 174
Jungian archetypes, 25, 62
Juno, 43

Kaddish and Other Poems (Ginsberg), 4
Kafka, Franz, 84, 113, 171
Kerouac, Jack, 174
KING, 189–190
King James Bible, 14, 35
Koestler, Arthur, 90, 91, 94, 194
'Kraken, The' (Tennyson), 63, 168
'Kubla Khan' (Coleridge), 174

Lady Chatterley's Lover (Lawrence), 83
language: ballads, 119; of creation, 13, 14, 15, 16;
    universal, of myth, 140
Larkin, Philip, 3, 116, 118, 183, 203
Last Judgement, 132, 172
laughter, 22, 89, 90–91
Lawrence, D.H., 48, 95, 144, 181, 202; *Lady
    Chatterley's Lover*, 83, 191
'Layla', 20
Leach, Edmund, 1
'Leda and the Swan' (Yeats), 199
Lempriere, John, 9, 40
Lessing, Doris, 36
Letters to a Young Poet (Rilke), 86

Lewis, C.S., 189
LIGHT, 190
literary criticism, 14
Literature and Evil (Bataille), 64, 124, 177
Literature and Western Man (Priestley), 82
Llewellyn-Williams, Hilary, 29–34, 53–54, 191
Lodge, David, 20
logic, 2
Logue, Christopher, 107, 112–113
Lonely Are the Brave (Miller), 75
Lord of Misrule, 89, 91, 92, 94, 97
loss, works of, 75
Loudermilk, John D., 84
love, 95
LOVE, 191
'Love Itself' (song by L. Cohen), 14, 15
Lucifer, 173; *see also* Devil

MADNESS, 192
madness, mythic, 89–98
Maeterlinck, Maurice, 83
magic, 25, 36, 39, 94, 151–155
Magical Name, The (Andrews), 193
Magician, The, 60–61, 75
man, as image, 15, 16
Managing Monsters (Warner), 103
Manchester, Phil, 164
Mandela, Nelson, 70
Marvell, Andrew, 120
Maxwell, Glyn, 114, 117, 119
May, Rollo, 94–95
Medusa's head, 187
Melville, A.D., 16, 52, 181
MEN, 192–193
Men Without Women (Hemingway), 193
mermaids/mermen, 198
Metamorphoses (Ovid), 9, 16, 42, 52, 53, 107, 166;
    incest in, 188
Metzner, Ralph, 48, 49, 50
Michell, John, 177
'middlebrow' writers, 82
Midsummer Night's Dream, A, 53, 95, 108
Miller, David, 75
Milligan, Spike, 87
Milton, John, 71, 124, 172
misbehaviour, 102
misery, 80
Mitchell, Adrian, 118–119
Moby-Dick (Melville), 181
Mock Heroic, The (band), 71
mock-happiness, 88
modernising myths, 99–111; developing,
    107–109; growing, 106–107; meanings,
    100; ways of beginning, 101–106;
    writing, 109–110
Modernism, in arts, 5
Money (Amis), 193

monotheism, 173
monsters/monstrosity, 16, 62, 64, 65, 66, 168; heads of monsters, 187
More English Fairy Tales (Jacobs), 151
Murder Ballads (Cave), 120
Muses, 16, 20, 44
music-making, 15–16
Mysteries, The (Harrison), 117
mystery, 2, 13
myth, concept, 1–2
Myth (Coupe), 3
'Myth and Education' (Hughes), 48–50
myth texts, 8–9
Myth-Browser, 99
mythical method, 101
Myths, Dreams and Mysteries (Eliade), 152
Myths of the Greeks and Romans (Grant), 8

nakedness, in dreams, 174
NAMES, 193
Narcissus, 142, 144
narrative truth, 35
narratives, 1, 6, 7
nature, 3, 51, 87–88, 123
nature worship, 129
navigation devices, 47–57
nectar, 184
neuroses, 64
New Maps of Hell (Amis), 171
New Princeton Encyclopaedia of Poetry and Poetics, The, 114
New Testament, 35, 123, 125; Gospels, 173, 182, 189; 'last supper', 183; *see also* Christ
news, 112, 119, 120, 121
nicknames, 193
Nietzsche, Friedrich, 81, 129, 190
Nigger of the Narcissus, The (Conrad), 44, 142–143
nihilism, 129
1984 (Orwell), 124, 168, 171
Noah's ark, 182, 183
Notes from Underground (Dostoevsky), 76–77, 84
nothingness, 16
Nova Express (Burroughs), 42
'Novel and the Feelings, The' (Lawrence), 48
novels, use of myth in, 3
'Now Zero' (Ballard), 126
nuclear bomb, 180

ode, 114
Odysseus, 67, 68, 73
Odyssey, The (Homer), viii, 20, 38, 56, 73, 113, 160; Cyclops in, 166; lotus eaters, 175; and gods, 173; Proteus in, 167; Sirens' song, 165; Telemachus, 205
Oedipus (Sophocles), 36, 187–188
'Oedipus Complex', 187
O'Heffernan, Mahon, 146

Old Testament, 123, 174; Exodus, 185; *see also* Adam and Eve; Bible; Genesis
Olympic Games, 112
On Heroes and Hero-Worship (Carlyle), 78
Opening to Inner Light (Metzner), 48, 50, 56
openings of texts, 20–21
Operation Shylock (Roth), 35
opposites, 60
OPPOSITES, 193–194
optimism, 87
originality, 4, 5, 37, 38
Origins (Partridge), 67, 203
Origins of Love and Hate (Suttie), 84
Origins of the Sacred (Young), 17, 132, 195, 197
Orpheus, Greek tale of, 6, 187
Orwell, George, 124, 162, 168, 171
Osborne, John, 44
otherness, 167
Out Loud (Mitchell), 119
outer world, 51
Ovid, 81, 116, 142, 188; *Metamorphoses*, 9, 16, 42, 52, 53, 107, 166
owl, 165
'Ozymandias' (Shelley), 63, 116

Pan, 173
Paradise Lost (Milton), 71, 124, 172
Paris' Judgement, Greek story of, 163, 164
Parliament of the Birds, The (al-Din Attar), 165
Partridge, Eric, 67, 203
pastoral writing, 87–88
pathetic fallacy, 198–199
patterns of myth, 6, 47–57, 115
peace, 112, 113
Pegasus, 160
Pentheus, 205
personal nature of mythic work, 4, 5
PERSONAL, 194–195
pessimism, 81, 82, 83, 84
Peter Pan (Barrie), 168
Phillips, Adam, 96
Philosopher's Stone, 168
Picasso, Pablo, 5
poets and poetry, 3, 5, 33, 38, 44, 51, 55, 63, 146–147; ballads, 119; purpose, 82; Victorian, 73, 74; *see also particular poets, such as* Blake, William
pollution, 132
POLLUTION, 195–196
Polti, Georges, 50
Polythemus, 166
Poseidon, 198
post-heroic texts, 75, 77
pregnance, 100
Priestley, J.B., 82
Primitive Mythology (Campbell), 140
'Private Life, The' (James), 28

'Professor of Fables, The', 148–151, 152
Prometheus, 69, 153, 180–181, 184, 196
Prometheus on his Crag (Hughes), 181
Proteus, 167
psychology/psychoanalysis, 35, 36, 174–175
psychoses, 64
publication, 139–147
Pudney, John, 161
Pullman, Philip, 3, 144, 145
puritans, 92

QUEST, 196

Raeben, Norman, 27
Rake's Progress (Stravinsky), 59
rap poetry, 33
Rape of the Lock, The (Pope), 71
Redgrave, Michael, 161
religious myth, 13
renewal, 60, 66
resistance problems, 28
Revelation, 129; Revelation of St John the
    Divine, The (New Testament), 125; and
    writers, 124–128
Rexroth, Kenneth, 145–146
Rilke, Rainer Maria, 86
Rimbaud, Arthur, 125
RINGS, 196–197
Rite of Spring (Stravinsky), 5
ritual space, 39
Rolling Stones, 173
romantic novels, 144
Romanticism, 25, 51, 61
Roth, Philip, 35, 44
Rowling, J.K., 3

Sage, Lorna, 70
Sallust (Roman writer), 1
Sampson (biblical story), 186
Sampson, John, 61
Samuel (Biblical prophet), 39–40
Sandars, N.K., 183
'Sane Revolution, A' (Lawrence), 95
Satan, 173; *see also* Devil
satire, 21, 141
Saturday Night and Sunday Morning, 141
Satyrs, 162
scepticism, 21
Schniewind, J., 1
science and scientists, 17
SCIENCE, 197
science fiction, 115, 134
Scintilla (Llewellyn-Williams), 54
sea, 63, 160
SEA, 197–198
'Sea Song' (Wyatt), 198
Season in Hell, A (Rimbaud), 125

SEASONS, 198–199
'Second Coming, The' (Yeats), 117, 132
Secret History, The (Tartt), 108, 205
seduction, 64
self, 101–103
self-consciousness, 87
self-renewing song, 141
Self-Renewing Song, The, viii, 6, 9
'separation-initiation-return' (Campbell), 60, 68
Seriously Funny (Jacobson), 91, 95
seriousness, 51, 82
Seven Basic Plots, The (Booker), 50
Seventh Seal, The (film), 124
SEX, 199
Sexton, Anne, 179
sexual initiation, 60
Shadow archetype, 62, 64, 65, 66
SHADOW, 199–200
Shakespeare, William, 4, 6, 85, 107, 178; *Hamlet*,
    83, 205; *Julius Caesar*, 182; *Midsummer Night's
    Dream*, 53, 95, 108; Shakespearean comedy, 80,
    81; *Tempest*, 161; *As You Like It*, 118, 177
Shelley, Percy Bysshe, 63, 116, 117
Sibling Society, The (Bly), 177
Silas Marner (Eliot), 151–152, 168
silliness, 87, 94
Sillitoe, Alan, 141
Simmonds, Ralph, 71
sin, 123
Sir Gawain and the Green Knight (Arthurian mythic
    poem), 3
Sirens, 162
Six Memos for the Next Millennium (Calvino), 190
Smith, Stevie, 44, 100, 179
Smyth, Jack, 149–150, 151
snakes, symbolism of, 42–43, 172
Snow White, 163, 164
Song of the Earth, The (Bate), 51, 177
songs, 85
Songs of Experience (Blake), 24
Songs of Innocence (Blake), 24, 169
songwriters, 27, 77, 85
Sophocles, 36, 187–188
Southwark, Bishop of, 97
Sphinx, the, 162, 171
Standon Morris, 198
Star Trek, 49
Stevenson, Robert Lewis, 174
stories, 2–3, 5, 6, 7–8; fairytales *see* fairytales;
    good, 47; myths as, 99–100; old, 141; within
    stories, 108; timeliness/timelessness, 115;
    ways of beginning, 104–105; *see also particular
    stories, such as* Iphigenia story
storms, at sea, 160
Stravinsky, Igor, 5, 59
structure, mythic, 47–57
sun worship, 190

superhero, 77
supernatural, 1, 36
superstition, 171
Suttie, Ian D., 84
symbolism, 2, 6, 48, 105–106, 128

tabloids, 114
taboos, 2, 36, 82, 124, 195; sex as, 199
Tales from Ovid (Hughes), 52, 107, 183
Taliesin, story of, 29–34
Tarot cards, 60–61, 96, 105, 154, 155
Tarot Speaks, The (Gardner), 105
Tartt, Donna, 108, 205
Telemachus, 205
Tempest, The, 161
tenderness taboo, 84
Tennyson, Alfred (Lord), 63, 71–73, 75, 77, 168
tension, 83, 87, 91
Terry, Philip, 135–137
Thanatos, 172
Theogony (Hesiod), 15, 16
Thirty-Six Dramatic Situations, The (Polti), 50
Thompson, Richard, 93, 186
Threshold Guardians, 28, 29, 62, 64, 201
time, 114–117, 121
TIME, 200
Time Machine, The (Wells), 117
timeliness/timelessness, 115
Tiresias (blind seer), 42–43, 44, 93, 142
Titans, 184
'To His Coy Mistress' (Marvell), 120
'To You' (Mitchell), 118–119
Tolstoy, Leo, 80, 83
'Tongue of Mist' (poem), 13
Touched with Fire (Jamison), 28
'Tradition and the Individual Talent' (Eliot), 5
traditionalism, 5
tragedy, 81
tragic comedy, 81
tragic hero, 70
trance-states, 39
traps, mythic, 6–7
Tricksters, 94
Trickster Makes This World (Hyde), 94, 96–97
TRICKSTERS, 200
Trojan War, 41
'Trouble's Coming Home' (poem), 19
Trumbo, Dalton, 75
truth, 1; myth as metaphor for, 32; narrative and factual, 35
Truth Game, 45–46
truth-lies, 35–46
Turing, Alan, 164
twin self, 60

UFOs, 171
Ulysses (Joyce), 5, 101, 169

'Ulysses' (Tennyson), 71–73
uncertainty, 16–17
unconscious, 27–28, 36, 37, 38, 39, 43; collective, 113; relationship to the concious, 142; sea representing, 63, 197
underworlds, 172
UNDERWORLDS, 200–201
uniqueness of individual, 4
Uruk, city of, 183
use of myth *see* writers' use of myth
Utopia, 84

Valéry, Paul, 38
Vaughn Williams, Ralph, 145
Vellacott, Philip, 40, 42, 93
Virgin Mary, 180
Vogler, Christopher, 4, 50, 62, 64, 76, 94
void, 16
'Voluntary Service' (Pullman), 144
Vonnegut, Kurt, 122–123

Wager, Chris, 37
Walcott, Derek, 3
Walker, Barbara, 179
Wallace, Robert M., 100
war, 112–113, 122–123
WAR, 201–202
War and Peace (Tolstoy), 83
War Music (Logue), 107, 113
Warner, Marina, 3, 103, 179, 180
warrior-hero, 68
Waste Land, The (Eliot), 101
WATER, 202–203
Waterson, Norma, 93
way, the, 68–69
ways of beginning: self, 101–103; story, 104–105; symbol, 105–106
Wells, H.G., 117, 178
Wender, Dorothea, 15
Westerns, 75
White Goddess, The (Graves), 60
Whitsun Weddings, The (Larkin), 203
Wilde, Oscar, 154
Wilson, Brian, 186
Wind from Nowhere, The (Ballard), 161
wish fulfilment, 83–84
witchcraft, 129, 161
Wodehouse, P.G., 78
Wolfe, Tom, 153
Woman's Encyclopedia of Myths and Secrets (Walker), 179
Women Who Run with the Wolves (Estes), 76
wonder, 13, 14, 16, 17
Woolf, Virginia, 162
WORDS, 203–204
WORK, 204
Work on Myth (Blumenberg), 100, 181

world, changing, 86
world wars, 122–123
'writer's block', 26, 33
Writer's Journey, The (Vogler), 4, 50, 62, 64, 76, 94
writers' use of myth: reasons for, 1–3; techniques of use, 3–6
writing: beginnings, 19–22; and birth myths, 33–34; and darkness, 66; difficulties for writers, 26; double nature of writer, 25; and happiness, 85–88; and heroism, 79; intention, 142; and modernising myths, 109–110; modernising myths, 109–110; and myth madness, 97–98; mythic nature of, 1; mythic structure, 47–57; as personal, 194–195; Revelation and writers, 124–128; rites of passage, 167; split personality of writer, 28;

and truth, 45–46; two-places-at-once element of, 114; and war, 112–114
Wyatt, Robert, 198

XENOPHOBIA, 204

Yeats, William Butler, 117, 132, 161, 164; 'Leda and the Swan', 199
Young, Dudley, 1–2, 5, 7, 93; *Origins of the Sacred*, 17, 132, 195, 197
Young, Neil, 27
YOUTH, 205

Zappa, Frank, 103
Zealtor, The (Hedsel), 56
Zeus, 164
ZOMBIES, 206